EIGHT DAYS IN MAY

Also by Volker Ullrich

Hitler: Ascent 1889–1939

Hitler: Downfall 1939–1945

EIGHT DAYS IN MAY

The
Final Collapse
of the
Third Reich

VOLKER ULLRICH

Translated by Jefferson Chase

Liveright Publishing Corporation

A Division of W. W. Norton & Company
Celebrating a Century of Independent Publishing

For information about permission to reproduce selections from this book, write to
Permissions, Liveright Publishing Corporation, a division of
W. W. Norton & Company, Inc., 500 Fifth Avenue, New York, NY 10110

For information about special discounts for bulk purchases, please contact
W. W. Norton Special Sales at specialsales@wwnorton.com or 800-233-4830

Manufacturing by Lakeside Book Company
Book design by Beth Steidle
Production manager: Beth Steidle

Library of Congress Cataloging-in-Publication Data

Names: Ullrich, Volker, 1943– author. | Chase, Jefferson S., translator.
Title: Eight days in May : the final collapse of the Third Reich / Volker Ullrich;
translated by Jefferson Chase.
Other titles: Acht tage im Mai. English | 8 days in May
Description: New York, NY : Liveright Publishing Corporation, a division of W. W. Norton
& Company, [2021] | "Originally published in German as "Acht Tage im Mai: Die letzte
Woche des Dritten Reiches." | Includes bibliographical references and index.
Identifiers: LCCN 2021027618 | ISBN 9781631498275 (hardcover) | ISBN
9781631498282 (epub)
Subjects: LCSH: World War, 1939–1945—Germany. | Germany—Social
conditions—1933–1945. | Hitler, Adolf, 1889–1945—Death and burial.
Classification: LCC D757 .U45 2021 | DDC 943.086—dc23
LC record available at https://lccn.loc.gov/2021027618

ISBN 978-1-324-09288-9 pbk.

Liveright Publishing Corporation, 500 Fifth Avenue, New York, N.Y. 10110
www.wwnorton.com

W. W. Norton & Company Ltd., 15 Carlisle Street, London W1D 3BS

1 2 3 4 5 6 7 8 9 0

CONTENTS

PREFACE

The Last Week of the Third Reich

On May 7, 1945, the German author Erich Kästner wrote in his diary, "People walk through the streets, numbed. The short pause in history lessons makes them nervous. The gap between no longer and not yet bewilders them."[1] This book is about the phase between "no longer" and "not yet" in Germany. The old order of National Socialist rule had collapsed, and the new order under the occupying powers had yet to be established. Many contemporaries experienced the days between Hitler's death on April 30 and Germany's unconditional surrender on May 7 and 8, 1945, as a profound caesura in their own life stories, as the oft-invoked German "zero hour."[2] During this period, the clocks literally seemed to be standing still. "It's so strange living without papers or calendars, clocks or monthly accounting," one Berlin woman noted on May 7. "A timeless time, which slips by like water, its passing measured only by the comings and goings of men in their foreign uniforms."[3] This feeling of living in a kind of temporal "no man's land" lent the first days of May their unique character.[4]

At the same time, these days were exceedingly dramatic. "Sensation upon sensation!" wrote a legal official from the western German town of Laubach in his diary on May 5. "Events rush in! Berlin conquered by the Russians! Hamburg in the hands of the English! . . . German troops in Italy and western Austria have surrendered. This morning the German army's surrender in Holland, Denmark, and Northwest Germany came into force. Disbanding on all fronts."[5]

The process of dissolution happened so suddenly that contemporary observers had trouble orienting themselves and keeping abreast of events. Germany's dramatic collapse left many who lived through it with a feeling of disbelief, of having witnessed something fantastically unreal. "Again and again, you take your head in your hands to convince yourself that all of this isn't a dream," remarked the pro-democracy politician Reinhold Maier from southwestern Germany on May 7.[6]

Contributing to the confusion was the fact that the end of the war came differently to different parts of the disintegrating Third Reich, and people in each region perceived it in divergent ways.[7] Whereas in the west the Allies were often welcomed as liberators, fear of the Soviets prevailed in Germany's eastern provinces. This was partly because for years the Nazis had cultivated an image of "the Bolsheviks" as mortal enemies and partly because Germans were aware of their own crimes against humanity in Hitler's genocidal war against the Soviet Union. While many German soldiers more or less voluntarily surrendered to the British and Americans, the Wehrmacht continued its fierce resistance to the very end against the Red Army in the east. Hamburg was handed over to British forces without a fight on May 3 while German soldiers kept trying to defend the so-called fortress city of Breslau (today's Wrocław) until May 6. Even as liberated cities and regions in Germany were taking the first measures to rebuild political life, the German occupation of parts of the Netherlands, Denmark, and Norway continued into the first days of May. In the Protectorate of Bohemia and Moravia, the German occupation did not end until the insurrection in Prague on May 5.

Notwithstanding many Germans' subjective perception that time had come to a halt, the first days of May witnessed frantic activity in the streets. Huge masses of people were on the move. Death marches of concentration-camp inmates crossed paths with retreating Wehrmacht units and groups of refugees; columns of POWs encountered those of liberated slave laborers and bombed-out people returning home. Allied observers spoke of a veritable migration: British diplomat Ivone Kirkpatrick compared all the movement to a giant anthill that had been disturbed.[8] One of the main ambitions of this book is to depict this chaotic and often contradictory sequence of events.

Essential to the intermezzo from April 30 to May 8 was Karl Dönitz, the grand admiral whom Hitler named as his successor, and his regime in the northern German city of Flensburg. Dönitz was responsible for the war continuing for a full week after Hitler's suicide. The admiral's strategy of partially surrendering in the west while fighting on against the Soviet Union in the east was intended not just to allow the greatest number of German civilians and soldiers to flee behind British and American lines, but also to sow discord within the anti-Hitler coalition. One of the narrative threads of this book examines how Dönitz sought to turn this strategy into reality, the steps he took, and the illusions under which he labored.

The short-lived Dönitz government is also instructive because it featured an almost uncanny continuity with the Nazi regime in terms of both its personnel and ideological statements. Dönitz and his ministers showed no willingness to take responsibility for the crimes against humanity the Nazis had committed. In this regard the government's attitude was typical not just of the entire Nazi elite but also of large segments of the German populace.

Yet as the final remnant of autonomous German statehood, the Dönitz government influenced only a small portion of events in those fateful eight days. Thus, this book trains its sights far beyond the narrow confines of the Flensburg enclave. The aim is to provide a broad panorama of major political, military, and social events and developments: the final military battles; the death marches; the suicide epidemic at the end of the war; the continuing horrors of German occupation for foreign peoples; Germans' own first encounters with their occupiers; the mass rapes in Berlin; the fate of POWs of various nations, concentration-camp inmates, and displaced persons; the early, "wild" expulsion of Germans from parts of Eastern Europe; everyday life among the ruins of war; and the tentative new beginning for the German people and the start of meteoric postwar careers for some among them.

The events described here had causes stretching back into the past and consequences reaching well into the future. For that reason, this book repeatedly travels beyond the boundaries of those eight days. Further, the book traces the origins and careers of its main protagonists. Biographical miniatures alternate with historical closeups. The aim is to create a vivid portrait of the dramatic transitional phase between the apocalyptic demise of the Third Reich and the beginnings of the Allied occupation.

This book allows historical eyewitnesses to be heard in the words of their own diaries, correspondence, and memoirs. In particular, daily journals are an essential source because they most directly express the ambiguous experiences of the end of the war.[9] They reflect the contradictory sensations and feelings of early May 1945: the impression of apocalypse on the one hand and of a new beginning on the other.

EIGHT DAYS IN MAY

PROLOGUE

April 30, 1945

In the early hours of April 30, 1945, devastating news arrived in the bunker deep beneath the Old Reich Chancellery in Berlin. The head of the Wehrmacht Supreme Command (Oberkommando der Wehrmacht, or OKW), Wilhelm Keitel, reported that the advances of the 12th Army under General Walther Wenck had been halted at Schwielowsee, a lake southwest of Potsdam, dashing the final hope of relief for the German capital, which had been surrounded by Soviet troops since April 25. With that defeat, Adolf Hitler finally decided to take his own life, as he had repeatedly threatened to do over the course of his political career.[1]

Before sunrise, he began bidding farewell to some of his underlings, including the medical staff of the provisional infirmary below the New Reich Chancellery. The physician Ernst-Günther Schenck, who saw Hitler for the first time up close, recalled feeling "almost unbearably disillusioned." The man before him was nothing like the energetic Führer of the early days of the Nazi regime. "He still wore the grey uniform with the golden epaulettes and the Iron Cross on his left breast and the same long black trousers, but the human being clothed in these garments had sunken into himself to an unimaginable extent," remembered Schenck. "I looked down upon his bent back and hunched shoulders, from which his head protruded almost torturously."[2] Hitler shook hands with everyone present and thanked them for their service. He was going to kill himself, he told them, so they were released from their personal oath of loyalty to him. They should try to break through to the American and British lines in the west so as not to be captured by the Soviets.

By 5:00 a.m., the chancellery was once again being relentlessly pounded by Soviet artillery. One hour later, Hitler called Wilhelm Mohnke, the commander of the "citadel," as the final defensive ring around the government district and Hitler's bunker was called, and asked how long he could hold out. At most for two days, answered the SS Brigadeführer. The Soviets had already taken most of Berlin's central Tiergarten park, and the battle had reached Potsdamer Platz, only four hundred meters away. Time was of the essence.

Around noon, General Helmuth Weidling, whom Hitler had put in charge of defending Berlin only a few days before, arrived from his headquarters on Bendlerstrasse for a final situation meeting. His report was even grimmer than Mohnke's. In all probability, the battle for Berlin would be lost that evening. Ammunition was running out, and it was impossible to bring in any further supplies by plane. Hitler took this news calmly. He still rejected any suggestion of surrender, but after consulting his chief of the army general staff, General Hans Krebs, he did agree that the soldiers defending Berlin, if all reserves had been exhausted, should attempt to escape the city in small groups and hook up with German troops still fighting in the west. Upon returning to Bendlerstrasse, Weidling received a final "Führer order" to this effect.[3]

After the situation meeting, Martin Bormann—the powerful director of the Nazi party chancellery and the "Führer's secretary"—summoned Hitler's personal adjutant Otto Günsche and told him that that afternoon the dictator would take his own life as would his new wife, Eva Braun. The Führer had ordered their bodies to be burned,

Bormann said, and Günsche was to procure the necessary quantity of gasoline. A short time later, Hitler made his adjutant swear to carry out his order to the letter, explaining that he did not want his remains to be taken to Moscow and put on display. Hitler was likely thinking of Benito Mussolini's fate in Italy. Italian partisans had arrested Mussolini and his lover, Claretta Petacci, on Lake Como on April 27 and executed them the following day. On the morning of April 29, their bodies were brought to Milan, where they were strung up by the heels at a filling station on the Piazzale Loreto. News of Il Duce's sorry end had arrived at Hitler's bunker late that evening, and it no doubt reinforced Hitler's determination that nothing should remain of his body or that of his longtime consort.[4]

Günsche immediately set about preparing to burn the bodies. He called Hitler's chauffeur and head of the state vehicle fleet, Erich Kempka, and ordered him to scrounge up ten canisters of gasoline and bring them to the bunker's emergency exit in the chancellery courtyard.

Between 1:00 and 2:00 p.m., Hitler had his last meal. In his company were his secretaries Traudl Junge and Gerda Christian and his dietitian Constanze Manziarly. As had been the case for weeks at such lunches, the conversation consisted of small talk. No one spoke about the imminent end of the war. In her memoirs, written in 1947 but not published until 2002, Junge remembered this final lunch as a "funeral banquet under the guise of relaxed good cheer and acceptance."[5] Eva Braun did not join them. In early March 1945, she had made a final return to Berlin from Munich and had decided to follow Hitler to the grave. Out of gratitude for her unconditional loyalty, Hitler had married her on the night of April 28. He had decided, he wrote in his "private testament," to take "that girl as a wife who after years of loyal friendship came of her own free will to the virtually surrounded city to share her destiny with mine."[6]

It was now time for Hitler to say goodbye to his entourage. He gave his chief pilot Hans Baur the portrait of Frederick the Great by

Anton Graff that had hung over Hitler's desk in his small office in the
bunker. "My generals have betrayed me and sold me out, my soldiers
have lost the desire to continue, and I am done!" he told Baur. He was
well aware, Baur recalled him saying, that "by tomorrow . . . millions
of people would curse him," but that was his destiny.[7] He advised his
valet, Heinz Linge, who had served him every day for ten years, to join
a group trying to break out to the west. In response to Linge's dumbfounded question—for whose sake was it worth surviving?—Hitler
replied, "For the man to come!"[8]

At around 3:15 p.m., Hitler's closest associates congregated in
the corridor of the bunker: Bormann, Minister of Propaganda Joseph
Goebbels, Foreign Ministry attaché Walther Hewel, Krebs, Wehrmacht chief adjutant Wilhelm Burgdorf, Junge, Christian, and Manziarly. Hitler appeared before them together with Braun. "He emerged
from his quarters very slowly, more hunched than ever, and stood in
the doorway and shook everyone's hand," Junge recalled. "I felt the
warmth of his right hand in mine, and he looked at me without seeing
me. He seemed very far away. He said something, but I didn't hear
what it was. . . . Only when Eva Braun approached me was the spell
broken somewhat. She smiled and gave me a hug. 'Please try to escape.
Maybe you'll get out. Say hello to Bavaria for me.' "[9]

Immediately afterward, Magda Goebbels came and asked Günsche for permission to speak with the Führer one last time. She and
her husband had also decided to commit suicide and to take the lives
of their six children. They had been living in the bunker for six days in
order to "give their National Socialist lives the only possible honorable
end," as she had written in her farewell letter of April 28 to her son
from her first marriage, Harald Quandt. "The world to come after the
Führer and National Socialism is not worth living in, and for that reason I have brought the children here as well. They are too precious for
the life that will follow us, and God in His mercy will understand if I
release them from it myself." She and her husband had sworn "loyalty

unto death" to the Führer, and she considered it a "grace of destiny we had never dared hope for" to be able to end their lives alongside him.[10] Nonetheless, she tried at the last minute to convince Hitler to attempt to escape from Berlin. Visibly irritated at being disturbed in his final minutes alive, Hitler sent her away.[11]

About ten minutes later, Linge opened the door to Hitler's office, looked inside, and told Bormann, "Mr. Reich Director, it has happened." The two men entered the room, where they saw a grisly scene. On the left of the sofa from their vantage, Hitler sat with his head drooped slightly. There was a bullet hole about as large as a ten-pfennig coin in his right temple, and blood was running down his cheek. The wall and sofa were also spattered with blood, and a pool of blood roughly the size of a plate had collected on the floor. The pistol had dropped from his hand and now lay next to his right foot. On the right of the sofa sat Eva Braun with her legs tucked up under her. The bitter almond scent coming from her body suggested that she had poisoned herself with cyanide.[12]

Günsche went to the situation room and announced to those waiting there, "The Führer is dead!" Krebs, Burgdorf, Hitler Youth leader Artur Axmann, and Reich Security Service director Johann Rattenhuber proceeded to the antechamber of Hitler's office, where Linge was removing Hitler's body with the help of two SS men. The body was wrapped in a blanket, with only Hitler's dark trousers, black socks, and boots visible. Hitler's and Braun's bodies were carried upstairs and placed on the ground three to four meters from the bunker's exit. Bormann approached one final time, folded the blanket back from Hitler's face, and stood silently for a moment.

All the while artillery fire was raining down on the chancellery. During a brief pause, Günsche, Kempka, and Linge ran out and emptied the canisters of gasoline over the bodies. At first they had trouble lighting a fire because the wind kept blowing out their matches. In the end, Linge made a torch out of some paper and threw it atop the bodies.

Flames immediately shot skyward. Those assembled at the entrance to the bunker raised their arms one final time in a Hitler salute and quickly retreated to safety below. That evening, on Günsche's commands, two members of the former Führer's SS bodyguard buried what was left of Adolf and Eva Hitler in a bomb crater in the chancellery courtyard.[13]

EARLIER, AS HITLER WAS preparing to commit suicide, Soviet troops were storming the Reichstag. For Russian commanders, the massive neo-baroque building on the Königsplatz, constructed by Frankfurt architect Paul Wallot between 1884 and 1894, was the central symbol of the hated Hitler dictatorship. They believed that the National Socialists themselves had started the Reichstag fire of February 27, 1933—the event that had not only provided the pretext for brutally persecuting Communists throughout Germany but that, thanks to the Reichstag Fire Decree of February 28, 1933, had been a cornerstone of the Nazi reign of terror. Thus, capturing the Reichstag—and not the Reich chancellery and the Führer bunker only a few hundred meters distant—was made the primary objective in the decisive battle for Berlin. Soviet commanders had ordered that the building be taken by May 1, the international day of the working classes.

On April 29, a Soviet vanguard had secured the Moltkebrücke over the Spree River and occupied the Reich Interior Ministry. In the early morning hours of April 30, the assault on the Reichstag began.[14] German defenders—a motley assortment of Wehrmacht and SS soldiers and a few hundred navy men—had turned the building into a fortress, blocking all the windows and doors, except for firing slits, and placing mines in the surrounding area. Machine-gun nests and newly dug, water-filled moats made for difficult obstacles, causing the first Soviet assault to fail amid heavy return fire from the German defenders. The Red Army brought reinforcements in the form of assault guns and tanks across the Moltkebrücke to the square, but a second attack in the late morning and early afternoon also failed, resulting in major casual-

Red Army soldiers raise the Soviet flag atop the Reichstag
in Berlin in a restaged photo by Soviet photographer
Yevgeny Khaldei on May 2, 1945.

ties. Soviet commanders decided to wait for nightfall before launching a final assault originally scheduled for 6:00 p.m. This time, Red Army soldiers succeeded in reaching the Reichstag's steps and forcing open the main door. Inside the building, the scene became one of bloody hand-to-hand combat. As Red Army soldiers with machine pistols and hand grenades fought their way up the Reichstag steps to the entrance, the German defenders retreated to the subterranean floors.

At roughly 10:40 p.m., a group of Soviet soldiers led by Mikhail Petrovich Minin reached the Reichstag roof. They carried a sheet of red cloth but no flagpole, and so they improvised with a pipe they found, affixing their makeshift flag to a half-destroyed sculpture of a woman.[15] But the battle for the Reichstag had not yet ended. German soldiers continued to put up fierce resistance. Not until the afternoon of May 2 did the last German units surrender.

The fighting was still going on when, that morning, the Soviet photographer Yevgeny Khaldei entered the building with his camera and restaged the flag-raising of some thirty hours ago. Two Red Army soldiers, ostensibly the original ones, raised a real Soviet flag with the hammer and sickle above the Reichstag. The photo that resulted became iconic, a unique symbol of the Red Army's triumph over Nazi Germany. Several months later Khaldei was required to retouch the image to remove the second watch worn on the right wrist of the soldier supporting the bearer of the banner. Soviet authorities wanted to suppress any hints of looting by Germany's conquerors, and watches were coveted bits of plunder.[16]

In the days that followed, the Reichstag effectively became a pilgrimage site.[17] The tide of visitors never stopped. Many Red Army soldiers wrote slogans in chalk and scratched messages on the building's walls, putting the euphoria of triumph into words.[18] The messages in Cyrillic lettering can still be seen today.

"IN THE EVENING we saw several American vehicles. They took up posts in the streets. It all transpired astonishingly peacefully." These words were written in a pocket calendar on April 30, 1945, by Marianne Feuersenger, a secretary in the war history division of the Wehrmacht Supreme Command.[19] It was significant that American troops occupied Munich at the same time Hitler and his wife were taking their own lives in Berlin: the obscure private from the First World War had begun his political career in the Bavarian capital of Munich in 1919. In the incendiary climate of the counterrevolution against the Bavarian Soviet Republic, the brief, unrecognized socialist state declared after the First World War, the ambitious would-be demagogue found the perfect soil for his vicious rabble-rousing to take root. The National Socialist movement swiftly blossomed in 1920s Munich, tolerated and even approved by the Bavarian police and judicial authorities. As Reich chancellor and Führer, Hitler expressed his abiding gratitude by con-

American soldiers marching into Munich, the "Capital of the Nazi Movement," on April 30, 1945, take along a road sign as a trophy.

ferring on the city in 1935 the title "capital of the movement." When they marched into the city, American soldiers proudly carried a road sign they had taken down bearing that slogan. A photo of that moment would become nearly as iconic as Khaldei's image of the raising of the hammer and sickle above the Reichstag in Berlin.[20]

In the final days of April 1945, as the Americans took Nuremberg, the site of the notorious Nazi party rallies, and advanced upon the Bavarian capital, US warplanes dropped leaflets calling on the men and women of Munich not to resist: "It is in your own interest and the interest of the entire populace to help reason prevail. For this reason, take control from the hands of the fanatics. Summon your courage and act!"[21]

Nonetheless, Paul Giesler—the fanatical local Nazi party leader, or Gauleiter, of Munich—and his followers were not about to surrender the city, which had largely been reduced to rubble, without a fight.

They wanted to defend it for as long as possible, in accordance with Hitler's wishes. To that end, Giesler commanded that the major bridges across the Isar River be destroyed. It was one of many senseless, last-minute orders of destruction, but an officer in the battalion responsible for the demolition defied Giesler and refused to carry out the order.

In Munich and its environs, several groups of Hitler opponents were determined to act and over the course of April 1945 coalesced into the Bavarian Freedom Initiative (Freiheitsaktion Bayern, or FAB). These groups consisted predominantly of conservative Bavarian regional patriots, whose initial goals were to arrest high-ranking Nazi functionaries and deliver Munich to the Americans. On the night of April 27, officers led by Captain Rupprecht Gerngross, the head of the translation corps of Defense District VII, gave the signal for the uprising to start. The action was code-named "Pheasant Hunt," a reference to the derogatory term "golden pheasants" used to describe Nazi bigwigs with their gold-laced brown uniforms. The insurgents succeeded in storming Munich's Rathaus and occupying the offices of two radio broadcasters, the Wehrmacht station in Freimann and the major broadcasting facility in Ismaning.

Radio listeners in the greater Munich area could not believe their ears when they heard the news in the early morning hours of April 28 that the FAB had "seized the authority of government." In a ten-point program, the insurgents announced the "eradication of the bloody rule of National Socialism," which had "violated the laws of morality and ethics to such an extent . . . that every upstanding German must turn away in revulsion." They also demanded an end to militarism, the restoration of the rule of law and of human dignity, and the creation of a "modern social state" in which "everyone would have a right to the place he deserved on the basis of his abilities."[22]

But Gerngross and his allies had miscalculated. The people of Munich did not join the rebellion, opting to wait and see what would come next. Franz Ritter von Epp, the Reich's main representative in

Munich, rebuffed the insurgents' demands to engage with them in surrender negotiations with the Allies and form a transitional government.
Even less successful for the FAB was an attempt to arrest Giesler. After
an initial phase of confusion, Nazi authorities launched countermeasures. On the morning of April 28, in a flyer addressed to "the populace
of Munich and southern Bavaria," Giesler proclaimed, "All positions
in Munich are firmly in our hands. We stick by our Führer Adolf Hitler. . . . Gerngross will not escape punishment. This shadow will soon
pass."[23] The insurrection was put down within hours. Gerngross was
able to escape, but many of his allies were executed by a firing squad
in the courtyard of the Central Ministry. Among them was Günther
Caracciola-Delbrück, a Wehrmacht liaison officer and a close associate
of Ritter von Epp.

In many communities in southern Bavaria where the FAB's call to
action had inspired rebellion against local Nazi functionaries, fanatics
and SS men loyal to Hitler carried out brutal acts of revenge. More
than fifty people were killed. One of the most horrific crimes took
place in the small mining town of Penzberg. Nazi murderers shot and
hanged sixteen men and women, including the former Social Democratic mayor, during the night of April 28.[24]

Before American soldiers entered Munich on the morning of April
30, Giesler fled to Berchtesgaden, where several days later he shot him-
self. The Americans took the Bavarian capital almost without a fight,
encountering nothing more than isolated resistance from units of the
SS and the Volkssturm militia. Shortly after 4:00 p.m., the deputy of
Munich mayor Karl Fiedler, who had also fled, handed over the city's
Rathaus to a major in the 7th US Army. In his daily orders, General
Dwight D. Eisenhower wrote, "The whole Allied Expeditionary Force
congratulates the 7th Army on the seizure of Munich, the cradle of the
Nazi Beast."[25]

Many Munich residents lined the streets to welcome the GIs. "Their
march into the city is the strangest thing I've experienced up until

now," wrote one outraged young National Socialist, nineteen-year-old Wolfhilde von König, in her diary. "Hardly had the first Americans appeared in our street, than white flags were flown from individual windows."[26] Ernst Langendorf, an émigré German journalist who served as a sergeant in a US psychological operations company, recalled how quickly the Marienplatz, Munich's central square, filled with people once GIs entered the downtown area: "They inspected our vehicles with great interest. Others touched the material of our uniforms and praised its quality. Girls fell around our necks, and the prohibition against fraternizing with the enemy was thoroughly disregarded. There was a truly cheerful atmosphere. Everywhere I heard people saying: now it's over. Now we can sleep easily again. Now no more warplanes will come."[27]

ON APRIL 30, ONE DAY after the Dachau concentration camp near Munich was liberated by American soldiers, the newly freed inmate Edgar Kupfer-Koberwitz observed from his bed in the infirmary, "Everywhere in the camp, flags fly with the colors of all the countries represented here. Where did they come from? As always, there are many inmates pacing up and down the camp street. But now they walk instead of shuffling their feet, moving more freely, less weighed down. . . . Everyone is very reassured that the Americans are now protecting us. I think for all of us the word 'American' will have a golden ring to it for the rest of our lives."[28]

The Dachau camp was built in March 1933 and quickly became synonymous with state terror. It functioned almost as a laboratory in which the SS experimented with various forms of torture and inhuman violence that would subsequently be exported to other concentration camps. Rumors circulated among the general German populace about what went on in the camp, deterring any thoughts of revolt, much to the satisfaction of the Nazi regime: "Dear God, strike me dumb, so that to Dachau I will not come" became a popular saying in the Third

Reich.[29] Thus the liberation of Dachau—much more so than that of Buchenwald on April 11 and Bergen-Belsen on April 14—symbolized the end of the Nazi system of terror, just as the raising of the hammer and sickle above the Reichstag stood for the final defeat of Hitler's Germany.

The conditions at Dachau had worsened dramatically in the final months of the war. People evacuated from the concentration camps in Eastern Europe arrived constantly, and the main camp became hopelessly overcrowded. The already insufficient food rations were cut even further, and sanitary conditions beggared description. Many prisoners succumbed to typhus. From December 1944 until the camp was liberated, more than 14,000 people died in Dachau. "Exhausted, malnourished and louse-infested, inmates dropped like flies," testified a former camp record-keeper at the end of 1945 at the trial concerning the crimes committed in Dachau. "Corpses piled up between inmates who were still alive in the barracks. Some were left lying around in the streets . . . for so long that they rotted."[30]

In the latter half of April, with artillery fire audible in the distance and low-flying American warplanes appearing overhead, the prisoners became almost unbearably anxious, and it became increasingly apparent that the SS was preparing to abandon the camp. To cover up the evidence of their crimes, SS men burned countless documents. Among the inmates, the mood vacillated between hope for liberation and fear that they would be killed in a last-minute massacre.

Starting on April 26, no new work details left the camp. Instead, inmates were ordered to line up for inspection, and toward the evening, 6,887 of them were forced to march in three huge groups, followed by SS men with attack dogs. Additional groups of inmates from satellite camps joined the march so that in total some 10,000 people trudged, under threat of dogs and guns, around 65 kilometers south to Bad Tölz. Residents of the towns through which these columns passed reacted variously with indifference and with shock and fear. This was the first time some Germans were directly confronted with the regime's crimes. SS guards usually intervened when someone showed pity and proffered a piece of bread or something to drink to the exhausted marchers. On the morning of May 2, having spent the night in a forest near Waakirchen, the prisoners could finally breathe a sigh of relief. The guards had disappeared. No one knows how many people died or were executed during the forced march. Estimates run from 1,000 to 1,500.[31]

By that point, the 32,000 inmates who remained in Dachau, including more than 4,000 in the infirmary, had already been liberated. Around noon on April 29, members of the 157th Infantry Regiment of the 45th Thunderbird Infantry Division under Lieutenant Colonel Felix Sparks reached the gigantic campgrounds. KupferKoberwitz described that moment in his diary: "Suddenly there was running and scurrying around outside, and cries came: 'The Americans are here! The Americans are in the camp! They're at the assembly ground!' Everyone sprang into motion.—The ill left their beds. Convalescents and personnel ran to the barracks street, leaping out windows and climbing over the wooden boards of walls.—Everyone ran to the mustering ground.—Yelling and cries of 'hurrah' could be heard from afar.—There were yelps of joy.—Everyone was still moving, running around.—The sick ones had excited faces, full of delight: 'They're here. We're free. We're free!'"[32]

Before the American soldiers reached the camp proper, they discovered an abandoned cargo train car on a side track containing the bodies of two thousand inmates who had died of starvation and thirst in transit from Buchenwald to Dachau. The shock at this horrific sight only increased when they found the bodies of several hundred other people scattered throughout the grounds of the camp itself. "Dante's Inferno seemed pale compared to the real hell of Dachau," Sparks would later recall. "A number of company men, all battle-hardened veterans, became extremely distraught. Some cried, while others raged."[33] Disgusted GIs shot some of the SS soldiers they captured, and only

Sparks's decisive intervention put a stop to the spontaneous executions.[34] By nightfall, the situation had calmed. Together with members of the International Concentration Camp Committee, the Americans set about tending to the seriously ill. But even after the camp's liberation, former inmates continued to die. In the final entry in his chronicle of the camp on May 2, Kupfer-Koberwitz wrote, "I desperately need to get out of the infirmary area and see what it looks like in the camp. . . . But above all, it is important to take my manuscripts, diary, book about Dachau and other writings from their hiding place, in the presence of the Americans, so that later no one will be able to say that they might not have been written here."[35]

AT 6:35 P.M. ON APRIL 30, a telegram from Martin Bormann arrived at the headquarters of the supreme commander of the German navy, Grand Admiral Karl Dönitz, in the northern German town of Plön. It read, "The Führer has appointed you, Herr Grand Admiral, to replace Reich Marshal Göring as his successor. Written authorization is on its way. As of right now, you should order all measures necessary in the current situation."[36] Bormann did not mention that Hitler had been dead for three hours and seems to have purposefully worded his telegram such that Dönitz would believe the Führer was still alive.

In his "political" testament, dictated on the night of April 28, Hitler had named Dönitz his successor as head of state—not as "Führer and Reich chancellor" but as "Reich president," a title he had abolished in August 1934 after the death of Paul von Hindenburg. At Dönitz's side, Hitler made Goebbels Reich chancellor and Bormann "party minister," a newly created title. Hitler had also ordered that three copies of the testament be dispatched from Berlin that very night. One was to go to Dönitz, the second to the supreme commander of the army, Field Marshal General Ferdinand Schörner, and the third to Nazi party headquarters in Munich. But none of the couriers carrying the documents reached his destination.[37]

In his memoirs, published in 1963, Dönitz stated that he had been unprepared to take over from Hitler: "No one had given me the slightest hint that he was considering making me his successor. . . . I would never have imagined I would be called upon to meet such a challenge."[38] But Hitler's decision was hardly surprising. Hermann Göring, the supreme commander of the Luftwaffe, whom Hitler had officially named his successor in case of his death in his speech to the Reichstag at the start of the Second World War on September 1, 1939, had fallen greatly in Hitler's esteem as Allied warplanes and bombers established absolute supremacy over the skies of Europe. And it had not escaped notice that the Reich marshal was the first of Hitler's paladins to seek refuge in southern Germany, on April 20, 1945. His disgrace became complete three days later, when he asked in a telegram from Obersalzberg whether the succession order had now come into force since Hitler had apparently lost his "capacity for action." The dictator interpreted the query as an act of disloyalty, placing Göring under house arrest and stripping him of his sundry titles.[39]

The second most powerful man in the Third Reich, Heinrich Himmler, had also fallen from Hitler's favor. On the evening of April 28, the Führer's bunker received word that the leader of the SS had tried to initiate negotiations with Eisenhower via the Swedish diplomat and vice president of the Swedish Red Cross Count Folke Bernadotte for a German surrender in the west. Hitler was beside himself with rage when he was informed. Of all people, how could Himmler, whose SS soldiers had sworn to uphold the principle "our honor is loyalty," have gone behind his back and act as though he were the Führer's successor? In his testament, Hitler expelled Himmler and Göring from the party and the government, fuming that they had "done inestimable damage" to their country by secretly negotiating with the enemy and trying to seize power. Himmler was replaced as Reich interior minister by Giesler and as Reichsführer SS and head of the police by Breslau Gauleiter Karl Hanke.[40]

On the morning of April 30, Bormann informed Dönitz that enemy radio was broadcasting the news of Himmler's surrender offer and that the Führer expected "lightning-quick and iron-hard" action to be taken against all traitors. At 3:00 p.m., the grand admiral went to the police barracks in Lübeck, where Himmler had quartered himself, and interrogated him. Himmler claimed that the Reuters report about him negotiating with Bernadotte was a lie, an explanation Dönitz initially accepted.[41]

With Göring and Himmler scratched off the list as potential successors to Hitler, Dönitz was the only ranking military commander the dictator completely trusted. Hitler had named him to replace Erich Raeder as supreme commander of the German navy in January 1943, and Dönitz had repaid this act of faith with scrupulous loyalty. Even when put on trial in Nuremberg after the war, he insisted on his unconditional fealty to his Führer, testifying that he regarded Hitler as an "overwhelming personality of extraordinary intelligence and drive, with a near universal education, a character that radiated strength and uncanny powers of persuasion."[42] Hitler treated Dönitz, unlike many of his other commanders, with respect, addressing him as "Herr Grand Admiral" and rarely butting into naval affairs.

Up until the spring of 1945, Dönitz still believed that Germany could turn the war at sea in its favor by developing and deploying submarines undetectable by enemy sonar. On April 7, ever the fanatic believer, he ordered his naval officers to hold out at all costs: "Our military duty, which we will fulfill unflinchingly, regardless of what may happen to the right or to the left, allows us to stand as a bulwark of resistance, brave, hard and true. Whoever does not act in this way is a lowly dog who must be strung up with a sign around his neck reading, 'Here hangs a traitor!'" Three days later, faithful to the Führer's orders, he told naval commanders to fight "to the very end," with the only options "to be victorious or fall."[43] In the very final days of the war, Dönitz still sent navy troops to fight in the hopeless battle for Berlin.

On April 15, Hitler issued an order for the eventuality that troops of the western Allies and the Red Army should meet in central Germany, splitting the Reich in half. In the "northern space," Dönitz was to assume command, and in the "southern space," Field Marshal Albert Kesselring. Hitler had decided some time previously that he himself would remain in Berlin instead of fleeing to Obersalzberg, as his entourage was urging. Holding out amid the rubble of the Reich capital was in his eyes a far more dramatic way of staging a "heroic downfall" than by decamping to the remote idyll of his Alpine retreat.

On the afternoon of April 21, with Berlin already being shelled by Soviet artillery, Hitler and Dönitz spoke for the final time. Early the next day, the admiral and his staff headed northwest from the Reich capital in a convoy, making slow progress because the roads were jammed with retreating Wehrmacht units and long columns of German refugees. Around midday they reached their destination: the town of Plön in the Holstein region, where military buildings had been freed up for a new headquarters.[44] Navy radio operators were able to maintain connections with all command centers in the "northern realm" as well as Berlin. One operator was Siegfried Unseld, later the owner of the Suhrkamp publishing house. In 1995, fifty years after the end of the war, he remembered, "We broadcast the most important reports of the final days of the war. I was a twenty-year-old private first class, and my orders were to use new, never-before-employed codes to encipher and decipher messages going to and from Dönitz. Unseld's station was thus the first one to receive Bormann's telegram on April 30, naming Dönitz Hitler's successor."[45]

That evening, once Dönitz had recovered from his initial surprise, he summoned Himmler from Lübeck. The two men met after midnight, with Himmler appearing with six armed SS officers as though to demonstrate that he was still a force in the party and in Germany. For his part, Dönitz, if his memoirs are to be believed, kept "a loaded pistol at the ready under some papers" just in case. He gave Bormann's radio message to Himmler and watched as the former SS leader's face fell: "It was . . . full of amazement, even dismay. Somewhere within him a hope seemed to collapse. He went very pale. He stood up, bowed and said: 'Let me be the second man in your state.'"[46] Dönitz seems to have answered evasively. Himmler still commanded significant numbers of SS and police forces, and there was no guarantee he would not refuse to acknowledge Bormann's telegram and declare himself Hitler's successor. It was thus important for Dönitz to secure the support of the military. Late in the evening, he told his adjutant Walter Lüdde-Neurath to summon the heads of the Wehrmacht Supreme Command and Wehrmacht Command Staff, Field Marshal General Wilhelm Keitel and Colonel General Alfred Jodl, to Plön the following day.[47] As April 30, 1945, drew to a close, it was completely unclear what would become of Germany after Hitler.

MAY 1, 1945

Hitler's death did nothing to diminish the intense fighting in Berlin. "May 1 dawned," remembered Colonel Hans Refior, who had taken refuge with his staff inside Wehrmacht headquarters in the Bendlerblock complex. "Artillery thunder rolled over the city from early morning to late evening. Incoming shells howled, and machine-gun fire crackled from the ruins and remnants of buildings, providing, together with intermittent bursts of rifle shots, the terrible soundtrack to the significance of the day."[1]

Early that morning, at 3:50 a.m., General Hans Krebs, Colonel Theodor von Dufving, and an interpreter arrived at Schulenburgring 2 in the Tempelhof district, where General Vasily Chuikov, the commander of the Soviet 8th Guards Army, had his headquarters. With a grave expression, Krebs announced, "You are the first foreigner I am informing of this. On April 30, Hitler voluntarily took leave of us and committed suicide." Chuikov seemed to be unmoved by the sensational news. "We already know that," he lied. Krebs then read out a message from Goebbels to the Soviet commander, confirming that Hitler had taken his own life at 3:30 p.m. on April 30 and had transferred governmental authority to Dönitz, Goebbels, and Bormann. As the new

Reich chancellor, Goebbels was authorized to contact the Soviet leadership to begin negotiations between the two European powers that had suffered the greatest losses in the war.[2]

In sending Krebs on this mission, Goebbels was pursuing an idea he had repeatedly, but previously in vain, suggested to Hitler since the fall of 1943. If Germany could reach a separate peace agreement with Stalin, the propaganda minister speculated, the nation might emerge from the war bruised but not beaten.[3] Goebbels hoped that the conflicts of interest between the western Allies and their Soviet partner would come to a head and that the Soviet leadership might be inclined to desert the anti-Hitler front. If there was any way out after the Führer's death, Goebbels believed, it would be due to an arrangement with the Soviet Union. On the evening of April 30, after the Führer's and his wife's remains had been buried, a lengthy conference had taken place in Hitler's office in the bunker. Also in attendance, along with Goebbels and Bormann, were the army commanders Krebs, Burgdorf, and Weidling, Vice Admiral Hans-Erich Voss, Hewel, and Axmann. It was decided that Krebs, the general chief of staff, would lead the negotiations given that as a former member of Germany's military commission in Moscow, he spoke some Russian.

It took a while to establish a telephone connection to Chuikov's command and then to agree on a time and place for the peace envoys to meet the Soviet side.[4] A nervous Goebbels paced around the situation room. "Previously smoking was not allowed there, but now he lit one cigarette after another," Axmann observed. "Sometimes he whistled one of his favorite songs from the party street-fighting days."[5] The others passed the time drinking coffee and schnapps and discussing in great detail whether it was better to commit suicide or attempt a breakout from the bunker. With Hitler's death a spell seemed to have been broken. Underlings who had been willing to follow the Führer's every command without a second thought, Traudl Junge recalled, suddenly become "autonomously thinking and acting people again."[6]

Not until shortly after midnight did Krebs, Dufving, and the interpreter set out on their arduous journey through the ruins of Berlin. At the prearranged meeting point, they were surrounded by Red Army soldiers, who brought them via numerous intermediary stations to Chuikov's headquarters.[7] The general later described his incredulity on speaking with the German peace envoys: "Did the leaders of the Third Reich really believe that our memories were so short that we had already forgotten the millions of dead and millions upon millions of widows and orphans? The gallows and crematoria? Majdanek and the other death camps?"[8]

Once Krebs had read out Goebbels's message, he presented his authorization to negotiate along with a copy of Hitler's testament listing the leaders of the new German government. But the ensuing discussions left no doubt that the two sides' positions were irreconcilable. In Goebbels's name, the German general chief of staff suggested an immediate ceasefire so that the cabinet members Hitler had named could meet under Dönitz in Berlin to discuss the situation. Afterward, negotiations could commence with the Soviet Union about the surrender of German forces.

Chuikov recognized immediately that the Germans were trying to buy time in hope of driving a wedge between the Soviet Union and its allies. Without any further ado, he declared that the only possibility was neither a ceasefire nor separate negotiations, but rather a total unconditional surrender to the Soviet Union as well as the United States and Britain.[9]

During a break in the talks, Chuikov called Marshal Georgy Zhukov, the commander of the 1st Belarussian Front, and informed him of the situation. Zhukov dispatched his deputy General Vasily Sokolovsky to Chuikov's headquarters and then sent a telegram, which arrived in Moscow at 5:05 a.m., telling Stalin that according to General Krebs, Hitler had ended his life by suicide.[10] A short time later, Zhukov phoned Stalin in his country house near Moscow. The Soviet dictator was still asleep and was irritated at being awakened. "So that's the end of the bastard," Stalin is supposed to have said. "Too bad it was impossible to take him alive." He also reemphasized to Zhukov that no negotiations were to be carried out with Krebs or anyone else about anything short of a total unconditional surrender.[11]

But the two German negotiators were not authorized to assent to an absolute capitulation. With the talks making no progress, it was agreed that Dufving and the interpreter would return to the chancellery to give Goebbels a preliminary report. A Soviet major accompanied them, and when they came under SS fire en route, this officer was seriously wounded. It took hours for Dufving to arrive at the chancellery and relay the news that the Soviets were insisting on immediate unconditional surrender, which Goebbels exclaimed he would "never ever" accept.[12]

Between 1:00 and 2:00 p.m. on May 1, Krebs—completely exhausted from his twelve-hour negotiating marathon—also returned and confirmed that the mission had been an utter failure. Yet again, Goebbels was outraged, fuming, "I am not going to use the final few hours I have left to live as Reich chancellor to sign a capitulation document."[13] For all of those who were not prepared to follow the Goebbels family in committing suicide, the time had come to plan an attempted escape from the bunker.

AT 1:22 A.M. ON THE morning of May 1, as Krebs was making his way to Chuikov's command post, Dönitz sent a radiogram message to the chancellery. Written on the assumption that Hitler was still alive, it was another effusive confirmation of Dönitz's unbroken subordination: "My Führer, my loyalty to you will always be unconditional. I will thus undertake all attempts to relieve you in Berlin. If destiny nonetheless compels me as your chosen successor to lead the German Reich, I will wage this war to the sort of end a unique heroic struggle of the German people demands."[14] Albert Speer, the Reich's armaments minister, had drafted the telegram.[15] He had also sought refuge in the "northern realm" after flying to the embattled capital to see Hitler for a final time, and was thus also present on the evening of April 30 when Bormann's news arrived that Dönitz had been named Hitler's successor. At this point, Speer was unaware that Hitler's testament had dismissed him as armaments minister in favor of his rival Karl-Otto Saur. That was payback for the refusal of Speer—Hitler's former favorite—in the final months of the war to carry out to the letter the Führer's orders to leave nothing behind in Germany but scorched earth.[16]

At 10:53 a.m., as Krebs was still negotiating with Chuikov, the regime in Plön received a second radiogram from Bormann: "Testament is in effect. I will come to you as soon as possible. Until then, not to be made public."[17] Again there was no explicit acknowledgment that Hitler was dead, although the phrase "testament is in effect" allowed for the conclusion that he must no longer be alive. But Bormann was keeping Dönitz in the dark as to when and how the Führer had died. In any case, Bormann seems already to have been convinced that negotiations with the Soviets would come to nothing and was thus preparing to travel to Plön to assume his new office as "party minister" in Dönitz's government. Whereas Goebbels left no doubt as to his intention to stay in Berlin and end his life there, Bormann was determined to save his skin and to continue to play a leading role in the German government.[18]

Once Krebs returned to the chancellery and the idea of a separate arrangement with the Soviets had been definitively buried, Goebbels no longer saw any reason to conceal Hitler's suicide. In a third radiogram sent from the chancellery at 2:46 p.m. and received in Plön at 3:18 p.m., he told Dönitz what had happened: "Führer passed on yesterday at 3:30 p.m. Testament of April 29 bequeaths to you the office of Reich president, to Reich Minister Dr. Goebbels that of Reich chancellor, to Reich Director Bormann that of party minister, and to Reich Minister Seyss-Inquart that of Reich foreign minister. On orders from the Führer, the testament was sent from Berlin to you, to Field Marshal Schörner, and for safekeeping for the general public. Reich Director Bormann will try to reach you today to inform you about the situation. The form and timing of an announcement to the troops and the public is left up to you."[19]

Now that he was certain Hitler was dead, Dönitz no longer felt bound by his oath of loyalty and refused to commit himself to choosing a cabinet. He told his adjutant Lüdde-Neurath to keep Goebbels's radiogram under lock and key and issued a general order that Bormann and Goebbels were to be arrested if they showed their faces in Plön. That at least was what both Dönitz and Speer claimed in their memoirs.[20]

On April 30 Dönitz was already considering whom he could appoint as foreign minister. Initially, he chose Konstantin von Neurath, who had occupied that post in the final two presidentially appointed governments of the Weimar Republic and in the Nazi regime until 1938. But Neurath could not be reached, having fled with his wife and son-in-law Hans-Georg von Mackensen, a former state secretary in the foreign ministry, to their remote hunting lodge in Vorarlberg, Austria. There, on May 6, they would be arrested by a unit of French soldiers. "A gang of dwarflike little African soldiers" surrounded the house, giving the two men only a quarter of an hour to get dressed and pack a knapsack, Neurath's wife would complain. "Our farewell was very difficult, but we kept a stiff upper lip. We didn't want to let this riff-raff see any weakness."[21]

After fruitless attempts to reach the former foreign minister, Dönitz asked Neurath's successor, Joachim von Ribbentrop, who was residing near Plön, if he knew where Neurath was. Ribbentrop was unaware he had been left out of Hitler's testament, which had replaced him as foreign minister with the Reich commissioner for the Netherlands, Arthur Seyss-Inquart. Ribbentrop insisted on a personal meeting with Dönitz. It took place late in the evening on May 1. As Himmler had before him, Ribbentrop offered the admiral his services, but Dönitz rejected him, supposedly saying, "He's too stupid for my liking."[22] Instead Dönitz decided to entrust the office of foreign minister to Count Lutz Schwerin von Krosigk, the longtime finance minister, who had survived all changes in government since Franz von Papen's 1932 "cabinet of barons" and had been confirmed in his post by Hitler's testament. Dönitz considered him a technocrat relatively unsullied by association with Nazism who might be better able to initiate contact with Germany's enemies. He knew there were "no laurels to be reaped" from the post of foreign minister, Dönitz told Krosigk, but he "needed a man who could advise him politically during the decisions to come." Krosigk asked for some time to think the matter over and ultimately accepted the office the following day.[23]

Originally, Dönitz had intended to make changes at the top of the Wehrmacht Supreme Command. The head of the OKW, Wilhelm Keitel, was generally mocked as a lackey for his subservience to Hitler, and Dönitz would have liked to replace him with Field Marshal Erich von Manstein, whom Hitler had dismissed from that post in late March 1944. But after Alfred Jodl, the Wehrmacht's chief of operations staff, threatened to quit his post should Keitel be fired, the admiral relented and left things as they were.[24]

Dönitz also rejected the idea of an immediate, unconditional surrender on all fronts. He saw his main task as to continue the war on the eastern front long enough to allow as many soldiers and refugees as possible to escape capture by the Red Army. To achieve this goal, he wanted to end the fighting in the west as quickly as he could, although again he still thought in terms of a partial surrender of individual army groups and not a complete capitulation.[25] Dönitz expressed this intention in the radio address he gave on the evening of May 1 in which he announced to the nation that Hitler was dead.

Between 9:00 and 10:25 p.m., the state radio station in Hamburg and its subsidiaries in Flensburg and Bremen proclaimed that a major piece of news was to be broadcast three times, with selections from Wagner's operas *Tannhäuser*, *Das Rheingold*, and *Die Götterdämmerung* and Bruckner's Seventh Symphony aired in between. Each time the music suddenly broke off, there was a drum roll, and an agitated speaker said, "There are reports from the Führer's headquarters that our Führer Adolf Hitler fell this afternoon in his command center in the Reich chancellery fighting until his last breath against Bolshevism. On April 30, the Führer had named Grand Admiral Dönitz as his successor."[26] The German public was given false information about not just the time but also the circumstances of Hitler's death. Covering up Hitler's suicide concealed the reality that through the act he had evaded responsibility for the regime's crimes.

Dönitz repeated the lie when it was his turn to speak. In its tone and diction, his speech was entirely in keeping with the fanatic declarations of loyalty with which the Hitler-worshipping grand admiral exhorted his navy seamen to hold out in the final weeks of the war. "German men and women, soldiers of the German Wehrmacht!" Dönitz said. "Our Führer Adolf Hitler has fallen. The German people bow their heads with the greatest sadness and respect. Early on, he recognized the terrible danger of Bolshevism and devoted his life to combating it. At the end of this, his struggle and his unflinching adherence to his life's path, was his heroic death in the capital of the German Reich. His life was one long act of service for Germany. His efforts in the fight against the flood of Bolshevism were directed on behalf of Europe and the entire cultured world as well."[27]

Dönitz did not just adopt the myth of Hitler's "heroic death." He also voiced without reservation a core element of Goebbels's propaganda, the lie that Germany's war of annihilation against the Soviet Union was a crusade for Europe and the whole of human civilization. Invoking the specter of Bolshevism, Dönitz also justified his refusal to end the war immediately: "My first task is to save Germans from destruction by the advancing Bolshevik enemy. It is only for this purpose that the military battle is continuing. As long as the British and Americans hinder us from reaching this goal, we will also defend ourselves against them and keep fighting. The Anglo-Americans are no longer fighting the war for their own people but to spread Bolshevism in Europe." Dönitz essentially tried to shift blame for the continuation of the war in the west to the British and Americans. Just as Goebbels had sought to use a separate arrangement with the Soviets to drive a wedge into the anti-Hitler coalition, Dönitz was obviously attempting to exploit the differences between the Allies in order to avoid an unconditional surrender.

Dönitz had no qualms about extolling the senseless sacrifice of soldiers and civilians in a criminal war, saying, "What the German people achieved in launching the struggle of this war and on the home front is unique in history." Dönitz promised that as far as he was able to do so, he would "create tolerable conditions of life" for the "brave women, men and children" of Germany and even suggested that God would be on their side: "If we do everything in our power, the Lord our God will not desert us after so much suffering and sacrifice."

When Dönitz had finished speaking, the German national anthem, the "Deutschlandlied," was played, followed by the hymn of National Socialism, the "Horst-Wessel-Lied." Then came three minutes of silence that gave way to mournful music, including Beethoven's *Eroica*. The radio broadcast concluded in the small hours of May 2 with the words, "We send a German greeting out to our listeners in Germany and abroad, our soldiers on the seas, on the battlefields, and in the air: Heil Hitler."[28]

Dönitz's first daily orders to the Wehrmacht on May 1 had touched on the same themes as his radio address. In them, he pledged to "continue the battle against the Bolsheviks as long as it takes for the fighting troops and hundreds of thousands of families from the eastern German realms to be saved from enslavement and destruction." He would only continue to fight the Americans and the British insofar as they hindered Germany in these aims. As Germany's new head of state and commander in chief, Dönitz demanded "uncompromising commitment," adding that the oath of loyalty sworn to Hitler applied "with no restrictions" to himself as Hitler's chosen successor.[29]

The writer Erich Kästner, who together with his colleagues from the German film company Ufa had sought refuge from the fighting in Berlin in the Tyrolean valley Zillertal, recorded in his diary the effect Dönitz's address had on him and those around him. Kästner deemed the words of the new German head of state "an act of desperation," adding, "He wants to beat back the Bolshevist tide while merely shadowboxing with the western Allies, if that indeed is what they want. The man cranking the organ may have changed. But it still plays the same old song. People jokingly say 'Heil Dönitz!' when they see one another. The new head of state expects the troops to abide by the same oath they swore to the Führer and apply it to his designated successor as well. Solely in terms of numbers, that will be difficult. Since the [1944 Allied] invasion, 3 million men and 150 generals have been taken prisoner. The disoriented, retreating remnants face imminent captivity too. The oath is becoming a solitary one."[30]

The reaction among the German military commanders held as POWs in the Trent Park estate in Cockfosters, London, was similar. Dönitz was a "stupid ass" and a "charlatan"; his cabinet would be "here today, gone tomorrow"; and his speech had sounded like something from "Hitler junior," they scoffed. How could "any reasonable person in possession of his senses" produce such nonsense and depict Hitler as "the purest of angels," knowing full well how the Führer had treated his military commanders? Although Dönitz had no real power behind him, he was still "playing the role of emperor." POWs asked sarcastically, "Are we supposed to say 'Heil Dönitz' now?" In their eyes, the new head of state had "no legitimacy whatsoever to lead and speak for others."[31]

Dönitz's speech was "extremely weak," noted the Berlin journalist and Hitler opponent Ursula von Kardorff, who had fled the capital for the southern German village Jettingen near Augsburg in February. "So this is the moment I've been desperately longing for all these years, the one I've prayed with all my heart would come. And now! When they played the Deutschlandlied, I got choked up for the first time in many years. Is it sentimentality?"[32]

Speer was also in a sentimental mood after the radio broadcast, if his memoirs are to be believed. Late that evening, he placed on his desk a small, personally dedicated portrait of Hitler that the dictator had given him six weeks previously for his fortieth birthday, and a "fit of weeping" overcame him: "That was the end of my relationship with Hitler. Only now was his spell broken, the magic extinguished. . . . I fell into a deep, exhausted sleep."[33] But Speer's relationship with the Führer, whom he had once so admired, was by no means over. On the contrary, he now redoubled his efforts, ongoing since February, to obscure his status as one of Hitler's most powerful associates and his participation in the Nazis' crimes against humanity.[34]

William L. Shirer, the American newspaper correspondent in Berlin who had left Germany in December 1940, received word of Hitler's death in San Francisco, where the founding conference of the United Nations had been meeting since April 24. He considered Dönitz's address a "fitting end" to Hitler's reign: "The whole Hitler regime, the whole Hitler legend, were built on lies. Now lies surround him in death. His successor, like him, wallows in them."[35]

Like Shirer, Thomas Mann, from his Californian exile, very much doubted the account of Hitler's death Dönitz had put out into the world. "Fallen as a hero in the fight against Bolshevism . . . the whole thing very suspicious and dubious," Mann wrote in his diary on May 1, adding that the "most probable thing" was Hitler having committed suicide.[36] The Nobel Prize winner had been a fan of Sebastian Haffner's book *Germany: Jekyll and Hyde*, which had appeared in English in the spring of 1940 and described Hitler as "the potential suicide par excellence."[37]

INFORMING DÖNITZ OF Hitler's death was in a sense Goebbels's last official act, and he now began preparing himself for his own end. Alongside Hitler, the propaganda minister had expended enormous effort in the final months of the war to stage for posterity the apocalyptic finale of the Third Reich as a heroic struggle to the very end. Both men repeatedly invoked the example of Frederick the Great. Just as the Prussian king had held out against an overpowering coalition in the Seven Years War, Germany would never capitulate—and perhaps it would ultimately turn the tide. "The Führer agrees with me completely, when I say to him that our ambition should be to ensure that in 150 years our grandchildren are able to cite the heroic example of our persistence, should a comparably great crisis befall Germany," Goebbels wrote.[38]

The final issue of the *Panzerbär*—the "Fighting Newspaper for the Defenders of Greater Berlin"—published on April 29, 1945, had spoken of a "great struggle unique in history."[39] Goebbels had stressed more than once that he would stay by his Führer's side in Berlin and follow him with his own family into death should there be no other way out. In his "Supplement to the Führer's Political Testament," dictated on the night of April 29 to Traudl Junge, he explained why for the first time in his life he would potentially have to disobey a command from Hitler—the order "to leave Berlin in the event of a collapse of the city's defenses and to take part as a leading member of a designated Reich government." For the rest of his life, Goebbels wrote, he would feel like "a dishonorable traitor and a common scoundrel" if he were to desert Hitler in his hour of greatest need: "In the delirium of betrayal that surrounds the Führer in these critical days, there must at least be a few men who stand by his side unconditionally and until death."[40]

In his few remaining hours on the afternoon of May 1, Goebbels seems to have brought his diary, which he had abruptly discontinued on April 10, to a conclusion, writing his parting message for history. He gave what he had written to his deputy Werner Naumann, whom Hitler had named Goebbels's successor, with the request that it be taken out of Berlin. But in the confusion of people fleeing the bunker, Goebbels's final written words were lost.[41]

While Goebbels was issuing some last orders, his wife, Magda, was preparing their children—five daughters ranging in age from twelve to four and their nine-year-old son—for their deaths. They had moved into the bunker with their parents on April 22, and Magda rejected all attempts by those who remained in the subterranean catacombs to persuade her to spare her children. Indeed, she fully backed her husband's decision. "My wife and I are in agreement that our children should follow us into death," Joseph Goebbels told Axmann. "We don't want them to see their father dragged through the international scandal sheets."[42]

Late in the afternoon of May 1, the telephone operator Rochus Misch watched Magda Goebbels with her children. She draped each of them in long, white sleeping gowns and spoke to them in soothing tones. Only her oldest daughter, twelve-year-old Helga, suspected what was about to happen and started crying.[43] Magda then summoned Helmut Kunz, an adjutant to the head physician in the SS hospital administration who had promised several days previously to help her kill her children, and told him that the decision had been made. He had offered to shelter the children in the sick bay under the New Chancellery building and hand them over to the protection of the Red Cross, but their father, Germany's chancellor for one day, arrived and brusquely dismissed the suggestion: "That won't work—they're the children of Goebbels!"[44]

In the antechamber to their apartment in the bunker, Magda Goebbels gave Kunz a syringe filled with morphine. "Then we entered the children's room," Kunz testified on May 7 during his first interrogation by the Soviet intelligence service SMERSH. "The children were already lying in bed, but they weren't asleep yet. Frau Goebbels told them: 'Children, have no fear. The doctor is going to give you a shot all children and soldiers are getting now.'" Over eight to ten minutes, Kunz injected all the children. As he remembered it, when he finished, the time was 8:20 p.m. He left the room and waited with Magda Goebbels until the children had fallen asleep for good.

In his first interrogation, Kunz testified that after around ten minutes Magda Goebbels had reentered the room in his presence and placed a crushed cyanide capsule in each of her children's mouths. When questioned again on May 19, he changed his story. Magda Goebbels, he now said, had asked him to administer the poison, but he had not been able to gather the necessary "psychological strength." Thereupon Magda had summoned Hitler's attending physician, Ludwig Stumpfegger, who apparently accepted the sad task of poisoning the children.[45]

Once the deed was done, Magda and Kunz returned to the deeper recesses of the bunker, where Goebbels was anxiously awaiting them. There was no time to lose. The first Red Army soldiers could appear in the Reich chancellery at any minute. Goebbels made his adjutant Günther Schwägermann promise to have his and his wife's bodies burned. Even in death, Hitler's head propagandist, who more than any other person had been responsible for inventing and popularizing the Führer mythology, wanted to emulate his great idol. Goebbels then took leave of those who remained in the bunker and who were furiously preparing to leave. "Perhaps you'll make it through," he told Junge with a crooked smile. Meanwhile he instructed Hitler's pilot Baur that if the latter succeeded in reaching Dönitz, he was to tell the admiral "that we knew not only how to live and fight but how to die as well."[46]

"Les jeux sont fait"—the game is up. Those were Goebbels's last words, spoken to Misch before he was relieved of his duties. Misch recalled a feeling of "salvation" and immediately pulled all the cables from the switchboard: "I practically tore them out, yanking them back fiercely, with a cable in each hand. Right, left, right, left. I couldn't do it fast enough. I didn't forget a single connection. . . . There was a coil of cable on the switchboard console. It was the last one. Over and out."[47]

There have been conflicting accounts of how Joseph and Magda Goebbels committed suicide. In Hugh Trevor-Roper's *The Last Days of Hitler*, published in 1947, which was based primarily on statements by Schwägermann, the couple ascended the stairs to the bunker's entrance and had an SS soldier shoot them in the Reich chancellery courtyard.[48] By contrast, Hitler's valet, Heinz Linge, and Hitler's adjutant, Otto Günsche, testified, as Russian POWs, that Goebbels and his wife shot themselves in the bunker.[49] Both stories were false. An examination of the Goebbels's bodies by Soviet physicians on May 7 and 9, 1945, found splinters of glass from crushed cyanide capsules in their mouths.[50] After poisoning their children, they had poisoned themselves. It is possible that to be on the safe side, Goebbels had ordered members of the SS to put a bullet in their heads after he and his wife had bitten down on the capsules. Investigators found two gunpowder-stained Walther pistols near the heads of the bodies.[51]

In British captivity in the Libyan port of Benghazi, Harald Quandt—Magda Goebbels's son from her first marriage to the industrialist Herbert Quandt—learned via the BBC about the deaths of his mother, stepfather, and half-siblings. There is no record of his reaction, but he is known during his time as a POW to have distanced himself from his stepfather. Nonetheless, that did not prevent him from later giving jobs in his family business to people with National Socialist pasts, including Goebbels's deputy, Naumann, who in the early 1950s along with other unrepentant fascists tried to infiltrate the business-friendly, individual rights–oriented Free Democratic Party in postwar West Germany's most populous regional state, North Rhine-Westphalia.[52]

"BREAK-OUT ATTEMPT" READ THE last entry in Martin Bormann's pocket calendar, from the evening of May 1.[53] While Joseph and Magda

Goebbels were readying themselves for suicide, the rest of the bunker's denizens were preparing to flee. Almost to a person, they had only one thing on their minds: how to get out of the bunker alive and make their way through Russian lines. Hitler's closest followers destroyed their identity papers to conceal who they were in case of arrest. Many ripped their insignias of rank from their uniforms. Equipped with pistols and steel helmets, like footsoldiers in the field, they waited for darkness.[54]

The commander of the "citadel," Wilhelm Mohnke, drew up the escape plan. Divided into groups that would leave the basement of the New Chancellery building at intervals of a few minutes, they would sneak across Wilhelmplatz to the Kaiserhof subway station and trek through the tunnel under Russian lines to Friedrichstrasse station. There they would join up with the remnants of Mohnke's forces and try to cross the Spree River and get to the Stettin train station, from there leaving Berlin for the northwest in an attempt to link up with German units still capable of fighting.[55]

Shortly after 10:00 p.m., Mohnke led the first group out. It included Günsche, Hewel, Vice Admiral Voss, Hitler's secretaries Christian and Junge, Bormann's secretary Else Krüger, and Hitler's nutritionist Constanze Manziarly. Bormann, Stumpfegger, and Bauer joined the third group, which was led by Naumann. Among the notable figures who departed the bunker after that were Linge, Hitler's chauffeur Erich Kempka, Schwägermann, the leader of the Reich Security Service Johann Rattenhuber, and Axmann.[56] Krebs, Burgdorf, and the commander of the SS Escort Command of the Führer, Franz Schädle, chose to commit suicide rather than flee—apparently because they thought the latter option had so little hope of success.

Indeed, Mohnke's plan quickly proved unworkable. The groups scattered in the darkness of the subway tunnels, in which countless wounded people, soldiers, and civilians alike had taken refuge. When the first individuals from the bunker reached Friedrichstrasse, they found themselves in a truly dangerous situation. Fighting was still

Soviet soldiers in the "marble gallery" of the New Reich Chancellery
in Berlin in early May 1945.

fierce, fires smoldered everywhere, and Russian sharpshooters targeted
anything that moved. Amid the inferno, the groups of fleeing Hitler
associates dwindled in number, until in the end every person was on
his or her own. "For hours, we crawled through filthy cellars, burning
buildings and unfamiliar, dark streets," wrote Junge two years later,
while memories of the events were still fresh. "Somewhere in an abandoned basement we stopped to rest and slept for a couple of hours.
Then we continued until Russian tanks blocked our path. . . . The
night passed, and in the morning everything was still. The shooting
had stopped. . . . Finally we arrived at an old beer cellar of a brewery. . . . This was our final station."[57]

Only a handful of Hitler's associates—Kempka, Naumann,
Schwägermann, Axmann, Junge, and Christian—succeeded in escaping Berlin. Manziarly disappeared without a trace. Most of the others, including Baur, Linge, Günsche, Voss, Rattenhuber, and Misch,
were captured by the Russians. Others, such as Hewel, Bormann, and

Stumpfegger, escaped capture by killing themselves. The skeletons of the latter two were found in December 1972 when excavation work was being carried out at the Lehrte train station in West Berlin. Both had taken cyanide. Bormann's remains were cremated in April 1999, and his ashes were scattered over the Baltic Sea.[58]

SOMETIME ON MAY 1, a teacher from the town of Demmin noted in her diary, "Suicides driven mad questioning the sense of life."[59] Behind these brief words was a tragedy that was for decades shrouded in a mantle of silence in Communist East Germany and that has only recently become part of Germany's collective historical memory. Nowhere did more people commit suicide in Germany in early May 1945 than in Demmin, a small Hanseatic city in the northeast on the Peene River. Until shortly before the end of the war, it had been spared aerial bombardments. While sirens had repeatedly forced the town's fifteen thousand inhabitants into air-raid shelters, Allied bomber squadrons had always flown on to drop their deadly payloads on Stettin (today Szeczin), Anklam, or Berlin. But starting in January 1945, constant streams of refugees began making their way through the city. Many private dwellings and public buildings were crammed full of newly homeless people resting for a bit during their arduous treks to the west.

In late April 1945, with the Red Army approaching, the party and state functionaries who had always demanded that their fellow Germans hold out until "final victory" was secured became the first to turn tail and flee. Nor did the Wehrmacht units stationed in and around Demmin think for a moment about applying slogans about a "heroic downfall" to themselves. They hastily deserted the city after demolishing the bridges across the Peene and its tributaries, the Trebel and Tollense. That had fatal consequences for those left behind, whose route to the west was now blocked. Residents who had not fled in time were trapped along with hundreds of refugees. All they could do was fearfully wait for Soviet troops to arrive.

Their fear was justified. Many people had heard stories about the crimes the Wehrmacht and the SS had committed in occupied areas of the Soviet Union. Hitler and his generals had always conceived of Operation Barbarossa, the German invasion of Soviet territory that had begun on June 22, 1941, as a war of annihilation in which large portions of the civilian population were to be murdered or enslaved. In the first months of the campaign, hundreds of thousands of Soviet POWs had been allowed to starve to death. Almost a million residents of Leningrad had died during Germany's siege of the city from 1941 to 1944. Millions of young Soviet men and women had been taken as "eastern workers," brought to the Third Reich and forced into slave labor. During their retreat on the eastern front beginning in 1943, German soldiers had applied a scorched-earth strategy, leaving behind nothing that could be of value to the enemy. Entire regions had been transformed into "dead zones."[60]

In October 1944, Red Army troops advanced into East Prussia and thus for the first time into the Reich proper. Everywhere they had gone, they had seen the aftermath of German troops' destructive frenzy. Almost every Red Army soldier had lost family members. Their hatred for the fanatical invaders and their thirst for revenge were further stoked by Soviet propaganda and put into action during a first wave of violence, of which the village of Nemmersdorf became a symbol. There, German soldiers who reconquered the town found traces of a massacre that had claimed the lives of numerous citizens, predominantly elderly men and women.[61]

Goebbels had exploited the massacre in a major propaganda campaign, releasing pictures of the bodies to newspapers and weekly newsreels. The idea, as he noted in his diary on October 26, was to show the German populace what they could expect "if Bolshevism in fact got hold of the Reich."[62] In late October 1944, the Wehrmacht succeeded in pushing the Red Army back beyond the Reich's borders, but the German military did not have enough men in reserve to resist the major offensive launched by the Soviets on January 12, 1945. Within three weeks, Soviet troops advanced five hundred kilometers westward, liberating the parts of Poland that Germany had occupied and annexed and seizing the majority of eastern Germany. The violence that had characterized the Red Army's first incursion into East Prussia returned. The pitiless war of extermination the Wehrmacht and the SS had conducted against the Soviet Union now created a backlash the civilian German population was forced to endure. "May the German mother curse the day she bore a son!" wrote one Red Army soldier from Tiraspol in western Ukraine to his family on January 30, 1945. "May German women now feel the terrors of war! May they now experience what they wanted to inflict on other peoples!"[63] Those who had been unable to flee to the west bore the brunt of Soviet retributions. Accounts of atrocities spread like wildfire, and the people who remained behind in Demmin knew only too well what was in store as they waited for the first Red Army soldiers to appear.

April 30 was a bright, clear spring day. That morning the thunder of artillery could be heard, and the sounds of approaching tanks grew louder and louder. Residents of Demmin and refugees sought shelter in basements. Women blackened their face with ashes and wrapped their heads in torn bandages to make themselves as unattractive as possible. A handful of citizens braved potential repercussions and hung white sheets and towels from their windows as a sign the city would surrender without a fight. A vanguard of two Soviet tank brigades reached the southern edge of town before noon, where they found the destroyed bridges, which prevented them from quickly pressing on toward Rostock as originally planned. By midday, tanks and other vehicles were backed up into the city's historic center. By afternoon, following two brief gun battles, Demmin was completely in the hands of Soviet troops. Twenty-one city residents had already taken their own lives before the soldiers arrived.

After darkness fell, the true nightmare began. "The tanks, armored

personnel carriers, trucks and huge amounts of military hardware had
transformed the city into a seething army camp," writes historian and
documentary filmmaker Florian Huber in his depiction of events in
Demmin. "Hundreds of soldiers, halted in the middle of their march to
victory, swarmed out looking for watches, jewelry, schnapps, women,
and opportunities for sex and violence. . . . In addition to their feelings
of triumph over the Nazis, Soviet soldiers were celebrating May Day.
That night the first buildings in Demmin were burned down."[64] The
town's closely huddled beam-and-mortar houses fed the flames, which
continued for several days, largely destroying the historic city center.

Much worse was the terror inflicted by marauding, often drunk Red
Army soldiers. Hundreds of women and girls were raped, a number of
residents murdered, and many dwellings plundered. These actions were
followed by an act of mass suicide, the dimensions of which exceeded
anything that transpired in other German cities and towns in the final
days of the war. Collective panic—a kind of mass hysteria—seemed
to seize the city's population, with whole families ending their own
lives. Huber writes, "Among the dead were infants and small children,
schoolkids and adolescents, young men and women, affluent couples,
people in the prime of life, pensioners and the extremely aged. There
was no pattern to the suicides' backgrounds, careers, and social status.
The victims included hundreds of refugees from Pomerania, East and
West Prussia, and other regions in addition to hundreds of people from
Demmin and the surrounding area. They were laborers and white-
collar workers, state officials and artisans, doctors and apothecaries,
wives and widows, merchants and policemen, bosses and bookkeep-
ers, pensioners and teachers. . . . The suicides of Demmin were a cross-
section of small-city life in German society."[65]

Those who were able ingested poison or put a bullet in their brain.
Others slit their wrists or hanged themselves. The greatest number
however, drowned themselves. Women filled knapsacks with rocks,
tied their children's and their own hands together at the wrists, and

waded into the water. Weeks later, corpses were still floating in the waters of the Peene and its tributaries.

There are various estimates of the number of people who committed suicide in Demmin. An improvised registry begun on May 6 by the daughter of a cemetery gardener contained the names of 612 people, of whom 400 killed themselves. In November 1945, the regional council of the area around Demmin put the number of suicides at 700, and eyewitnesses spoke of more than 1,000.[66] A stone in the Demmin cemetery commemorates them. It bears as an inscription the note in the teacher's diary: "Suicides driven mad questioning the sense of life."

The mass suicides of Demmin were a unique event. Nonetheless, the chaos of the end of the war prompted people in many places across Germany to take their lives in what can accurately be called a "suicide epidemic."[67] It was not always fear of the Red Army that drove people to desperation. Leading Nazi functionaries and highly decorated Wehrmacht officers were not the only ones who had surrendered themselves to the mythology of the Führer and the norms of his regime. Many ordinary Germans could no longer imagine a life without Hitler and National Socialism. Suicide seemed to them the only solution to a situation in which defeat was inevitable and a future for themselves and their families was impossible to envision. The SS Security Service was already reporting in March 1945, "Many people are getting used to the idea of killing themselves. The demand for poison, pistols, and other means of ending one's own life is great everywhere. Suicides born of desperation at the catastrophe certain to come are the order of the day."[68] Many Germans experienced the imminent end of the war as an apocalypse and saw it as the complete collapse of a social order that had given their lives structure and a foundation. Along with a collective loss of faith in the future, anxiety over the fate of family members provided a common motivation for suicide. The suicide rate among refugees from eastern parts of Germany, many of whom had left their families behind, was notably high. The number of suicides in western Germany also rose, albeit not nearly as dramatically as in eastern regions, where hopelessness and grief over what had been lost mixed with terror of the Soviets.

"WHEN WE ARRIVED IN Berlin, you could barely find a path through the ruins for all the smoke," recalled Communist leader Walter Ulbricht about returning to the German capital on May 1.[69] Ulbricht headed a contingent of ten Communist functionaries from Moscow, the so-called Ulbricht Group, who were charged with assisting the Soviet occupiers. Berlin was familiar terrain for the fifty-one-year-old trained carpenter. From 1929 to 1932, Ulbricht had been a secretary of the German Communist Party (Kommunistische Partei Deutschlands, or KPD) regional leadership in Berlin and Brandenburg and was thus well acquainted with the labor movement in the city. He had left Germany in 1933 for Paris and Prague, heading in late January 1938 to Moscow. When he arrived in the Soviet capital, Stalin's purges were still in full swing, and leading German Communists who had fled the Third Reich for the Soviet Union got caught up in the machinery of persecution. Of the nine members and candidates of the KPD's Politburo in 1932–33, five were murdered, two died of natural causes, and only two survived Stalin's secret police, the NKVD (People's Commissariat for Internal Affairs): Ulbricht and party chair Wilhelm Pieck.[70]

It took special skills to survive the waves of purges, and Ulbricht possessed them in abundance. He was a classic emotionless apparatchik who subjugated himself without resistance to Stalin's domination and supported all Stalinist changes in policy. "He was characterized by a certain pragmatic cleverness, an instinct that allowed him to anticipate Soviet changes in the political line and adapt to them," Ulbricht Group member Wolfgang Leonhard recalled. "He had no scruples about enforcing Soviet orders, at times showing cunning, severity, and ruthlessness toward his own comrades."[71] These were precisely the qualities that made Ulbricht particularly suited to playing a leading role in the postwar order in the Soviet occupation zone, which later became the Communist German Democratic Republic (GDR).

Ever since July 1943 and the tank battle at Kursk, when the Wehrmacht had been put on the defensive and the initiative had passed once and for all to the Red Army, German Communists exiled in Moscow had begun preparing for the end of the war. In February 1944, the KPD leadership under Pieck, Ulbricht, and Communist functionary Anton Ackermann created a "working commission for political problems," which was intended to determine the basic plan for rebuilding postwar Germany. The result of their discussions was an "action program for battle-ready democracy," produced in October 1944. It called for, among other things, the immediate "arrest and conviction of the Nazi murderers and warmongers for their crimes against their own and other peoples"; a "fundamental cleansing of the entire state apparatus and local administrations of all fascist elements"; the "commencement of reparation measures to other peoples, particularly the Soviet one, for damage done during the war"; and the "energetic development of a true democracy that guarantees the civic liberty of all members of the people without regard to origin, class, race and religion."[72]

But the KPD leadership in exile was hardly free to make its own decisions. Indeed, they were always required to balance their ideas with the interests of their Soviet bosses. The role of mediator was played by Georgi Dimitrov, the former general secretary of the Executive Committee of the Communist International, who since December 1943 had been the director of the Division for International Intelligence (foreign department) of the central committee of the Communist Party of the Soviet Union. Stalin's wishes were clear. The Soviet dictator assumed that a long period of occupation would follow Nazi Germany's defeat. He did not consider the immediate introduction of socialism in the Soviet occupation zone either possible or desirable. On the contrary, it was the task of antifascist forces to pave the way for a bourgeois-democratic restructuring that would in a sense continue and complete the German revolution of 1848. At this point, Stalin did not push for the division of Germany and the establishment of a separate Communist satellite state. He wanted to secure his influence over Germany as a whole and did not want to alienate the western Allies by openly encouraging regional Communist rule in Germany's east.[73]

Parallel to its preliminary work on protocols for rebuilding Germany, the KPD leadership made plans for German exiles in the Soviet Union to return to their home nation. In July 1944, in view of the "fact that the Red Army will soon be on German territory," Pieck suggested to Dimitrov that "large cadres be sent to the country to organize the struggle of Hitler opponents."[74] That August, at Dimitrov's behest, Pieck drew up a list of comrades to be considered for the task. To prepare them for their mission in Germany, the KPD leadership set up training courses, in which twenty-five to thirty German participants were schooled in the ABCs of Marxism-Leninism and the general line of the Soviet Communist Party.[75]

Following the Yalta Conference in February 1945, which confirmed the Allies' decision to divide Germany into occupation zones, ideas about how the Communist cadres should be deployed took more concrete form. They were to be transported in small groups to occupied territories and subordinated to the Main Political Administration of the Red Army (PUR). These groups were explicitly charged with assisting occupation authorities. In a later second phase they would be given "expanded tasks," such as rebuilding the KPD.[76] Accordingly, the guidelines the KPD agreed on in early April 1945 read, "The antifascists active in occupied German areas will work in complete conjunction with the occupation authorities, and their work will ensure among the populace that the orders and instructions of the occupation authorities will be unconditionally carried out in the interest of the German people."[77]

By mid-April thirty cadres were selected for assignment to the commands of the three Soviet armies, the 1st and 2nd Belarussian Fronts and the Ukrainian Front.[78] Leading the way was the Ulbricht Group, which was to be deployed to follow Zhukov's 1st Belarussian Front as it bore down on Berlin. The cadre comprised a number of functionaries who would later occupy high offices in the GDR, including Karl Maron, editor of the newspaper *Free Germany* in Moscow and later deputy editor in chief of the main organ of the East German Socialist Unity Party (Sozialistische Einheitspartei Deutschlands, or SED), *New Germany*; Otto Winzer, a longtime member of the Communist International and later the East German foreign minister, who was the head of the private chancellery of Pieck as the president of the GDR; Richard Gyptner, another longtime member of the Comintern apparatus in Moscow and later the main departmental director in the GDR foreign ministry and an ambassador to numerous countries; Hans Mahle, deputy editor in chief of the Free Germany broadcaster, who in the summer of 1945 was named the first chair of the Berliner Rundfunk broadcaster and who was, until he was dismissed in 1951, the general director of all broadcasters in the Soviet occupation zone and the GDR; and Fritz Erpenbeck, who worked at the Free Germany broadcaster and was later the editor in chief of the *Theater des Tages* (Theater of the Day) newspaper and the head dramaturg at Berlin's Volksbühne theater. The youngest member of the group was twenty-four-year-old Wolfgang (Wladimir) Leonhard, a graduate of the Comintern Academy and a broadcaster for the Soviet-based, German-language radio station Free Germany. In 1949, he would break with Stalinism and flee to West Germany via Yugoslavia. His book *Die Revolution entlässt ihre Kinder* (The Revolution Dismisses Its Children) is one of the most important sources of information about the Ulbricht Group's activities and the rise of the GDR.[79]

On April 25, the German Communists had a final meeting with Dimitrov. Once again it was stressed that in going about their work they were to obey instructions from the PUR. While they were allowed to make suggestions, they were not to undertake any initiatives on their own. They were dispatched with the commands, "Destroy the legend that the Red Army wants to annihilate and enslave the German people." Hitler was done for and would be killed. The German people would be allowed to exist but would have to learn how to be peaceful members of the international community.[80]

As Leonhard reported about their final days in Moscow, "Ulbricht didn't seem impressed or happy at all—at least if he was, he didn't show it. He spoke to us as though it were the most natural thing in the world to be returning to Germany after so many years."[81] Each member of the group was given a thousand rubles to purchase necessities in Moscow and two thousand rubles to cover initial expenses in Germany. On the evening of April 29, there was a small farewell celebration in Pieck's room at the Hotel Lux, the home of the international Communist movement in the center of Moscow, where almost every night during the Great Purge Stalin's secret police had apprehended people and taken them to the dungeons of the infamous Lubyanka Building prison.

At 6:00 a.m. the following morning, the Ulbricht Group gathered in a side street near the hotel and took a bus to Moscow Airport. An American-made Douglas transport plane was waiting for them there. After a short stop in Minsk, the aircraft landed in the early evening at a provisional landing strip not far from Calau (Calewa today) around seventy kilometers east of Frankfurt an der Oder. The group was met by a Soviet officer and brought to their quarters for the night. On the morning of May 1, the journey westward continued by car via Küstrin (Kostrzyn) and the battlefields of the Seelow Heights. Only two weeks before, they had been the scene of incredibly fierce fighting, after which Zhukov's army overran the last German line of defense before Berlin. The convoy of vehicles stopped in the small village of Bruchmühle near Strausberg some thirty kilometers east of Berlin, where the main political division of the 1st Belarussian Front had its headquarters. The Ulbricht Group was shown to a three-story building, the so-called Pillar House. It was to be their domicile until Germany's unconditional surrender on May 8, when they moved to Berlin's Friedrichsfelde district.[82]

On the evening of May 1, Ulbricht returned from an initial brief foray into Berlin, relating his impressions and announcing the agenda for the coming days. "It will be our task to build organs of self-administration in Berlin," he said. "We will go to the various Berlin districts and select from the antifascist-democratic forces those who are suitable for the establishment of a new German administration."[83]

There had been much speculation that the first of May would lead to a "great festival of fraternity between German and Soviet Communists," but there was no sign of anything like that taking place, noted Norwegian columnist Theo Findahl, who was in Berlin. "In the evenings, you see soldiers intoxicated by a mixture of victory and alcohol saunter down Podbielskiallee, yelling and looking for 'young women.'"[84]

THAT SAME EVENING, a group of socialists who had dubbed themselves the "Small International" convened in Stockholm to celebrate the international day of the labor movement with their Swedish comrades. Among the one hundred or so participants was a thirty-one-year-old by the name of Willy Brandt. Born Herbert Frahm in Lübeck in 1913, Brandt had joined the Social Democrats (Sozialdemokratische Partei Deutschlands, or SPD) at the age of sixteen but had quit the party two years later in October 1931 to protest its tolerance of the conservative Brüning government. He became a member of the Social Workers' Party of Germany (Sozialistische Arbeiterpartei, or SAP), a left-wing splinter group. In April 1933, Willy Brandt—originally a pseudonym—fled Nazi Germany on a fishing boat, landing first in Denmark, then in the Norwegian capital Oslo after learning Norwegian astonishingly quickly. There he worked as a journalist for an SPD organization in exile and authored numerous articles for newspapers connected with the Norwegian labor movement, which tried to inform people about current developments in Nazi Germany. In November 1940, when the Wehrmacht invaded Norway, Brandt was forced to flee again, this time to Stockholm. His experiences in Swedish exile stayed with him his entire life. In the free atmosphere of the Norwegian and Swedish Social Democratic movements, he distanced himself from the dogmatic positions of his early years, going from young revolutionary socialist to pragmatic left-wing Social Democrat, a process essential to his meteoric postwar career that saw him become the leader of the Berlin SPD and in 1969 the chancellor of West Germany.[85]

As the festivities were drawing to a close on May 1, 1945, Brandt hastened up to the speaker's podium and read out a resolution: "We socialist refugees would like to thank the Swedish labor movement and the Swedish people for the hospitality we've been shown. We also want to express our gratitude for the help Sweden has provided for victims of the war." But while he was speaking, he was handed a news agency report, which he immediately shared with the other guests: "Dear friends, it can only be a matter of days now. Hitler has evaded responsibility by committing suicide." He concluded with the words, "We will be parting from one another with profound emotion."[86]

Brandt would not return to German soil until November 1945, when the Norwegian newspaper *Arbeiderbladet* sent him to Nuremberg to report on the war-crimes trials. But Brandt did not restrict his reporting to the trials, instead undertaking several journeys across his destroyed home country. On returning to Oslo, he collected his impressions in a book published in 1946—*Forbrytere og andre tyskere* (Criminals and Other Germans). In his political campaigns during the 1960s, Brandt's far-right and conservative-nationalist enemies would twist that title into "Germans and Other Criminals" to depict the book as the opposite of what it truly was. As someone who had left Germany, Brandt, they claimed, wanted to hold all Germans collectively responsible for the crimes of National Socialism. To the contrary, Brandt's true agenda had been to discredit the thesis of British diplomat Lord

Vansittart, a prominent Germanophobe, by showing that a "different Germany" existed and arguing that not all Germans should be viewed as criminals.[87]

"YESTERDAY IT WAS COLD and rainy, but today is spring, a special spring, not just an ordinary one, but the spring in which peace arrived—heavens, how marvelous!" When the children's book author Astrid Lindgren wrote these words in her diary on May 1, peace had in fact not yet arrived, but an end to the war was imminent. The thirty-seven-year-old, who lived with her husband and two children in Stockholm, was at the time working in the letter censorship division of the Swedish intelligence service. She had yet to publish anything aside from a few short stories, but she had invented the character of Pippi Longstocking for her daughter, Karin, and had begun composing the central story. The first Pippi Longstocking book would appear in late 1945 and make Lindgren famous the world over.

That evening, at the same time Brandt was speaking in front of the group of international socialists, Lindgren was sitting in front of her radio listening to the state German radio station in Hamburg announce Hitler's death. "This is a historical moment," she noted. "Hitler is dead. Mussolini's dead, too. Hitler died in his capital, in the ruins of his capital, amid the ruins and rubble of his country. . . . Sic transit gloria mundi!"[88]

MAY 2, 1945

Between 12:50 and 1:50 a.m. on May 2, 1945, the Grossdeutscher Rundfunk radio station on Berlin's Masurenallee ended its program with the following words: "We send our regards to all Germans and commemorate the brave German soldiers on land, on the sea, and in the air. The Führer is dead. Long live the Reich!"[1] For the majority of the German populace, the news of Hitler's death seems to have elicited more apathy than sadness. "What we hear is accepted with a mere shrug of the shoulders," Count Christian von Krockow, a seventeen-year-old soldier in Denmark, wrote in his diary.[2] Staff officer Gerd Schmückle, who would become a general in the postwar West German Bundeswehr and a deputy NATO supreme commander, heard the news at an inn in the Tyrolean village of Hinterriss. "If instead of this radio bulletin, the innkeeper had walked through the door and said that one of his animals had perished in its stall, the sympathy would not have been any less," Schmückle recalled. "One young soldier jumped up, stuck his right hand in the air and cried, 'Hail to the Führer!' Everyone else kept spooning soup into their mouths as if nothing important had happened."[3]

The mythic aura surrounding the Führer, which had experienced a brief renaissance after the failed assassination attempt of July 20,

1944, decayed dramatically in the final months of the war, and with it, National Socialism lost a fundamental source of appeal. The magic was indeed gone, and the spell broken. "People here are completely indifferent to whether Hitler, their once so fervently worshipped Führer, is still alive or already dead—he's played out his role," wrote Ursula von Kardorff on May 2, adding that "millions died because of him, and now his death is unmourned by millions. How quickly the Reich that was supposed to last one thousand years has passed."[4]

Journalist Ruth Andreas-Friedrich, who was a member of a Berlin resistance group that had aided people persecuted by the regime, described a similar reaction among her acquaintances: "Hitler is dead! And we . . . we act as though that were of no consequence, as if this concerned the most insignificant person in the world. What has changed? Nothing! Only that we have forgotten Mr. Hitler in the inferno of the past few days. The Third Reich has dissipated like an apparition."[5]

In a diary entry about her experiences in Berlin, musician and writer Karla Höcker related an incident she witnessed in a Berlin air-raid cellar during the early morning of May 2. After those taking refuge there finally settled down to sleep, the local Nazi block leader appeared and announced with a "strangely cold voice . . . that Hitler is reportedly dead." A woman shot back, "Well everything's okay then," eliciting "thin laughter."[6]

As an eighteen-year-old schoolgirl from a Social Democratic family in a working-class section of Hamburg observed on her way to school on the morning of May 2: "Strange. No one was crying or even looked sad, although the beloved, venerated Führer these idiots considered almost a god was no longer alive. . . . So this was the popular community they kept invoking, which was supposedly prepared to sacrifice everything for the Führer!" Yet the reactions of the pupils at her girls' school revealed a different attitude. Many of her schoolmates wept when the "Deutschlandlied" and "Horst-Wessel-Lied" were played after the principal's eulogy in the assembly hall. As the girl wrote, "How can this be? These are supposed to be clever, talented people!! Laughable!"[7]

Among the German military commanders being held as POWs in Trent Park outside of London, Hitler's death dominated conversations, but here, too, opinions diverged. The majority were in agreement that the Führer had been a man of "great services" to the German people and a "historic personality" who would "only first get his full due" from later generations. At the same time, he had tragically failed in his mission because he had surrounded himself with "unable, criminal people." The minority had come to the view that they had served a system in opposition to "all laws of morality." As one of the penitent prisoners put it, "You repeatedly clutch your head in disbelief that we all followed this lunatic."[8]

Captain Ernst Jünger, the conservative thinker who left the staff of Germany's military commander in Paris after D-Day in June 1944 and was transferred that September to the "Führer reserve" in the town of Kirchhorst near Hanover, wrote in his diary on May 1, 1945, "In the evening Hitler's death was announced on the radio. It is as obscure as much of what went on around him. I had the impression that the man, like Mussolini, has been for quite some time a marionette moved around by other hands and forces. Stauffenberg's bomb may not have taken his life, but his aura was gone. You could hear it in his voice."[9]

Quite a few people were relieved at the news of Hitler's death since it meant that the end of the war had to be imminent. The diplomat Erwin Wickert, who worked as a radio attaché at the German embassy in Tokyo, recalled feeling as though a heavy burden had been lifted: "Now there was no one up there who would continue the war and whose commands were beyond appeal. I wouldn't call it glee, but it was a strange, unaccustomed sense of lightness."[10]

By contrast, Hitler's most fervent followers, who had believed in his promised "miracle weapons" and "final victory" up to the very last, were shocked. The editor in chief of the *Hamburger Zeitung*, Hermann Okrass, appealed to them in his obituary of the Führer, published on May 2 under the headline "Farewell to Hitler." "A great man has departed from this world," he wrote, a man who "wanted the best for his people" and had been "so very beloved" in return. Adolf Hitler had encapsulated and encompassed "the most wonderful virtues, the most passionate desires, the most noble longing and the entire wonderful aspiration of our people," Okrass gushed, adding that the final judgment of Hitler could be "comfortably left up to posterity."[11]

Often sadness over the loss of the beloved Führer was mixed with self-pity. A twenty-six-year-old student of German literature, Lore Walb, noted on May 2, "Now he's at peace, which is without doubt the best thing for him. But what about us? We're abandoned and left to face everything, and there's no way we will be able to rebuild in our lifetimes what this war has destroyed." Originally Hitler had wanted to realize "positive ideas," and "some good" had been achieved in domestic politics, Walb thought, but Hitler had completely failed in his foreign policy and as commander in chief. "Now the people have to pay!" complained Walb. "If Papa had lived to see this!"[12] The same day, a clerk from Hamburg, also twenty-six years old, wrote in his diary, "Our Führer, who promised us so much, has achieved what no German leader before him was able to and is leaving behind a completely destroyed Germany. . . . He allowed millions to die and created terrible chaos. And once again we, the poor German people, are going to pay the price."[13]

Such lamentations reflected the ambivalence with which many of Hitler's followers received the news of his death. The credulous trust they had shown in their Führer for years now transformed into disappointment and anger—or cynicism, as was the case with nineteen-year-old Erika Assmus, once a fervent group leader in the Nazi League of German Girls, who was from the Baltic Sea spa town of Ahlbeck on the island of Usedom and who had to flee with her family toward Wismar.

She leavened her initial pain after the hopes she had placed in Hitler were dashed with a dispassionate metaphor: "The company is bankrupt. Its founder has deserted it, leaving it behind in the mud. That's not the way the game is played! That was not the basis for doing business! Sadness was immediately transformed to cynicism, the expression of those deceived and without hope."[14] In postwar West Germany, under the pseudonym Carola Stern, Assmus would make a name for herself as one of the country's most important left-wing authors.

In the air-raid bunker of the radio station on Masurenallee in Berlin, sixteen-year-old Hitler Youth member Lothar Loewe, who like many boys his age was called up to join the last-ditch Volkssturm militia to defend the city, felt nothing but an immense inner emptiness and bewilderment when he learned of Hitler's death. "What now, I thought. Who's leading Germany now? And what will become of us, the Hitler Youth, without Hitler?"[15] In West Germany, Lothar Loewe would become one of state television's most recognizable journalists and serve as a foreign correspondent in Washington, Moscow, and East Berlin.

The judicial official Friedrich Kellner, from the small West German town of Laubach, spoke for many of the isolated clusters of Hitler opponents who had predicted the coming catastrophe when he cautioned his countrymen not to place all the blame on Hitler and the underlings around him. Every one of the millions of Nazi Party members, Kellner argued, was also culpable for Germany's disaster. Kellner, who until 1933 had been a member of the SPD, began keeping a diary after the start of the Second World War. Day after day, in ten notebooks, he recorded what he overheard or was told by acquaintances. By reading the Nazi press with a critical eye, he was able to see through the propaganda and draw accurate conclusions about the criminal nature of the regime. On hearing the news of Hitler's death, he wrote in his diary, "The craziest of all political systems, the unique-leader state, has found its deserved end. History will note for eternity that the German people were not able on their own initiative to shake off the National Socialist yoke. The victory of the Americans, English, and Russians was a necessary occurrence to destroy the National Socialists' delusions and plans for world domination."[16]

William Shirer drew similar conclusions. "The war, which had destroyed so much and which had almost been lost, was ending in total victory. Mussolini was hanging by his heels in a square in Milan. Hitler was dead, undoubtedly by his own hand. . . . Fascism, which had almost overwhelmed our world, which had almost ruined it, and which had caused more obscene misery to more human beings than any other movement in recorded time, was being buried with the men who had made and led it."[17]

DURING THE EARLY MORNING of May 2, the radio operators of the 79th Soviet Guards Division received a message in Russian. "Attention! Attention! This is the 56th German Tank Corps. We request that you cease your fire. At 0:50 hours Berlin time, we are sending negotiators to Potsdam Bridge. They will be identified by white flags. We await your response." A short time later the Soviets sent their answer: "Understood! Understood! We are passing on your request to our commander."[18] General Vasily Chuikov ordered a ceasefire in places to allow the German emissaries safe passage and nominated an officer from his staff and an interpreter to receive them. Once again he issued strict instructions only to engage in negotiations over an unconditional surrender and not to budge from the demand that the Germans immediately lay down their arms.

The German forces had gradually concluded that it was senseless to keep fighting in Berlin and that there was no alternative to surrender. On the evening of May 1, at approximately 11:00 p.m., General Helmuth Weidling, the commander of the 56th German Tank Corp and the latest of many officers appointed to oversee the defense of Berlin, had summoned all the troop commanders he could reach to the

Bendlerblock. When he announced that Hitler was dead and explained the necessity of surrendering, one eyewitness reported an "audible groan from the men." Even those who had long realized or suspected that the end was near were overwhelmed when they were confronted with reality: "For them, a world collapsed."[19]

Ultimately, all of the military commanders present supported Weidling's decision. Theodor von Dufving, who had accompanied General Krebs on his mission the previous day, was tasked with communicating an offer of surrender. Together with an interpreter and a soldier waving a white flag he set off toward the agreed meeting point. In contrast to the previous day, negotiations this time around concluded quickly. The Soviet representative, one Colonel Semchenko, declared that his superiors had authorized him to accept the offer of surrender. He assured the Germans that they would be granted "honorable conditions," with officers being allowed to keep "small side arms" (rapiers and daggers but not pistols) and to leave the city with as much as they could carry. The Soviets also pledged to "protect the civilian population and treat the wounded." Where the timing of the surrender was concerned, Dufving pointed out that almost all long-distance communication facilities had been destroyed and messengers would have to be sent out to all units still fighting, which would take three or four hours. Thus, 6:00 a.m. was agreed on as the start of the ceasefire. At around 3:00 a.m., Dufving returned to the Bendlerblock and reported to those assembled there the result of the negotiations.[20]

Between 5:30 and 6:00 a.m., Weidling and his staff left the Bendlerblock and allowed themselves to be taken prisoner. Weidling was brought to Chuikov's headquarters in Tempelhof. There he assured the Soviets that he had given the ceasefire order but that because of the poor connections he could not guarantee it had reached all the German units still fighting. At Chuikov's request, at 7:50 a.m., Weidling wrote out a formal order to surrender. It read, "On April 30, 1945, the Führer took his own life and thereby deserted those of us who had sworn loyalty to him. Acting on the Führer's orders, you believe that you must keep fighting around Berlin, although the lack of heavy weaponry and ammunition as well as the general situation make further fighting senseless. Every hour you keep fighting prolongs the terrible suffering of the civilian population of Berlin and our wounded. Anyone who now falls in battle for Berlin is making a sacrifice for nothing. With the agreement of the supreme command of the Soviet troops, I thus demand that you immediately cease fighting."[21]

A young Soviet political officer from a German family, twenty-year-old Stefan Doernberg, typed out Weidling's order on his portable machine. In 1935, Doernberg had emigrated with his Jewish parents to the Soviet Union. After the German invasion in 1941, he had volunteered for the Red Army and at the end of the war served as an interpreter during the negotiations over Germany's surrender. (He would later make a career as a historian in Communist East Germany.)[22] Weidling was sent with a copy of the surrender order to a recording studio in the Treptow-Köpenick district, where he read it aloud. The recording was played back over loudspeakers on trucks driven throughout Berlin.[23]

Nonetheless, fighting continued at various flashpoints even on May 2. SS units in particular still offered fierce resistance. But by 5:00 p.m. that day, the general ceasefire was finally in place. The remnants of the defeated Wehrmacht assembled for the long march to become POWs. "Many soldiers are still wearing their steel helmets, although they serve no purpose," observed Soviet interpreter Yelena Rzhevskaya. "They march now, exhausted, betrayed, with blackened faces, downcast. Some pull down their heads between their shoulders, others seem relieved, but the majority seem both defeated and indifferent."[24] General Weidling and twelve other members of the Wehrmacht and the SS would be flown to Moscow on May 8. There Weidling was interned in several different prisons over the years before finally being put on trial in February 1952. He was sentenced to twenty-five years' incarceration, but he died in an infirmary in the Lubyanka Building in November 1955, the cause of death listed as coronary arrest.[25]

Slowly, with fearful disbelief, the residents of Berlin emerged from the cellars where they had been crammed together for days without electric light, gas, or water. They were confronted with a horrific sight. Clouds of black smoke hung in the sky, here and there fires still smoldered, and building façades were crumbling. The ruins piled up in mounds, between which lay the bodies of soldiers, Russian and German. Disabled tanks, upside-down artillery guns, and burned-out streetcars bore testament to the ferocity of the fighting that had just ended. Dead horses lay about everywhere and became a welcome supplement to Berliners' diets.

The journalist Margret Boveri, who unlike her colleague Kardorff had not sought refuge in the south of Germany but stayed in her apartment on Wundtstrasse in Berlin's Charlottenburg district, heard on the morning of May 2 that horsemeat was being handed out. "I . . . ran out and found half a horse, its body still warm, on the sidewalk and saw men and women sawing off pieces with knives and hatchets. I took out my large pocketknife, found a spot, and sawed along with them. It wasn't easy. I got a quarter of a lung and a piece of the joint with the horse's hair still on it. Spattered with blood, I withdrew."[26]

One common scene in the first days of peace in Berlin were masses of people plundering stores and food stocks. The situation was particularly turbulent in the Schultheiss brewery in Prenzlauer Berg, where the Wehrmacht had hoarded large amounts of supplies. "Men, women and children emerged from the brewery with butter, margarine, preserved goods, soap, cookies, bread, chocolate, candy, lozenges, wine, and lots of other things," recalled a schoolboy one year later. "The looting got so bad that Russian soldiers fired warning shots in the air."[27]

Literally nothing remained of the "ethnic community" that Nazi propaganda had never tired of promoting but that was always more wishful thinking than reality. With the defeat of the Reich, all were

After the end of the fighting on May 2, Berlin residents
cut pieces of meat from a dead horse.

preoccupied with trying to procure the necessities of life for themselves
and their family members. "People attacked one another and fought,
tearing clothes from bodies and grasping whatever they could get their
hands on," wrote another schoolchild.[28]

One of the main things people noticed when they emerged from
their basements was the unaccustomed and thus uncanny silence. The
thunder of artillery and the rattle of machine guns had ceased, and
there were no more air raids. "Unbelievable—no sirens will howl any
more, no bombs will fall, and we can slowly readjust to removing our
clothes before we go to sleep," wrote a happy Berlin woman, Marta
Mierendorff, on May 2. To her amazement, she realized that people
were already at work clearing the sidewalks of rubble. "A quiet sigh of
relief can be felt," Mierendorff recorded.[29]

For Red Army soldiers, May 2 in Berlin was a holiday. "The enormity of victory—a spontaneous celebration breaks out at the Victory Column," wrote author Vassily Grossman in a report about the situation.[30] "The tanks are flooded in an ocean of flowers and red flags. Everyone is dancing, singing, and laughing. Colored flares shoot up into the air. Automatic and regular pistols and rifles are fired in celebration."[31] A Russian lieutenant, Nicolai Belov, wrote to his wife, Lidiya, that "I haven't slept like I did just now for a long time—I was like a corpse. I don't know whether there will be another lot of fighting like we've just seen, but I doubt it. It's all finished in Berlin. It's all over." Belov would not live to see the end of the war. On May 4, he was deployed to the town of Burg on the Elbe River, where he was killed the following day.[32]

ON THE MORNING OF May 2, at the same time General Weidling was signing his order to surrender, the members of the Ulbricht Group drove in several vehicles into Berlin along with Soviet political officers. What they saw devastated them. Ulbricht Group member Wolfgang Leonhard wrote, "Fires, rubble, hungry people wandering around in torn clothing. Restless German soldiers who seemed to no longer understand what was going on. Singing, celebrating, and often inebriated Red Army troops. Groups of women, guarded by Soviets, clearing debris. Long lines of people patiently waiting for pumps to fill buckets with water. All of them looked terribly tired, hungry, worn out, and damaged."[33] White flags hung from the windows alongside red ones in working-class parts of the city. Many residents wore armbands of white, red, or both.

The group's first destination was the central Soviet command center at Alt-Friedrichsfelde 1–3. The man appointed commander of the city, Colonel General Nikolai Berzarin greeted the German emissaries from Moscow cordially and gave them some initial instructions. For the Soviets the top priority was restoring public order. Streets had to be cleared of rubble and military hardware; the bodies of people and horses removed; supplies of water, electricity, and gas secured; and shops and businesses reopened. "Help us get normal life moving again," Berzarin said. "Help us, the Red Army. You'll be helping your compatriots."[34]

The Ulbricht Group was tasked with rebuilding Berlin's twenty-one district administrations and forming a city council. Two members of the group were assigned to each district and saw to it that personnel decisions conformed to Soviet interests. Leonhard accompanied Walter Ulbricht to the Neukölln district where a group of Communist survivors of Nazi persecution had gathered in a badly damaged residential building. Leonhard vividly described his and Ulbricht's reception: "All of a sudden several men took to their feet and called out 'Ulbricht!' In no time, he was surrounded. Surprise and joy were written across these comrades' faces. But even then, Ulbricht remained severe and unemotional. He greeted them—his greeting sounded rather cool in my ears—and introduced me as his colleague. After one or two minutes, the discussion moved on, albeit steered by Ulbricht. . . . He asked questions, if not in the manner of a police interrogation, then by no means in a tone of voice I would have expected from an émigré meeting up for the first time in twelve years with comrades who had lived through Hitler's terror. When he finally laid out the political 'line' from now on, he did so in a tone that brooked no contradiction and in a fashion that left no doubt that he and not the Berlin Communists . . . would determine the policies of the party."[35]

That evening, the group convened again in the "house of pillars" in Bruchmühle. They discussed what they had seen that day; Ulbricht then issued instructions for how to reconstitute the district administrations. In working-class areas, Social Democrats were to be installed as mayors, while in the bourgeois areas—Wilmersdorf, Charlottenburg, and Zehlendorf—opponents of fascism, preferably with university degrees, were to be selected. The heads of the offices for food, economics, social affairs, and transportation were all to be Social Democrats. "They know a thing or two about local politics," Ulbricht proposed. German Communists would remain in the minority but receive key posts as deputy mayors and departmental heads for personnel issues, popular education, and the police. "The situation is quite clear," Ulbricht concluded matter-of-factly. "Everything has to look democratic, but we have to maintain complete control."[36] And indeed this was precisely how the group went about constructing a Communist-dominated city in the first ten days of May 1945.

Right from the start, Ulbricht worked closely with the head of the Main Political Administration of the Red Army in Berlin, General Galadchev, and his deputy General Serov. Ulbricht was the most important partner for Soviet occupation authorities, and because he could reliably guarantee that Stalinist policies would be loyally and effectively enacted, he usually got his way with his personnel suggestions for major posts. After only two weeks, he reported back to the chairman of the German Communist Party, Wilhelm Pieck, in Moscow: "It is already the case that, whenever complicated questions arise, the commanders of the various parts of the city will call us and ask for an instructor to clear up those questions and build up the administrative apparatus properly. Because we began by concentrating all our energy on district administrations, we have become acquainted with a sufficient pool of people to make commendations for a central administrative apparatus, a police force, and everything else that is necessary."[37]

The first days of the occupation in Berlin saw acts of violence by Red Army soldiers, particularly countless rapes of German women, but Ulbricht categorically forbade any frank discussion of this issue despite the demands of Berlin's Communists, who pressed it. He even came out against allowing women who had been raped and impregnated to get abortions.[38] Ulbricht deeply mistrusted those German Communists who had stayed in the Third Reich and joined the underground opposition. In his eyes, they remained too wedded to the Communist symbols and agendas inherited from the Weimar Republic, such as the immediate introduction of socialism, which contradicted the line dictated by Stalin. "We must take into account the fact that the majority of our comrades have sectarian attitudes," Ulbricht wrote to Pieck in mid-May. "Many comrades institute our policies while ironically winking, many have the right sort of will but cannot overcome 'Red Front' slogans, and many . . . talk about Soviet power plays and the like. We have battled energetically against the false attitudes in the ranks of our comrades, but new ones constantly appear who want to begin anew with the mistakes of old."[39]

Ulbricht put his complete faith in the group that bore his name, composed of men trained in Soviet exile who had internalized the imperative of subservience to Stalin. In his eyes, these were the only people who could be counted on to rigorously enforce the ideas of the Soviet occupiers.[40] The Moscow emissaries were just as distrustful when they encountered the "antifascist committees" that had formed in almost all of Berlin's neighborhoods once the Red Army had moved in. These committees were spontaneous associations of antifascists of various ideological schools that set about trying to coordinate initial cleanup operations, assign people places to live, and get businesses and public utilities working again. Ulbricht was profoundly suspicious of these initiatives from below, and in close conjunction with Soviet commanders, he did everything he could to nip them in the bud. By May 5, he was already reporting to Dimitrov that "we've closed down the offices, posted signs, and made it clear to comrades that all our efforts must now be concentrated in work in the city administration."[41]

At the same time that it was reconstituting district administrations, the Ulbricht Group was also charged with finding suitable candidates for Berlin's new citywide council. Here, too, the emphasis was on selecting Social Democrats and members of the bourgeoisie to personify the "antifascist, democratic revolution," while in reality the Communists would keep power. The first person willing to join the new council was the Social Democrat and former trade union secretary Josef Orlopp, and Ulbricht secured a coup when he persuaded former national government minister and well-known centrist politician Andreas Hermes to take over the department of food affairs. In January 1945, Hermes had been sentenced to death for his part in the July 20, 1944, attempted assassination of Hitler, but a fortunate set of circumstances had prevented his sentence from being carried out. He would go on to cofound the conservative Christian Democratic Union Party (CDU) in the Soviet occupation zone and, upon resettling in the West, would become an influential member of the West German CDU. Ulbricht made his expectations for Hermes clear in a missive to General Serov: "The crimes of the Hitler regime have made such a deep impression on him that he will support a thorough cleansing of Germany from fascism. . . . Our task must be to systematically and patiently influence Dr. Hermes and to use all means of cementing his friendship with the Soviet Union."[42]

Ulbricht also succeeded in locating two more bourgeoisie recruits: the surgeon and head of Charité Hospital Ferdinand Sauerbruch, brought on as the departmental head of health matters, and the architect Hans Scharoun, enlisted as head of the construction department. The mayor installed by the Soviets was the sixty-eight-year-old politically independent construction engineer Arthur Werner. He had few qualifications for the job, which suited Ulbricht and the Soviet commanders just fine. All the real work was carried out by Werner's deputy, Karl Maron, who held the reins of the city administration. In addition, Communists occupied two further key positions, with Arthur Pieck, Wilhelm Pieck's son, installed as head of personnel and Otto Werner as departmental head of popular education. On May 19, with Berzarin present, the new city council was sworn in.[43]

A few weeks later, on June 10, the KPD reconstituted itself. With that, the Ulbricht Group's work was done. Within the space of two months, Ulbricht had laid the foundation for Communist domination in the Soviet occupation zone.

DURING THE NIGHT OF May 1, the governmental district around Wilhelmstrasse was still the scene of heavy fighting. But when morning broke, the artillery fell silent there as well. A spectral quiet settled on the Reich chancellery, which had been subjected to days of Soviet bombardment. The few people left in the bunker who had not attempted a breakout anxiously awaited the arrival of the first Red Army soldiers.

At around 9:00 a.m., the bunker's head technician and the man who kept the power generators running, Johannes Hentschel, heard Russian being spoken. The speakers were not men but rather a group of women in uniform who were part of the Red Army's medical corps. Their leader, who could speak German, immediately asked Hentschel, "Where's Hitler?" The engineer responded truthfully, stating that Hitler was dead and describing how the Führer's body had been burned in the chancellery courtyard. The Russians' interest soon moved to the Führer's alleged lover and her wardrobe. "Where are the clothes?" one asked. Years later Hentschel recalled, "Finally I realized what these Russian women wanted. To the victor went the spoils. After fighting so fiercely for so long, these women of war wanted to obtain some respectable civilian clothes. . . . With a sigh of relief that everything had turned out so harmlessly, I led them down to Eva Braun's changing room."[44]

Over the course of the day, troops from the 3rd Assault Army of the 1st Belarussian Front occupied the chancellery. Scouts checked the catacombs for possible explosive booby traps. They were followed by a unit from the counterespionage division, SMERSH. Their mission was to find and identify Hitler's body. Although Krebs had told Chuikov about Hitler's suicide in their negotiations on the night of April 30, and Weidling had explicitly confirmed that the Führer was dead on the morning of May 2, the Soviets remained wary. What if this information was false and Hitler had been able to escape? The possibility was a nightmare to SMERSH operatives, who were under considerable pressure from Moscow. After all, *Pravda* had already reported that word of the Führer's death was a fascist trick.[45]

In the afternoon, the SMERSH division, led by Lieutenant Colonel Ivan Klimenko, started their search. After inspecting the labyrinth under the chancellery, they ascended to the courtyard. "Countless shells have dug up the ground and mangled the trees," wrote Yelena Rzhevskaya, who served as an interpreter. "We step on charred branches and walk across grass turned to black soot. Splinters of glass and broken bricks are everywhere."[46]

At around 5:00 p.m., officers near the entrance to the bunker discovered the half-charred remains of Joseph and Magda Goebbels: Schwägermann had been unable to procure enough gasoline to burn them thoroughly. The report filed by the head of SMERSH under the 1st Belarussian Front, Lieutenant General Alexander Vadis, stated that "the body of the man was of small stature, and the foot of the right leg was found in a semi-bent position (club foot) in a charred metal prothesis. On top of the body lay a burnt NSDAP [Nationalsozialistische Deutsche Arbeiterpartei, or National Socialist German Workers' Party] uniform and a singed golden party insignia. Near the charred body of the woman we found a singed golden cigarette case, and on it a gold NSDAP party insignia and a scorched gold brooch."[47] On May 3, Soviet troops also found the bodies of the Goebbels's six children in the bunker of the Reich chancellery. They were discovered lying in their beds in their nightshirts, just as they had been when they died two days previously.

To identify all the bodies, the Soviets brought in Vice Admiral Hans-Erich Voss, whom they had captured; the chancellery chef, Wilhelm Lange; and the manager of the chancellery garage, Karl Schneider. All three confirmed that the dead were the propaganda minister and his family. Voss remarked that Hitler had awarded Magda Goebbels the party's gold insignia three days before his suicide.[48]

But where was Hitler? Voss was interrogated about the body's whereabouts, and he told the Soviets that while trying to flee he had heard from Hitler's adjutant that the dictator had killed himself and that his body had been burned in the chancellery courtyard. On the evening of May 3, under a water basin for extinguishing fires, the Soviets discovered a pile of bodies, of which one bore a certain resemblance to Hitler. On closer inspection, however, they saw that the man was wearing patched socks and thus could hardly have been the all-powerful dictator.[49] The search for Hitler's remains continued. "Again and again, meter for meter, we comb through the abandoned bunker," reported Rzhevskaya. "Overturned tables and smashed typewriters lie around, and glass crunches and paper rustles under our feet. We search through the cells, the rooms, and the long corridors. We feel our way along the concrete walls and tiptoe through the puddles collecting in the hallways. The air is damp and oppressive. The ventilation fans no longer work. It's hard to breathe."[50]

On May 4, Klimenko's men dragged the bodies of a man and woman, burned beyond recognition, from a shell crater a few meters away from the entrance to the bunker, but because there was no reason to believe these were the remains of Hitler and Braun, they were quickly reburied. The following day, Klimenko began to have doubts and he ordered a platoon leader, First Lieutenant Alexei Panassov, to unearth the bodies. They were wrapped in blankets, placed in two munition crates, and taken to surgical field hospital number 496 in the Buch area on the outskirts of the city.[51]

By this point, Soviet intelligence officers had also captured Weidling and Hans Baur and subjected them to extensive interrogations about the fate of the Nazi leadership. On May 5, the SMERSH commandant of the 1st Belarussian Front, Major General Trussov, filed his report to the head of military intelligence general staff, Colonel General Fyodor Kuznetsov, who immediately forwarded it to Stalin. It reached the clear conclusion that Hitler had committed suicide and before killing himself had ordered that his body be burned.[52]

Between May 7 and 9, coroners supervised by Colonel Faust Iosifovich Shkaravsky examined the bodies of the Goebbels and their children. In all cases, the examiners determined the cause of death to be cyanide poisoning. Glass shards were also found in the mouths of the bodies suspected to be Hitler and Braun, which indicated they, too, had bitten down on capsules of cyanide.[53] But this possibility conflicted with Krebs's and Weidling's testimony that Hitler had shot himself. Further examination was necessary, and the teeth that had been recovered would play a central role.

From the chief physician of the Charité's ear, nose, and throat clinic, Professor Carl von Eicken, who had twice operated on Hitler's vocal cords, Soviet investigators learned the name of the dictator's dentist: Hugo Blaschke. He had fled Berlin for Hitler's Alpine retreat in Obersalzberg in southern Germany in the final days of the war. But on May 9, Blaschke's assistant Käthe Heusermann was located. She recounted from memory—Blaschke had taken his X-rays with him—Hitler's bridgework, which matched exactly the teeth from the body suspected to be the Führer's. Dental technician Fritz Echtmann then identified the artificial rubber bridgework worn by Braun. This was crucial evidence that the remains were in fact those of Hitler and his wife.[54]

On May 13, the Soviets finally located a witness who could describe what exactly had happened in the chancellery courtyard on April 30. SS Rottenführer Harry Mengershausen of the Reich Security Service had observed from his post the bodies of Hitler and Braun being brought out of the bunker, doused in gasoline, and set alight. When asked, he described the place where the charred remains had been buried.[55] There was no further reason to doubt that Hitler was dead and his body had been burned.

At that point Lieutenant General Vadis informed the Soviet intelligence service chief, Laurenti Beria, about the results of the investigation.[56] Stalin was still mistrustful. In a conversation with American special ambassador Harry Hopkins on May 26, he said he suspected that Hitler had been able to flee Berlin with Bormann and was hiding out in some unknown location. No stone should be left unturned, Stalin demanded, in order to find him. Perhaps Hitler had escaped to Japan in a submarine, he suggested.[57] At a press conference in Berlin on June 9, Marshal Zhukov said that he could say nothing definitive about Hitler's fate. It was possible the dictator had been flown out of Berlin at the last second and was now in Spain.[58] Even at the Potsdam Conference in July, Stalin still insisted that Hitler was alive. Soviet investigations, he claimed, had failed to turn up any trace of his remains or discover any conclusive evidence of his death.[59] Did the Soviet dictator really believe this, or was he trying to deceive the western Allies?

Whatever Stalin's intentions, the confusion sown by the Soviets continued for some time. In the fall of 1945, Hitler's valet Linge, his personal adjutant Günsche, his pilot Baur, and the switchboard operator Misch were taken to the Lubyanka Building and subjected to intensive interrogation. In early 1946, the NKVD leadership decided to convene a special commission, code-named "Myth," to review all known facts about Hitler's suicide. Those involved in the operation took the prisoners to Berlin in May 1946 to revisit the locations in question. The bloodstains on the sofa in Hitler's bunker office, still preserved, were carefully examined, and further excavations in the chancellery courtyard turned up two fragments of a human skull with damage characteristic of a ballistics exit wound. With that, it was conclusively found that the eyewitnesses who said Hitler had shot himself were telling the truth. In all probability, he also took a cyanide capsule.[60]

After the original forensic examination, the bodies of the Goebbels family, Hitler, and Braun had been packed in wooden crates and buried in the Buch district on Berlin's northern edge. But they were exhumed by a SMERSH unit and moved among locations where Soviet troops were stationed: from Finow to Rathenow to Stendal to Magdeburg, where they were reburied on military grounds in February 1946. There they rested for more than two decades. But in the spring of 1970, as the Soviet garrison in Magdeburg was about to be handed over to the GDR, KGB director Yuri Andropov sent a letter to Communist Party chair Leonid Brezhnev recommending that "the remains be unearthed and destroyed once and for all by incineration."[61] On April 4, 1970, KGB officers dug up the graves and removed what was left of the wooden crates and their contents. The final report stated, "The destruction of the remains was carried out by incineration on a pyre. The remains were completely incinerated and ground together with pieces of charcoal to pulverized ash and thrown in the river."[62]

ON THE EVENING OF MAY 2, the BBC reported the sensational news that on April 29 Germany's Army Group C had surrendered in northern Italy. Some six hundred thousand men had laid down their arms. It was the first German capitulation of this scope in the war and the only surrender of a German army that had taken place while Hitler was alive, although he had never learned of it. British prime minister Winston Churchill interrupted a session of the House of Commons to relay the news, calling it a historic event. In Washington, Secretary of War Henry Lewis Stimson wrote that he hoped the surrender would serve as an example to other German troops and lead to the entire Wehrmacht laying down its arms.[63]

This momentous development was preceded by months of complex, secret negotiations. The decisive initiative came from Himmler's former chief of staff, Karl Wolff, who had been named "supreme SS and police leader in Italy" in September 1943. Since July 1944, he had also served as the "plenipotentiary general of German Wehrmacht in Italy" and controlled rearguard Wehrmacht troops. Thus, together with the supreme commander in the southwest, Field Marshal General Albert

Kesselring, Wolff occupied a key position. As one of the leaders responsible for combating Italian partisans, a campaign that had cost the lives
of thousands of innocent civilians, he knew that he could be put on
trial for war crimes. His efforts to negotiate a partial surrender with the
Allies in the final months of the war were no doubt motivated in part
by his desire to keep his neck out of the noose. In any event, he was
called as a witness at the Nuremberg Trials but not charged himself.[64]

With the help of Italian and Swiss intermediaries, above all
Lucerne intelligence official Max Waibel, Wolff succeeded in contacting the director of the Bern branch of the Office of Strategic Services
(OSS), Allen Dulles.[65] But before Dulles would agree to meet Wolff,
he demanded as a show of good faith the release of two incarcerated
resistenza leaders, Ferruccio Parri and Antonio Usmiani. On March
8, 1945, after both were taken from SS imprisonment to Switzerland,
Wolff met Dulles and his assistant Gero von Schulze-Gaevernitz in
Zurich. Wolff immediately assured them that he was not there at the
behest of either Hitler or Himmler. For his part, Dulles emphasized
that talks only made sense if the Germans recognized the need for an
unconditional surrender. Wolff agreed to this stipulation and promised
to win over the still hesitant Supreme Commander Kesselring.

Dulles seems to have been impressed by the SS and police leader,
telling the head of the OSS, William Donovan, that he regarded Wolff
as a gentleman and a moderate. The opportunity to end the war in
northern Italy had to be seized, he argued. Donovan passed on a similar recommendation to Washington, and Dulles got the green light to
continue negotiations, which were code-named "Operation Sunrise."[66]

Senior negotiator Major General Lyman Lemnitzer; Field Marshal Harold Alexander, the deputy chief of staff of the Allied Supreme
Command in Italy; and Major General Terence Airey of Britain, head
of intelligence at Allied Main Headquarters, traveled to Switzerland.
On March 16, a top-secret meeting was held with the three Allied
officers, Wolff, and Dulles in the town of Ascona on Lake Maggiore. It

was the first time during the war that Allied and German military leaders had met at a bargaining table. Wolff made no attempt to bargain, Dulles reported, declaring instead that he would stand or fall with this enterprise. Using a map, Wolff told his negotiation partners how he envisioned the war could be ended.[67] A surrender agreement in northern Italy seemed imminent, but unexpected obstacles soon appeared.

On March 11, Hitler summoned Kesselring from Italy and named him Germany's supreme commander in the west. His successor as supreme commander in the southwest, Colonel General Heinrich von Vietinghoff-Scheel, did not arrive in Italy until late March, and it was anybody's guess what he would think of the secret plans to surrender. Moreover, the SS leadership in Berlin had gotten wind of Wolff's trip to Switzerland. On April 17, Himmler, who was staying in an SS infirmary in Hohenlychen, north of Berlin, ordered Wolff to account for his independent action to the head of the Reich Main Security Office, Ernst Kaltenbrunner. It seems to have cost Wolff considerable effort to convince Himmler that his contact with Dulles was in no way aimed at bringing about Army Group C's surrender.[68]

On April 18, Wolff also had to justify himself in front of Hitler. The dictator criticized the SS general for acting independently and, as always, rejected any suggestion of capitulation. However, he did allow Wolff to continue his negotiations with Dulles, which Hitler saw as a means of sowing discord among the Allies. "Two more months, and the break between the Anglo-Saxons and the Russians will come," Hitler declared. "Then I will join whoever approaches me first, no matter who it is."[69]

Of course, the negotiations in Switzerland did not lead to a break in the anti-Hitler coalition, but it did cause a crisis of confidence between the Soviet Union and its western partners. Stalin was wary of a British-American plot with the Germans and sent a strongly worded telegram to Franklin D. Roosevelt on April 3 complaining that the western powers were talking with their joint enemy behind his back. Germany, he fumed, had practically suspended fighting on the western front while it was still battling with all its might against the Soviet Union in the east. Roosevelt, irritated by the accusations, tried to mollify Stalin, pointing out that there had been no direct negotiations, only nonbinding talks without any political ramifications. Nonetheless the leadership in Washington and London were so unsettled that they decided to cancel the Swiss talks. After Roosevelt died suddenly on April 12, Churchill and FDR's successor, Harry S. Truman, agreed, in view of possible conflicts with the Soviet Union, to prohibit all further contact with German negotiators.[70]

In the meantime, Wolff had succeeded in winning Vietinghoff over to the plan for Army Group C to lead the way in surrendering. The final decision was made on April 23. Wolff and Lieutenant Colonel Viktor von Schweinitz, Vietinghoff's envoy, made their way to Lucerne. Dulles, whom Washington had prohibited from responding to any new feelers, initially refused to see them. But after the Swiss intermediary Waibel informed him that the German emissary was carrying broad authorization to bring about the capitulation of the German army in Italy, Dulles succeeded in getting Harold Alexander to lift the prohibition on contact with the enemy from April 20. On April 27, a message arrived that the German negotiators—Schweinitz and SS Sturmbannführer Eugen Wenner (Wolff's authorized representative)— were expected at Allied headquarters in Caserta. The next day, the pair flew to southern Italy, and on April 29, together with Alexander's chief of staff, General William Morgan, they signed the declaration of surrender. Two Soviet general staff officers were present at the signing.[71]

At the beginning of the ceremony, the inkwells and pens were carefully arranged on the table, recalled Schulze-Gaevernitz. Several reporters who had cast covetous eyes at the writing implements as historically valuable souvenirs were disappointed when another souvenir hunter, a young officer, handed the Germans his own pen to sign the surrender agreement. It was 2:17 p.m. when General Morgan ended the ceremony. The Germans were escorted out of the room, and the lights were turned out. Suddenly it was as dark and barren as an empty stage after the performance of a play.[72]

In the agreement's first article, the German supreme commander in the southwest agreed to unconditionally deliver up all land, sea, and air forces under his command or control and, again unconditionally, place himself and these forces at the disposal of the Allied supreme commander in the Mediterranean theater of war. The second article required the German side to ensure that all hostilities on land, sea, and air were halted at noon (Western European time) on May 2.[73] Nonetheless, there was still some resistance within the German ranks. The Gauleiter of Tyrol, Franz Hofer, withdrew his support for the agreement and told Kesselring in a phone conversation about the steps taken by Wolff and Vietinghoff. Kesselring, whom Hitler in one of his last official acts had named supreme commander of all German forces, was outraged. On April 30, Kesselring dismissed Vietinghoff and his general chief of staff, Hans Röttiger, replacing them with General Friedrich Schulz and Lieutenant General Johann Wetzel, but these officers, too, gradually arrived at the conclusion that all further resistance by Germany's army in Italy would be futile. When Hitler's death was announced on May 1, they no longer felt bound by their oath of loyalty or feared reprisals. On the night of May 1, in a telephone call lasting hours, Wolff finally succeeded in convincing Kesselring to agree to the surrender of Army Group C.[74]

The following day, Kesselring sent a telegram to Grand Admiral Dönitz and the Wehrmacht Supreme Command, taking responsibility for laying down arms in Italy, even though it had been initiated without his knowledge and approval. He was aware, he wrote, that it might mean "the most severe upheavals for the entire German front," but it would open the possibility of reaching a partial surrender of the army groups in the west on the same basis, "while the fight against Bolshevism will by no means be weakened and on the contrary possibly be strengthened."[75] Kesselring was adapting an idea Dönitz had put forth in his radio address and his daily orders to the Wehrmacht on the evening of May 1. Fighting in the west was to be ended as soon as possible while the "battle against Bolshevism" continued in the east. After overcoming some initial worries about possible effects of the surrender on troop discipline on other fronts, Dönitz approved Vietinghoff's autonomous action. After all, it fit with his own ideas for how to the end the war.[76]

AT 10:30 A.M. ON MAY 2, Dönitz summoned his newly appointed foreign minister Krosigk and his new head of the chancellery, Paul Wegener, the Gauleiter of Weser-Ems and the supreme commissar for the defense of northern Germany, to his provisional seat of government in Plön for an important meeting. They began by reviewing the situation in the various theaters of war. Coherent fronts no longer existed, and the territory under Wehrmacht control was shrinking. In East Prussia, the Courland Peninsula and a narrow strip of coastline at the mouth of the Vistula remained in German hands. In Courland, one army group was still holding out, but it could no longer be supplied with ammunition and fuel, so its days were numbered. "Like a dull grumbling of final collapse, our downfall is announcing itself," wrote a soldier stationed in the town of Windau (today Ventspils, Latvia) in his diary. "But our work and service continue. Bunkers are built, as if nothing special were imminent."[77] Further to the west, in Vorpommern and Mecklenburg, Army Group Vistula was completely disintegrating. South of those positions, the remnants of the 9th Army under General Busse and the 12th Army under General Wenck freed themselves from encirclement and were fighting their way westward across the Elbe River. In northwestern Germany, East Frisia and Schleswig-Holstein had yet to be occupied, but British troops had already established a bridgehead across the Elbe at Lauenberg and were ready to advance north.

Army Group C in Alpine Italy had surrendered, rendering the position of the adjacent Army Group G to the north under General

Friedrich Schulz untenable. Army Group South under General Lothar Rendulic was defending the majority of Austria, and Army Group Center, commanded by Field Marshal General Ferdinand Schörner, was holding onto its positions in the protectorate of Bohemia and Moravia. Meanwhile, Army Group E, under Colonel General Alexander Löhr, was in full retreat in the Balkans. German troops still occupied large parts of Norway, the Netherlands, and Denmark, as well as several outposts and ports in Biscay, Dunkirk, and the Channel Islands.[78]

"The military situation is hopeless" read the minutes of the meeting taken by Dönitz's personal adjutant Walter Lüdde-Neurath, but the admiral still rejected the idea of an "unconditional total surrender" because "millions of German soldiers and civilians would suddenly be delivered up to the Russians." The goal thus had to be "capitulation to the west only." In the wake of assurances made by the Allies to one another, such a surrender would be impossible to achieve "via the uppermost authorities through official channels," so Germany had to realize its ends "with partial measures, for instance, army group by army group." Fighting in the east was to continue "with any and all means" in order to "save as many German people as possible from annihilation by Bolshevism."[79] In line with this idea, Army Group Vistula was ordered to keep fighting so that the stronger segments of the group could withdraw to British- and American-controlled areas. By contrast, the supreme commander in the German northwest, Field Marshal General Ernst Busch, was instructed to put up only enough resistance to gain time for possible negotiations with the British.[80]

Krosigk spoke to the German people that day. He began by referring to an "iron curtain" that was approaching ever closer as the Red Army marched forward and "behind which, away from the eyes of the world, the work of annihilating those who have fallen under the power of the Bolshevists is continuing."[81] The new foreign minister was appropriating a phrase used by Goebbels in a February editorial for the weekly newspaper Das Reich about the Yalta Conference. In case of German surrender, Goebbels had written, "an iron curtain behind which the mass butchery of people would begin would immediately fall" in front of Soviet-occupied territory.[82] On May 12, only a few days after the Wehrmacht's unconditional surrender, Churchill would use the phrase in a telegram to Truman, writing, "An iron curtain is drawn down upon their front. We do not know what is going on behind."[83]

Krosigk made no mention of the crimes committed by the SS and the Wehrmacht in occupied Poland and the Soviet Union, as well as in Greece, the Balkans, Italy, and other countries. Instead, he verbosely sought to portray the Germans as the party that had actually suffered most from the war: "Among all peoples of this earth, we Germans have experienced most forcefully what war means in terms of the destruction of all culture. Our cities are destroyed, our cultural monuments in Dresden and Nuremberg, in Cologne and Bayreuth and other world-renowned cities of cultural creativity lie in ruins, and our cathedrals have fallen victim to bombs. Hundreds of thousands of women and children have been taken from us by the fury of war, while millions of German men and youths have fallen at the front." Like Dönitz in his speech of May 1, Krosigk attempted to conjure up the specter of "Bolshevist Europe," proposing to his audience that "the world can only be made peaceful, if the Bolshevist wave doesn't flood Europe. For four years, Germany has waged an unprecedented heroic battle, sacrificing its final reserves of strength to serve as a bulwark for Europe and therefore the world against this red flood. Germany could have protected Europe from Bolshevism, if its back had been kept free."[84] Krosigk's words were a none-too-subtle invitation to the western powers to change sides and make common cause with a defeated Germany against the Soviet Union.

In the afternoon of May 2, news arrived in Plön that British field marshal Bernard Montgomery's 21st Army was advancing from its bridgehead at Lauenburg and had already seized Lübeck. Meanwhile, American units had crossed the Elbe further to the east and reached the

Baltic Sea near Wismar without encountering meaningful resistance. "The gate enabling German people from Mecklenburg and Pomerania to flow into the region under our control has been closed," read the minutes of the situation meeting held at 4:00 p.m.[85] Dönitz and his advisers drew two conclusions. They decided to move their headquarters to Flensburg, as British tanks in Lübeck were only an hour away from Plön. And they would seek to initiate the plan discussed that morning of offering to negotiate with Montgomery about a partial surrender in northwestern Germany. Admiral General Hans-Georg von Friedeburg, the man chosen by Dönitz to replace himself as the supreme commander of the Germany navy, was named Germany's envoy.

At 9:00 p.m., on his way north, Dönitz met Friedeburg at the Levensau Bridge across the Kaiser Wilhelm Canal near the city of Kiel and gave him some instructions for his negotiations with Montgomery. The wartime logbook of the Wehrmacht Supreme Command summarized those instructions: "Attempt to save as many German soldiers and European people from being Bolshevized and enslaved. Therefore withdrawal of Army Group Vistula into the Anglo-Saxon area of power. Protection of people collected in Schleswig-Holstein from annihilation and starvation. Provision of this area with medical supplies. Prevention of larger places from being destroyed by bombs. Additionally, attempt to find agreement to shield central and northern Europe from further chaos."[86]

That night, Dönitz, Krosigk, and Lüdde-Neurath arrived in Flensburg in an armored limousine, then quartered themselves in a converted passenger steamship, the MS *Patria*. The following day, they established their new headquarters in the naval academy building in Flensburg-Mürwik, which Captain at Sea Wolfgang Lüth had hastily furnished with the necessities.[87] It would remain the seat of Dönitz's government until the arrest of its principal members on May 23.

A WISCONSINITE NAMED Fred Schneikert, the commander of an anti-tank unit of the 44th US Infantry Division operating on the border between Bavaria and Austria, received a bit of a surprise on the morning of May 2, when a German approached on a bicycle, introduced himself as Magnus Braun, claimed that the inventors of the V-2 rocket were currently staying in the Alpine village of Oberjoch, and asked to speak to General Dwight D. Eisenhower. The man was taken to US Army Counterintelligence Corps headquarters in the town of Reutte in Tyrol. After a short interrogation, Lieutenant Colonel Charles Stewart issued letters of consignment and ordered the emissary to return to where he had come from and fetch the men allegedly sheltering up in the mountains.[88]

The previous month, the team of rocket scientists led by Walter Dornberger and Wernher von Braun had been transferred from the Peenemünde Army Research Center to Oberammergau. They had spent the final days of the war in the relative comfort of the Ingeburg Sporthotel in Oberjoch. There, on the evening of May 1, they heard the reports of Hitler's death. Dornberger and von Braun decided to surrender to the Americans, convinced that their expertise would be of interest to the US Army. Von Braun's brother Magnus was charged with making contact since he spoke the best English. On his return at 2:00 p.m., the scientists packed their bags and drove down the mountain road. American soldiers escorted them to a villa in Reutte where Stewart received them and served a frugal meal. The next morning, they were presented to the press. Pleasantly surprised by the friendly treatment he was afforded, von Braun posed for photos with his arm in a cast: he had broken his arm and shoulder several weeks earlier in an automobile accident.

In a 1950 interview in the United States, von Braun said that he never expected to be "treated like a war criminal." He added, explaining why he surrendered, "No, it was all logical. The V-2 was something we had and they didn't. Of course, they wanted to know everything about it."[89] The German rocket scientist was only too willing to pro-

Rocket scientist Wernher von Braun (with arm cast) and the director of
the Peenemünde Army Research Center, Walter Dornberger (front left),
turned themselves in to the Americans on May 2, 1945.

vide the desired information. Right from the start, von Braun perfectly
played the role of the apolitical scientist who had never had any part in
National Socialism and its crimes against humanity. But his record was
hardly as clean as he tried to convince his audience and himself.

Born in Wirsitz in the eastern province of Posen in 1912, von
Braun had been raised in the jingoistic nationalist ethos of a Prussian
aristocratic family.[90] His father, Baron Magnus von Braun, who pre-
sided over a hereditary estate, had been the agriculture minister in the
"cabinet of barons" of Chancellor Franz von Papen, Hitler's predecessor
who had done so much to dismantle the Weimar Republic. As a young
boy Wernher had been interested in everything relating to rocket technology, and even before starting toward a degree at the Technical Uni-

versity of Berlin, he joined the Society for Space Travel and, together with other young tinkerers, began experimenting with small rockets powered by a mixture of gasoline and liquid oxygen. In 1932, at the tender age of twenty, he became a member of the rocket program of the Army Weapons Office. He carried out his experiments first at the Kummersdorf Research Center south of Berlin and, starting in 1936, in Peenemünde on the Baltic island of Usedom.

On the strength of his technological and managerial gifts, his rise was meteoric. In May 1937, he became the technical director of the Peenemünde institute. That same year, he applied for membership in the NSDAP. In 1940, he also joined the SS, and three years later, Himmler promoted him to the rank of Sturmbannführer. Among his most important tasks was the development of long-distance ballistic rockets. In October 1942, the first successful tests were carried out on the A-4—later known as the V-2 because it was designed to exact *Vergeltung* (retribution) against the Allies. In July 1943, when von Braun and Dornberger visited Hitler's Wolf's Lair field headquarters, the dictator was ecstatic about the possibilities offered by these new "miracle weapons," and he made the thirty-one-year-old von Braun a professor right then and there. Von Braun would insist on being addressed by that title until well into the 1950s.

On the night of August 17, 1943, the Royal Air Force bombed Peenemünde, causing considerable damage. After that, serial production of the V-2 was transferred to a discontinued mine near the town of Nordhausen in central Germany. There, prisoners from the Mittelbau-Dora concentration camp were forced to work under terrible conditions building V-2 rockets. Von Braun visited the "middle factory," as it was code-named, on numerous occasions and took part in meetings about the deployment of slave labor. When he claimed after 1945 to have known nothing about the prisoners' horrific fate, he was lying to protect himself.

Conservative estimates put the number of people who died in the Mittelbau-Dora complex between 16,000 and 20,000. Some 6,000 V-2 rockets were produced there, roughly half of which were fired, mostly at London or the port of Antwerp. V-2s killed almost 3,000 people in Britain and at least that many in Belgium.[91]

But the Americans were not interested in the human toll of the former Peenemünde rocket program. Their priority was to secure the services of the men who had come up with such a militarily significant technology. And rocket scientists were not the only experts the Americans sought to get their hands on. Starting in July 1944 with the Allied landing in Normandy, US Supreme Command set up snatch squads, independently operating units whose mission was to locate major weapons-producing sites and to capture the scientists and technicians who worked there and take them to America. Once the Allies had crossed the Rhine and occupied large parts of western and central Germany in late March 1945, the hunt for experts could begin in earnest. The operation was code-named "Overcast." Numerous specialists were captured in Saxony and Thuringia, regions of Germany that would become part of the Soviet occupation zone, so the Soviets would be unable to benefit from their knowledge and skills. Over the course of Operation Overcast and the expanded Project Paperclip, which ran from 1946 to 1952, 642 German and Austrian experts were "imported" to the United States.[92]

Von Braun and his team arrived in Fort Bliss, Texas, in September 1945. "My country has lost two world wars," he said. "This time I would like to be on the winning side."[93] Von Braun had little difficulty making a career among his former enemies. In the 1950s, he was named technical director of the US Space and Rocket Center in Huntsville, Alabama. In 1960, he joined NASA as one of the agency's leading experts. When the United States succeeded in putting a man on the moon on July 20, 1969, von Braun's public esteem was at its zenith. His fame as a genius rocket builder and the father of space travel would first be tarnished in the 1990s, well after his death in 1973, when critical historians began to more closely examine his Nazi past.

"TERRIBLE COLD, SNOW on the fields and roofs, more snow falling. This and the constant absence of electric current make life more than uncomfortable. Nevertheless, the feeling of having been saved is dominant."[94] The Jewish-German diarist Victor Klemperer wrote these words in a tiny attic in the Bavarian village of Unterbernbach, where he and his wife had taken refuge. Born in 1881, the onetime professor of Romance languages at the Technical University of Dresden had, like all his Jewish colleagues, been driven from his academic position by the Nazis and gradually, step by step, forced into social isolation. In May 1940, he and his wife were required to give up their home and move into one of the "Jew houses," where they and others who had shared the same fate vacillated every day between hope and worry, always afraid of raids and deportations. Klemperer owed his survival solely to the fact that he was married to a Gentile, the pianist Eva Schlemmer, since Jews in mixed marriages were exempted from deportation to the concentration camps. Despite being under pressure to leave him, Klemperer's wife stayed by his side and accepted the considerable risk of smuggling his diaries out of the house at regular intervals and taking them to a friend of hers, a doctor in Pirna, where they were kept in a trunk and remained for decades, until their publication in 1995. They bear witness more poignantly than any other document to the fate of Jews in Germany between 1933 and 1945, from their loss of all legal rights and exclusion from society to their eventual deportation and annihilation.[95]

On February 13 and 14, Dresden—which had previously been spared from Allied air raids—was nearly destroyed when incendiary bombs unleashed a firestorm in the city. For the Klemperers, the inferno meant salvation, and amid the general chaos, they decided to flee. Victor cut the yellow star from his coat, and that was the begin-

ning of an odyssey that eventually led them, on April 12, to Unterbernbach. On their journey, the couple witnessed Germans turning
their backs on National Socialism and the Führer they had loyally followed for so long. "The 'final victory' optimism has almost died away,"
Klemperer wrote while stopping in Munich in early April. "Everywhere
(people) sigh: 'If only the Americans come quickly!'" When he and his
wife reached Pfaffenhofen, he added, "Everyone says, and already said
in Munich, 'Grüss Gott' (Good day) and 'Auf Wiedersehen' (Goodbye)."[96] Previously, they had said "Heil Hitler!"

In late April 1945, before the Americans arrived, the mayor of Unterbernbach and the farmers' representative in the village of Flamensbeck,
who initially took the Klemperers in, removed the swastika that had
been affixed to the gable of the town hall. Similar scenes played out
in many towns as the Third Reich collapsed. Everywhere, portraits of
Hitler disappeared from public offices and private dwellings, editions
of *Mein Kampf* were removed from bookshelves, and uniforms, party
insignia, and swastika flags were burned. "To what extent are coats
now being turned, to what extent can one trust?" Klemperer asked in
his diary on May 1. "Now everyone here was always an enemy of the
Party. But if they really *always* were . . ." Several days later Klemperer
registered how increasingly mysterious it seemed that Hitler could have
been successful. "Here, e.g. in Flamensbeck, they sometimes talk as
if Hitlerism had been essentially a Prussian, militaristic, un-Catholic,
un-Bavarian cause."[97] But as Klemperer recalled, Munich had been the
place where the National Socialist movement had started and Hitler
had celebrated his initial triumphs.

On the afternoon of May 2, Klemperer walked four kilometers
from Unterbernbach to Kühbach to procure some necessities. There,
in the town's church square, he encountered Americans for the first
time, part of an "emergency or repair column." Klemperer wrote,
"Black, more precisely brown negro soldiers in indefinably grey-green
earth-colored jackets and trousers, all with steel helmets stuck on their

heads, bustled and swarmed around—village children stood close by and among them. . . . Later I also saw individual blond soldiers in dark leather jackets, revolver strapped on, rifle . . . slung over the shoulder." From a young German woman, Klemperer learned that the soldiers had emptied out shops but had otherwise behaved "altogether decently." "The blacks, too?" Klemperer asked. "They're even friendlier than the others, there's nothing to be afraid of," he was told. Two older ladies he engaged in conversation confirmed this view. "What has been said about the cruelty of these enemies, that was all nothing but slogans, that was only rabble-rousing," they told him. Klemperer was astonished at how enlightened ordinary Germans suddenly seemed to be.[98]

Many of Klemperer's contemporaries recorded similar impressions when they first encountered Americans.[99] The horror scenarios of Goebbels's propaganda, according to which the "Jewish plutocracy" of the West was bent on destroying the German people, apparently had not fooled all Germans. And most of those who did believe it soon learned better. Ursula von Kardorff, who witnessed the Americans marching into a Swabian village in late April 1945, noted, "The American soldiers are very friendly. Now and then, some of them peep over our fences. We enjoy talking to them. . . . They bring chocolate, and we talk—in utterly poor English—as objectively as possible about politics."[100]

MAY 3, 1945

Dönitz's headquarters in Flensburg began the morning of May 3, 1945, in pandemonium. The previous night, reports had arrived that British troops were accelerating their push forward in northern Germany, and the grand admiral was afraid they would soon reach Flensburg and arrest him and the other members of the government. At 4:00 a.m., he had ordered that the final line of resistance, the Kaiser Wilhelm Canal, "be defended by all means for as long as possible to ensure the government retains its freedom to move and act."[1] But during the day those fears proved unfounded. The Allies seemed to have no plans to take Germany's enclave in Flensburg as long as the Dönitz government was willing to negotiate the Wehrmacht's surrender.

Having sent Admiral General Friedeburg to Montgomery's head-quarters with the offer to surrender German armies across the entire north of the country, Dönitz now summoned the civilian and military commanders of the regions Germany still occupied. The state minister for Bohemia and Moravia, Karl Hermann Frank, and the chief of staff of the Army Group Center, Lieutenant General Oldwig von Natzmer, flew in from Prague. Frank, a Sudeten German politician from Karls-bad (today, Karlovy Vary), had been named a state secretary under the

Reich protector of Bohemia and Moravia, Baron Konstantin von Neurath, after Germany occupied the non–ethnically German parts of what is now the Czech Republic. Frank commanded the SS and the police in the area and was among those responsible for the orgies of vengeance wreaked by the Gestapo and the SS on the Czech populace following the assassination in late May 1942 of Reinhard Heydrich, the head of the Reich Main Security Office and deputy Reich protector of Bohemia and Moravia. The village of Lidice became a symbol of German-inflicted terror: all of the town's 196 male inhabitants were executed, its women deported to the Ravensbrück concentration camp, and most of its 96 children murdered in Chelmno, while the village itself was razed to the ground.[2]

Reich Commissar Josef Terboven and the Wehrmacht commander in Norway, Franz Böhme, arrived in Flensburg as well. As a commander general in Serbia in 1941, Böhme, who was Austrian, was responsible for numerous massacres of civilians, including thousands of Jews and Sinti and Roma.[3] Terboven, who had been a card-carrying Nazi since the party's earliest days, had been the Gauleiter of Essen and the president of the Rhine province before the war, and was named Reich commissar of Norway after the Germans occupied it. Until the end of the war, he possessed the true power in that country, while Prime Minister Vidkun Quisling was little more than a puppet of the German occupiers. With great vigor, Terboven went about economically exploiting Norway and crushed all signs of resistance among the Norwegian people with pitiless severity.[4]

Werner Best and Colonel General Georg Lindemann came to Flensburg from Copenhagen. Best, a doctor of law from the western German region of Hessen, had enjoyed a meteoric career after 1933 and had risen to become the third most powerful man, after Himmler and Heydrich, in the SS security and terror apparatus. After falling out with Heydrich in 1940, he worked for the German military commander in France before assuming the office of Reich plenipotentiary in Denmark in November 1942. Unlike Terboven in Norway, Best charted a moderate course, keeping the hardships of occupation to a minimum and seeking to make Denmark an example for the new National Socialist–dominated order in Europe. In 1943, with resistance growing among the Danish people and the number of labor strikes and acts of sabotage increasing, Best became more severe, although he did not, as Hitler demanded, answer every attack on German soldiers with brutal "counter-terror." In the final months of the war, Best was chiefly concerned with provisionally accommodating the tens of thousands of refugees from East Prussia and Pomerania pouring into Denmark.[5]

Arthur Seyss-Inquart came by speedboat from the Netherlands because every overland connection to northern Germany had already been severed. The son of an academy teacher and a trained lawyer, Seyss-Inquart had played a central role in the amalgamation of Austria into the Third Reich in March 1938. As the Reich representative in the "eastern march," as Austria was called under the Nazis, and a year later the deputy to the general gouverneur of Poland, Hans Frank, Seyss-Inquart had helped dramatically increase pressure on Jews. In May 1940, Hitler made him Reich commissar for the occupied Dutch territories. Seyss-Inquart was an efficient, bureaucratic sadist who put down all opposition with draconian retaliatory moves, oversaw the seamless deportation of Dutch Jews to the death camps, and sent hundreds of thousands of men and women to work as slave laborers in Germany. The fact that in his last will and testament Hitler had named Seyss-Inquart Germany's foreign minister shows how he and the dictator were of one mind.[6]

May 3 saw a series of separate meetings whose attendees depended on which territories were concerned. Along with Dönitz, the participants common to all of them included Krosigk, Wegener, Jodl, and Keitel, the head of the Wehrmacht Supreme Command, while Speer and Himmler sometimes took part. The day started at 9:30 a.m. with consultations about the "Bohemian question." Frank reported that the

Protectorate of Bohemia and Moravia—the parts of Czechoslovakia that Germany had de facto annexed—was on the "eve of a revolution" and would be "impossible to keep either militarily or politically" in the long term. To calm the situation, Frank proposed that Prague be declared an "open city." Frank also wanted to establish contacts with bourgeois Czech circles interested in seeing their homeland liberated by the Americans and not the Soviets. With these groups on board, Frank argued, an attempt should be made to offer Eisenhower the surrender of the Army Group Center and convince him to occupy Czechoslovakia. Neither Dönitz nor Krosigk thought this initiative likely to succeed: they assumed that the Allies had already decided the fate of Czechoslovakia among themselves. Nonetheless, they authorized Frank to investigate and, if possible, to send a German and a Czech emissary to Eisenhower.

A quarrel broke out over whether the Dönitz government should move to the protectorate to avoid a possible British attack. Keitel, Jodl, and Himmler favored the idea, especially as Natzmer assured them that the Army Group Center would be able to defend itself for two more weeks. Dönitz rejected the idea, though, saying that there was no way he could rule Germany from abroad and that the Bohemian political situation was too unstable.[7]

At 11:00 a.m., the focus shifted to the Scandinavian countries. Terboven characterized the state of play in Norway as still "favorable" since "most people's efforts" were directed at "emerging in one piece when Germany's expected collapse arrived and the war came to an end." Best offered similar conclusions concerning Denmark, where an uprising seemed unlikely "despite the strong liberation movement." On the state of the German military, the commanders Böhme and Lindemann were optimistic. The strength and will to fight remained unbroken, they said. "Come to North Schleswig, Mr. Grand Admiral, then we'll seal the bottleneck and fight the final proper battle of the war," Lindemann was said to have exclaimed. But both Krosigk and Best rejected the suggestion of bringing about a "heroic downfall" in one final battle. That, they argued, would provoke an uprising by Danish liberation fighters, leaving the many German refugees in Denmark at their mercy. For both occupied Norway and Denmark, Dönitz decreed the following to his subordinates: "Maintain calm and order since internal unrest will only be to our disadvantage. Maintain a strong and energetic impression but be prepared to compromise in individual instances."[8]

By 3:30 that afternoon, the group arrived at the "Dutch question." Back in April, Seyss-Inquart had sent out feelers to Eisenhower's general chief of staff, General Walter Bedell Smith, in an attempt to improve the catastrophic food situation of the Dutch people.[9] Now he reported that negotiations had "proceeded satisfactorily," with "all sides interested in an orderly transition." Nonetheless, Seyss-Inquart was skeptical about the idea of a German surrender in the west only. The Allies had pledged to accept only a total surrender, he pointed out, and that pledge was considered binding. Despite such doubts the commanders decided to continue preliminary surrender discussions. Dönitz instructed Seyss-Inquart to fulfill his "mission to fight" until a ceasefire was concluded but to refrain from flooding whole regions of the Netherlands by blowing up dikes. "An honorable transition will be a small credit in our account," Dönitz argued.[10] Seyss-Inquart was never able to carry out these instructions because bad weather kept his boat in port, and on May 7, during an attempt to reach the Netherlands by land, he was taken into custody by British military police in Hamburg.[11]

On the evening of May 3, a strange if ultimately inconsequential incident took place at the Flensburg naval academy. Himmler suddenly appeared together with the head of the Foreign Security Service, SS Brigadeführer Walter Schellenberg, and suggested to Dönitz that he make an offer to surrender Germany's troops in Norway to the Swedish government. Instead of becoming Allied POWs, these soldiers would be interned in Sweden. Schellenberg, it turned out, had already approached Swedish leaders with this proposal. But Dönitz saw little sense in it, asking, "How can we, in our hopeless situation, seek to lead the Allies around by the nose by offering to surrender in Norway not to them, but to a neutral country?" Under the influence of Krosigk, however, Dönitz did agree that Schellenberg could continue his efforts in Sweden, although without official authorization to negotiate anything final. In any case, Schellenberg's mission never yielded any results and was soon overtaken by events.[12]

Also on May 3, Flensburg's radio station broadcast a speech by Albert Speer, most of which had been recorded on April 21 during a visit to Hamburg Gauleiter Karl Kaufmann. The speech was an attempt by Speer to shore up his position for the post-Hitler period. In his memoir, Speer said he had given the speech to awaken the German people from their lethargy and to encourage them to energetically take control of the nation's reconstruction. In reality, Speer went far beyond that. He started his address in a tone that was as jingoist and racist as Dönitz's and Krosigk's speeches of May 1 and 2. "Never has a cultured people suffered such a heavy blow, and never has the devastation and destruction of war been so great as in our country, and never has a people borne the hardships of war with greater endurance, toughness and faith," Speer said, adding that "in future days the admiration of a just history" was assured.

Speer, likewise, did not utter a single word of regret for the devastation Germans had brought to the peoples of Europe—devastation for which he was significantly responsible insofar as his ruthless exploitation of all natural and human resources in the service of arms production had intensified and prolonged the war. Instead Speer appealed to the Allies to demonstrate understanding of the German situation and not to block Germans in their desire to rebuild their country: "It is entirely in the hands of the enemy to what extent they grant the German people the respect and the opportunities due to a vanquished but heroically battling foe and in so doing go down in history themselves as generous and righteous." Speer concluded his speech very much in the style of his beloved Führer by invoking "providence," which, he suggested, could give Germany's destiny a positive turn.[13] Anyone listening to these words on the Allied side would have gotten the impression that the malevolent Nazi spirit was alive and well in the Dönitz government.

THE WAR ENDED FOR Hamburg on May 3. Throughout the day, local radio stations broadcast the news that British troops were ready to march peacefully into the city. Large posters informed the populace that a general curfew would be in force beginning at 1:00 p.m., with exceptions made only for employees of the electricity, gas, and water utilities.[14] A spectral quiet settled over the city that afternoon. There was no traffic, and shops and businesses were closed. Hamburg police were posted at crossings and bridges, but otherwise the streets were deserted.

As recently as mid-April, there had been no indication that Hamburg was ready to surrender without a fight. The previous fall, construction had begun on an inner and outer defensive ring around the city. Trenches had been dug, and antitank fortifications put in place. On February 19, Gauleiter Kaufmann had told a group of party functionaries, business leaders, and top administrators in the unheated ballroom of the Hamburg Rathaus that Hitler had declared the city a "fortress" to be defended to the last bullet.[15]

Kaufmann was the most powerful man in the city. Born in 1900 as the son of a laundry business owner in Krefeld, he was one of the NSDAP's original "old-time streetfighters." In May 1929, Hitler had named him the Gauleiter of left-wing Hamburg at the tender age of twenty-eight. In 1933, he became a Reichstatthalter (a kind of regional governor), in which office he was responsible for the rigorous enforcement of Nazi policies in the city. Kaufmann completely overshadowed the city's mayor, Carl Vincent Krogmann, whom the Nazis had installed as a bourgeois figurehead. In 1936, Kaufmann was officially put in charge of the regional government, and at the start of the war he was given the additional title and responsibilities of Reich defense commissar.[16] On the one hand, as a diehard Nazi, he left no doubt that he intended to faithfully execute Hitler's orders even as the war ground to a close. On the other hand, he was enough of a realist to know that defending Hamburg to the last would ensure its complete destruction. By the spring of 1945, Hamburg had been subjected to more than two hundred aerial bombardments, the most severe of which, from July 25 to August 3, 1943, saw British and American bombers lay waste to broad stretches of the city. Thirty-four thousand people had perished in the firestorm, according to conservative estimates, and tens of thousands had been forced to flee for their lives.[17] By the start of 1945, around one million people still lived in the city, many in basements and emergency shelters. The public mood was at an all-time low despite government appeals to hold out. Wherever one went, regardless of social class, Hamburg residents were resigned, saying, "Let the Tommies come and put an end to it now, so that we can lead a reasonable and orderly life again."[18]

In these circumstances, Kaufmann began to search for ways to spare the people of Hamburg a senseless "final battle." Without question, he was also partially motivated by the desire to style himself Hamburg's "savior" and to offer a counterweight to the crimes he had committed during the previous twelve years of a regime whose days were clearly numbered. Kaufmann began by securing the support of Major General Alwin Wolz, who had been named, at Kaufmann's own request, on April 2 as the city's commandant. The following day, the Gauleiter set out with the supreme commander of Army Group Northwest, Field Marshal General Ernst Busch, to pay a final visit to Hitler in the Reich chancellery. The only surviving record of their meeting, also attended by Bormann, Keitel, Jodl, Dönitz, and Himmler, were notes Kaufmann made after the fact. If they are to be believed, the atmosphere was extraordinarily frosty. When Busch asked when Army

Group Northwest could expect reinforcements, Hitler brusquely waved him off, saying that all available reserves would be placed at the disposal of the newly formed Army Wenck, which was to play a central role in the decisive battle for Berlin. Kaufmann claims he then asserted that in view of the general situation, he could not countenance a defense of Hamburg. He explained that 680,000 women and children remained in the city, and Schleswig-Holstein was already overwhelmed by refugees from Germany's east; there was nowhere to evacuate them. Hitler, Kaufmann's notes state, dismissed his objections "in the sharpest terms" and insisted that his "fortress order" be carried out unconditionally.[19] Kaufmann is unlikely to have confronted the dictator as openly as he later claimed. But it is plausible that the encounter with the Führer, who had become palpably divorced from reality, opened Kaufmann's eyes and strengthened his resolve to hand over Hamburg to the British without a fight.

On April 20, Hitler's final birthday, Montgomery's 7th Tank Division under Major General Lewis O. Lyne had advanced to Hamburg's southern periphery. "Now we face the ultimate catastrophe," wrote Mathilde Wolff-Mönckeberg, the wife of a noted English literature professor and member of one of Hamburg's leading families, to her children. "You can't imagine the past few days! To have ruination approaching, a constant tension and agitation, rushing to the radio to get every bit of news among a thousand swirling bits of gossip, preliminary warnings and alarms alternating with one another from morning until late at night."[20]

With British artillerymen firing on the southern Hamburg district of Harburg from their advanced positions, several shells hit the Phoenix factory in which a reserve hospital had been set up in late 1944. The factory director, Albert Schäfer, and its head physician, Hermann Burchard, decided to set off for British lines to ask that the barrage be ended. Wolz approved the mission and gave the two men an interpreter, his staff lieutenant Otto von Laun, the son of a well-known international human-rights lawyer. On the evening of April 29, after losing their way for hours, they were received by the 7th Tank Division's intelligence officer, Captain Thomas Martin Lindsay. He promised to divert artillery fire from the hospital but demanded something in return. One of the three emissaries was to take a letter from his divisional commander, Lyne, to Hamburg's commandant. It called upon Wolz "in the name of humanity" to send an officer authorized to surrender the city.[21]

Wolz received the letter the following day and immediately discussed it with Kaufmann. Both agreed that they could not afford to lose any more time. In a telegram to Dönitz, Kaufmann indicated that he was going to hand over Hamburg to the British. This earned him a rebuke from the admiral, who insisted on the necessity of "defending our positions on the Elbe with extreme tenacity against the West." Hamburg, Dönitz added, could make "the greatest of contributions . . . in this battle for the destiny of our people."[22] But Kaufmann and Wolz were determined to act on their own authority. On the evening of May 1, two emissaries from Wolz's staff, Major Peter Andrae and Captain Gerhard Link, set off for the 7th British Tank Division's main headquarters and gave Lyne a message from the Hamburg battle commandant confirming his willingness to "discuss the issue of a potential surrender of the city of Hamburg and the broad-ranging consequences that would result."[23] Lyne replied that the German side would have twenty-four hours to accept an unconditional surrender. That night the emissaries returned to the city and informed Wolz about the negotiations. The battle commandant immediately ordered the withdrawal of all army and Waffen-SS units in Hamburg's south.

The people of Hamburg were still completely unaware of the developments that would determine their fate. But around noon on May 2, a special edition of the *Hamburger Zeitung* was delivered to the display case on the central Gänsemarkt square. It contained a message from Kaufmann to the city populace, informing them of the imminent capitulation: "Anyone whose soldierly honor demands that he continue to fight has the opportunity to do so outside the city. But my heart and my conscience, in clear recognition of the circumstances and in the consciousness of my responsibility for our Hamburg, require that I protect its women and children from senseless, irresponsible destruction. I am aware of what I am bringing upon myself. I am content to leave judgment about my decision to history and to you."[24] Originally, this entreaty was supposed to be published the following day to coincide with the entry of British troops into the city, and it has never been determined how it was made public prematurely. In any case, the news spread immediately throughout the city. "At Gänsemarkt, there were tumultuous scenes of joy," wrote one Hamburg resident. "People embraced, and many of them burst into tears."[25]

Dönitz was initially furious at Kaufmann's independent action. But by the afternoon of May 2, after Montgomery's troops had broken through German lines at the Elbe and advanced on Lübeck, the admiral acknowledged that there was no sense defending Hamburg and approved the city's surrender without a fight. Orders to that effect went out to Keitel and Busch in the evening.[26]

Meanwhile, Kaufmann addressed the people of Hamburg via radio and told them that their home had been declared an "open city." He said, "When tomorrow the enemy occupies Hamburg, it will be the heaviest hour of my life. For this hour, I demand from you dignity and discipline." State Secretary Georg Ahrens—Kaufmann's deputy as the director of the Hamburg city administration, whom residents had nicknamed "Uncle Baldrian" owing to the soothing quality of his voice during nighttime air raids—closed out the broadcast: "You have been listening to the monumental address of our Gauleiter to his Hamburgers."[27]

Kaufmann had spoken with "great shock, with heartfelt emotion, simply and honorably . . . as he has always been to his Hamburgers," wrote Wolff-Mönckeberg.[28] Kaufmann's attempt to portray himself as a responsible politician who had only wanted the best for "his" city was, at least at first, a success. "The legend of the good Gauleiter" who had gone from being a loyal Hitler follower to a rebel against his destructive fury spread far and wide. It laid the ground for another legend: that of Hamburg as an "island of relative reason" amid brown-shirted barbarism.[29]

Shortly after 9:00 p.m. on the evening of May 2, Wolz, accompanied by Andrae, Link, and former Hamburg mayor Wilhelm Burchard-Motz, set off for the frontlines. Brigadier General John M. K. Spurling, the commander of the 131st British Infantry Brigade, brought the delegation to Lyne's headquarters. When asked, Wolz confirmed that he was unconditionally surrendering and pledged to institute a curfew on May 3 and clear the mines from the streets of the city and the bridges over the Elbe. The actual surrender agreement, however, was first signed around noon on May 3 in the headquarters of the 2nd British Army in the town of Häcklingen near Lüneburg. Wolz had been required to accompany the delegation from the Wehrmacht Supreme Command under Friedeburg, sent from Flensburg, before returning to Hamburg just in time to see the British occupy the city.[30]

British forces began marching into Hamburg shortly after 4:00 p.m. on May 3, with three columns of soldiers from the 7th British Tank Division crossing the bridges over the Elbe River and arriving at the market square in front of the city's Rathaus about 6:00 p.m. At 6:26, Wolz and Burchard-Motz received Spurling and the members of his staff in front of the Rathaus entrance and formally surrendered the city. They then accompanied the British officers into the Kaisersaal ballroom, where they were greeted by Kaufmann and Mayor Krogmann.[31]

Most Hamburg residents did not take notice of their new masters until the following day. "Suddenly English soldiers teemed about, crawling through the streets like ants," Wolff-Mönckeberg observed in the wealthy district of Winterhude. "On their heels followed cars, tanks, armored vehicles, and motorcycles in huge numbers, and in

In front of the Hamburg Rathaus on May 3, 1945,
Major General Alwin Wolz surrenders the city to
British Brigadier General John M. K. Spurling.

no time, they established themselves, putting up large wooden signs everywhere: Army Post Office, Tailor, Furlough Application Centre, etc. . . . There were many curious people who stood on their balconies the whole day, watching what was going on down below. We kept ourselves occupied by emptying the cellar of everything that had collected there the past six months."[32]

By 7:00 p.m. on the evening of May 4, Radio Hamburg resumed broadcasting from its undamaged facility on Rothenbaumchaussee, becoming the first German radio station to go back on the air. The station's initial message was broadcast in both English and German: "Here is Radio Hamburg, a Station of the Military Government."[33]

That same day, members of the Giordano family crawled out from a cellar in the Alsterdorf district, where they had been hiding for almost three months. In early February, the Jewish mother, Lilly, who had been living in a so-called mixed marriage with a Gentile musician of Sicilian heritage, had been ordered to report to the former Talmud and Thora school at Grindelhof, where she was scheduled to be deported to the concentration camps. In his memoirs, Lilly's son Ralph, who was born in 1923 and later became a well-known German writer and journalist, described their moment of liberation: "When I passed by my mother, I saw what I hadn't noticed in the darkness of our hiding place—her hair, once so majestically black, had gone completely grey with the exception of a few strands. But I didn't cry until I saw [my brother] Egon in the light of day—some of his brown hair had turned silver."[34]

As the Giordanos glimpsed the light of freedom, the British were arresting Kaufmann. He remained incarcerated until October 1948, when he was released for health reasons. Hitler's man in Hamburg, who had pitilessly persecuted his political enemies and was responsible for the death of thousands of Hamburg's Jews, never had to answer for his crimes in court. In the late 1950s, he became a senior executive at an insurance company and a part owner of a chemical plant. Until his death in December 1969, he lived as an affluent, generally respected member of Hamburg society.[35]

WHILE MAJOR GENERAL WOLZ was signing Hamburg's surrender agreement in Häcklingen, one of the most significant sea catastrophes of the war was taking place in the Bay of Lübeck: the sinking of the SS *Cap Arcona* and the death of thousands of concentration-camp inmates onboard just as the war was about to end. The vessel was the flagship of the Hamburg–South American Steamboat Association, which had been launched by the Blohm & Voss shipyards in Hamburg in 1927. Before the war, it had been used for luxury cruises between Hamburg and Rio de Janeiro. In 1940, it had been sent as a navy residential vessel to Gotenhafen (Gdynia). In the spring of 1945, the *Cap Arcona* was one of many vessels used to transport refugees and wounded soldiers from Germany's eastern provinces, now under Soviet control, to Schleswig-Holstein and Denmark. During its final voyage, the ship's engine had broken down, and since April 14, it had been anchored, unable to maneuver, in Lübeck Bay closest to the town of Neustadt.[36]

In mid-April 1945, Himmler had instructed the commandants of the concentration camps that had not yet been liberated that no inmates were to be allowed to fall into enemy hands and that the camps should thus be promptly evacuated.[37] At Hamburg-Neuengamme, a large-scale facility with a broad network of satellite camps that had been operating since 1940 at a former brickyard, the evacuation began on April 20. Responsible for overseeing it were Kaufmann and the supreme SS and police leader in the North Sea, Count Georg Henning von Bassewitz-Behr. They had an interest in making sure British troops were not witness to crimes perpetrated just outside Hamburg. Because there was nowhere else to take the inmates, Kaufmann proposed housing them on ships. On his authority as Reich commissar for ocean sea travel, he requisitioned three vessels anchored in Lübeck Bay: the freighters *Thielbek* and *Athen* and the *Cap Arcona*.[38]

From April 21 to 26, more than nine thousand inmates were taken from Neuengamme to Lübeck, some on trucks and freight trains, others by foot. Under the command of SS Sturmbahnführer Christoph Gehrig, who had been the head of administration in Neuengamme, they were put aboard the vessels. What the SS intended to do with them is unclear. It is possible that they planned to get rid of their captives by sinking the vessels or that they hoped British warplanes would perform that task for them.[39] It is also possible that Himmler wanted to use the prisoners as a bargaining chip in negotiations for a partial peace in the west. Perhaps, amid the chaos of the time, the SS leadership never did decide what to do with their "floating concentration camps."

At first, the *Cap Arcona*'s captain, Heinrich Bertram, refused to accept the prisoners, but he relented when Gehrig threatened to have him shot.[40] By April 28, some 6,500 captives were already on board.

The conditions were almost indescribably horrid. "There was hardly anything to eat or drink," remembered a survivor, Rudi Goguel. "Exhausted inmates lay everywhere. Corpses were beginning to pile up onboard, thirty to fifty of them every day. Toward the end, the death count was rising steeply. The ill had a particularly harsh fate. They were stored in the belly of the ship, and there was no opportunity for helping them at all since there was no medication or dressings for wounds. No one emptied the heavy latrine buckets any longer, so a terrible stench hovered over the ship."[41] Because the *Cap Arcona* was so overcrowded, the SS ordered 2,000 prisoners to be moved to the *Athen*. Another 2,800 inmates were also crammed aboard the *Thielbek*, which had been towed into Lübeck Bay on May 2 and anchored near the *Cap Arcona*.

The collection of ships in the waters of Kiel and Lübeck had not failed to attract the notice of Allied air reconnaissance, and the British military leadership feared that the Dönitz regime and its remaining troops were about to flee to Norway to continue fighting. The decision was made to eradicate the remnants of the German fleet. Information from the Swiss Red Cross that the ships actually contained concentration-camp inmates was not communicated in time.[42]

At 2:30 p.m. on May 3, British bombers attacked the *Cap Arcona* and the *Thielbek*. Both vessels took a number of direct hits and quickly caught fire. Horrific scenes played out on board. The actor and Communist Erwin Geschonneck, who had been interned at various concentration camps, including Neuengamme, since 1933 and who would later star with Bertolt Brecht's Berliner Ensemble theater company and in a number of East German films, described the moment when the *Cap Arcona* was bombed: "There was a bang and then the sound of something splintering. Several bombs had hit us midship. I sprinted down the gangways, all of them were full of smoke, wounded were screaming, and bewildered prisoners were running to the stairs, completely panicked. People driven half-mad with fear were arriving from all directions and clamoring to get up on deck. Several were pulled to the floor and trampled to death. The so-called banana hold was full of Russians. There was no escape for them. Six hundred ill people in the sick bay below were also cut off."[43]

The *Thielbek* sank within minutes, while fire gradually consumed the *Cap Arcona*, which began listing to one side. Prisoners had little chance of survival because SS men, German sailors, and crew members claimed the few undamaged lifeboats and all the life vests. Some 6,600 prisoners burned to death or died while trying to swim to shore. Some drowned; others were shot in the water by the SS. About 450 people managed to escape the inferno, including Geschonneck, who survived only because he swam back to the wreck of the *Cap Arcona* and huddled on it with some other inmates until the British occupied the coasts and took them via motorboats to Neustadt.[44] Bodies continued to wash up on the beaches of Lübeck Bay for weeks afterward.

"SLOWLY BUT SURELY we're starting to view all the raping with a sense of humor—gallows humor." By the time a Berlin woman in her early thirties wrote these words in her diary, the mass rape of German women by Red Army soldiers had passed its initial high point. The diarist, who herself had been raped multiple times, was now able to put the unspeakable into words: "What does it mean—rape? When I said the word for the first time aloud . . . it sent shivers down my spine. Now I can think it and write it with an untrembling hand, say it out loud to get used to hearing it said. It sounds like the absolute worst, the end of everything—it's not."[45]

The diary written by an anonymous "woman in Berlin" is a remarkable document. From April 20 to June 22, 1945, the diarist recorded her experiences in the pauses between bombings, rapes, and the arduous trips outside to try to procure food. That July, she began to type out the handwritten notes that had filled three notebooks. The result was 121 single-spaced manuscript pages she later gave to a friend, the writer Kurt W. Marek, who penned the 1949 best-seller on archaeology *Gods,*

Graves and Scholars under the pseudonym C. W. Ceram. Marek convinced the diarist to allow the manuscript to be published, although she understandably insisted on remaining anonymous. In 1954, *A Woman in Berlin* appeared in the United States, with a German version, published by a small Geneva publishing house, following five years later. The book was widely read in the United States and United Kingdom, but it failed to attract a German readership. The time was obviously not right for people to confront its appalling subject, which remained taboo across Germany for many years to come.[46]

That changed in the spring of 2003, when the Eichborn publishing house reprinted the diary as part of a series entitled *Die andere Bibiliothek* (The Other Library) edited by Hans Magnus Enzensberger. The German version of the diary *Eine Frau in Berlin* became one of the successes of the season and attracted unanimous praise from critics as the most harrowing account of the violence against German women during the Red Army's conquest of much of the country. The book served as the basis for a film by director Max Färberböck starring the popular actress Nina Hoss in the lead role.

Perennial speculation about the identity of the author was put to rest in September 2003 when an editor for the *Süddeutsche Zeitung*, Jens Bisky, revealed that "Anonymous" was Marta Hillers, a woman who was born in 1911 in Krefeld and died in 2001 in Switzerland. After attending high school from 1925 to 1930, Hillers had traveled extensively abroad, including in the Soviet Union, where she learned Russian. This gave her an advantage during the occupation of Berlin. As of the summer of 1934, she was a freelance journalist for the *Berliner Lokalanzeiger* and other newspapers and periodicals. From April 1941 until the end of the war, she worked for the student newspaper published by the Nazi teachers' association, where she supervised short-story competitions. She also wrote articles for the magazine *Der deutsche Erzieher* (The German Educator). Hillers seems not to have been a fanatic Nazi. She was a small-time propagandist who helped stir up enthusiasm among young Germans for the war.[47] In her diary, she attempted to downplay her own role in the Third Reich, writing, "What about me? Was I for . . . or against? What's clear is that I was there, that I breathed what was in the air, and it affected all of us even if we didn't want it to."[48]

When her identity was revealed, doubts emerged as to whether the book truly was an authentic document of the period as the publisher claimed. Skeptics wondered whether the author might not have revised her original notes more significantly than previously assumed or whether Marek, who wrote the afterword to the original edition, had edited the text. These questions were fiercely debated but could not be answered because Marek's widow, who controlled his estate, refused to let anyone inspect the relevant documents.[49]

In the end, Eichborn hired the author Walter Kempowski, known as a painstaking collector and editor of diaries, to examine the case. His evaluation, finished in January 2004, confirmed that the original diary and Hillers's typescript were genuine. But Kempowski did not address the key question of how much the original text had been edited and to what extent its character as a diary had possibly been compromised.[50]

To fill in that particular blank, historian Yuliya von Saal examined Hillers's private papers, which the Mareks' son had given to Munich's Institute for Contemporary History. Saal concluded in her 2019 essay for an academic history journal that Hillers had been faithful in typing out her handwritten diary. Deviations were minimal and consisted of small stylistic corrections. The differences between the typescript and the book version, which was almost twice as long and which the author had put together in the 1950s, were far more significant. Hillers had thoroughly revised the text, making it more literary and, of course, adding new material. People's identities were consistently concealed; thoughts, observations, and emotions subsequently fleshed out; events reinterpreted; and scenes enriched with fictional elements to make them more dramatic. Among other things, all the passages that suggested any affinity on the author's part with Nazism were expunged. The diary was not an authentic contemporary source but an edited literary account in diary form of what the author had experienced.[51] Nonetheless, *A Woman in Berlin* remains an important historical source. Among other things, Hillers's description of rape in the printed version corresponded to her handwritten notes.[52]

With the appearance of Red Army soldiers in Berlin, it was open season on women, as Hillers found out. In remarkably laconic, unsentimental language, she described what happened to her: "I'm numb. Not with disgust, only cold. My spine is frozen: icy, dizzy shivers around the back of my head. I feel myself gliding and falling, down, down, through the pillows and the floorboards. So that's what it means to sink into the ground."[53] After being raped multiple times, Hillers reached a decision: "I have to find a single wolf to keep away the pack. An officer, as high-ranking as possible, a commandant, a general, whatever I can manage. After all, what are my brains for, my little knowledge of the enemy language?"[54] Hillers found a Russian major who not only protected her from other men but kept her supplied with food, blurring the boundaries between rape and prostitution. "By no means could it be said that the major is raping me. One cold word and he'd probably go his way and never come back. So I am placing myself at his service of my own accord."[55]

Hillers was hardly free of prejudice, but she did avoid collectively blaming "the Russians." Individual men with names and past histories—Petka, Anatol, Andrey—stood out from the masses of raping and pillaging soldiers. "I speak with them as one person to another, at least I can tell who's truly evil from who is bearable, can picture them as separate human beings, distinguish them as individuals."[56]

Hillers could not expect any help from German men, most of whom proved cowardly and hid behind the women. "Deep down we women are experiencing a kind of collective disappointment. The Nazi world—ruled by men, glorifying the strong man—is beginning to crumble, and with it the myth of 'Man.'"[57] A woman ahead of her in line at a water pump told of a male neighbor yelling out while she was being pawed by Red Army soldiers: "'Well, why don't you just go with them, you're putting all of us in danger!' A minor footnote to the Decline of the West."[58] When she showed her notes to her boyfriend, who returned from the front in late June 1945, he left her without a word. His behavior presaged the atmosphere of the 1950s in Germany, which maintained strict silence about the helplessness and violence German women had suffered at the end of the war.

TAKING NOTES WAS HILLERS'S way of reinforcing her sense of self, a method of dealing with the blows being dealt to her very identity. At the same time, and incredibly, in her diary she was able to depict her own individual suffering as a collective destiny. In the final days of the war and the first days after its conclusion, tens of thousands of Berlin women were sexually assaulted. In his book *Die Russen in Berlin 1945* (The Russians in Berlin in 1945), journalist Erich Kuby estimated that 80 percent of all the rapes committed in the greater Berlin area were perpetrated between April 24 and May 3.[59] Although Stalin and Marshal Zhukov had ordered Soviet troops to maintain discipline and concentrate on their military tasks, the conquest of Berlin was accompanied by an explosion of unconstrained sexual violence.[60] Even before the fighting was over, Red Army soldiers forced their way into basements and apartments and raped women, often multiples times and before the eyes of their husbands, children, and neighbors. Neither elderly women nor young girls were spared. "With uninhibited lust, the army of our conquerors has fallen upon the women of Berlin," noted Ruth Andreas-Friedrich on May 6. "'They are defiling our daughters and raping our wives,' the men say. It's all people talk about in the city."[61]

There were many reasons why Soviet soldiers behaved as they did. The extraordinary losses they had suffered in the battle for Berlin enflamed already powerful desires for revenge and retribution, and their hatred and fury were stoked further when Red Army troops saw the affluence in which many Germans lived despite the war. "Why did people who had such a good life feel the need to attack us?" many Soviet soldiers asked. A Russian officer quartered in a German railway worker's apartment in the town of Jahnsfelde in late April 1945 wondered, "Their pantries and storerooms are filled with self-smoked hams, jarred fruit, and strawberry jam. The deeper we advance in Germany, the more outraged we get at the opulence we encounter everywhere. . . . I feel like striking out with my fist at all of these orderly rows of cans and jars."[62]

It was also not unusual for acts of violence, sexual and otherwise, to be carried out under the influence of alcohol. "The Red Army soldiers were intoxicated by victory, intoxicated by their experience of Western civilization, and, in a literal sense, intoxicated as well," writes Kuby. "As a rule, there was a connection between drunkenness and acts of violence. In this uninhibited state, Soviet troops did what they lusted for (after years without leave and female companionship), but they didn't do it either in the name of Soviet honor or German shame. They did it in the crudest way imaginable."[63]

In addition, the desire to humiliate the vanquished by subjugating their women was encouraged by the obtrusive air of superiority with which many Germans behaved toward their occupiers, even in the very moment their defeat became concrete. More than a decade of anti-Soviet propaganda promoting distorted images of primitive "Asiatic subhumans" continued to have its effects.

But by no means did every Soviet soldier attack women in Berlin. Amid all the reports of violent transgressions, there were also examples of generosity and readiness to help. A Hitler Youth named Lothar Loewe recalled that after he was taken prisoner, an older Russian soldier gave him a field cooking pot full of beef broth and a spoon: "This was the first time I encountered Russians. I have never forgotten this encounter, this humane gesture."[64] Red Army soldiers were particularly prone to showing kindness to children. "Based on the propaganda, we expected the worst and were pleasantly surprised when a Russian commissar appeared in our courtyard and asked us to behave reasonably so that nothing bad would happen," recalled one woman from the working-class neighborhood of Prenzlauer Berg a few months after the fact. "They scooped the children up into their arms, and gave them sugar and chocolate. . . . In the days that followed, too, our children were given lots of food and sweets by the Russians."[65]

Moreover, it would be wrong to believe that the women of Berlin invariably resigned themselves to their fate without a fight. On the contrary, they came up with a wide variety of tricks and strategies to avoid being raped. Some women hid for days in attics, while others put on filthy clothing, blackened their faces with ash, and simulated the symptoms of infectious disease. Or, like Hillers, they found one Red Army soldier to protect them against the others. Berlin's women sought to filter their horrific experiences through the gruffness and cynicism Berliners were known for. When they visited acquaintances or stood in line in front of stores, they spoke of this most sensitive subject with unprecedented openness.[66] Conversations often began with the question "How often?" Journalist Margret Boveri, who herself escaped being raped but had heard from her female friends what they had endured, noted on May 6, "It is very curious what now gets talked about. Even Elsbeth who, despite her husband and two adult sons, was always holier than thou has temporarily become a bit more forthcoming. And of course, there's a lot to laugh about."[67]

While sexual violence was particularly common in greater Berlin, many cities and towns in the Soviet occupation zone were subjected to it as well. There is no way of knowing how many German women were victimized, but estimates ranged as high as two million.[68] Even after Soviet authorities stepped up their efforts to control soldiers and punish them for their crimes, the rapes continued. By 1947, the Soviet military administration tried to solve the problem by restricting soldiers to military camps and thereby separating them from the German populace.[69] For the German Communist Party (KPD) and later the Socialist Unity Party (SED) leadership, the mass rapes at the end of the war remained a stain on their reputation. The days during which German women lived in fear of Soviet soldiers had inscribed themselves on East Germans' collective memory and hindered Communist efforts to win new converts. "Even after three years, I constantly hear, the workers tremble with panic caused by the pillaging and rapes that followed the conquest of Berlin," wrote Bertolt Brecht in his "work journal" in 1948. "In working-class districts, people had awaited their liberators with desperate joy. Their arms were outstretched, but the encounter turned into an attack that spared neither seventy- nor twelve-year-olds and took place completely in public."[70] The KPD and SED functionaries in East Germany could never broach the subject without butting heads with their Soviet occupiers. The topic remained strictly taboo throughout the entire history of Communist East Germany.[71]

Nor were rapes restricted to Soviet-occupied areas. Soldiers of the western Allies also committed sexual violence against women in parts of Germany they invaded—and in greater numbers than was long assumed.[72] Troops from French Morocco were particularly brutal, raping numerous women, particularly in and around Stuttgart, at the start of the occupation.[73] Nor did American and British troops always behave with the morality and discipline still attributed to them in many of today's accounts of the period. But overall, sexual violence was far less common in the West than in the Soviet-occupied zone. Among other things, the Americans and British never suffered the terror of German occupation as Soviets had, nor had they absorbed anywhere near the number of casualties as the Red Army. Moreover, the Americans and British often had no need to use violence to get what they wanted. A not inconsiderable number of German women willingly traded sex for dollars, cigarettes, and chocolate.[74] Despite military prohibitions on fraternizing with the enemy, relationships quickly developed between GIs and "fräuleins," some of which even resulted in marriage.

ON THE MORNING OF MAY 3, a delegation from the Wehrmacht Supreme Command—Admiral General Hans-Georg von Friedeburg, General Eberhard Kinzel, Rear Admiral Gerhard Wagner, and Major Jochen Friedel—arrived at the headquarters of British general Miles C. Dempsey in Häcklingen. From there they were taken to nearby Timeloberg, where Field Marshal Montgomery had erected a small tent city surrounding his trailer. In his memoirs, Montgomery wrote, "They were brought to my caravan site and were drawn up under the Union Jack, which was flying proudly in the breeze. I kept them waiting for a few minutes and then came out of my caravan and walked towards them. They all saluted, under the Union Jack. It was a great moment; I knew the Germans had come to surrender and that the war was over."[75] Montgomery did not mention that before this encounter he had ordered that a line be drawn on the ground for the Germans to toe—a gesture they regarded as "dishonoring."[76]

Friedeburg read aloud a letter from Keitel, as the head of the Wehrmacht Supreme Command, offering the surrender of all German forces in northwestern Germany, including Army Group Vistula. Montgomery rejected the offer, saying that he could not accept the surrender of troops still fighting against the Red Army and that Army Group Vistula would have to surrender to the Soviets. To Friedeburg's objection that no German soldiers would voluntarily become Soviet prisoners because they feared being sentenced to hard labor in Siberia, Montgomery coolly replied, "The Germans should have thought of all these things before they began the war, and particularly before they attacked the Russians in June 1941." In a slightly conciliatory gesture, however, he promised that no soldiers in the east who raised their arms in surrender to British lines would be turned back.[77]

Montgomery also refused to negotiate about the fate of refugees in Mecklenburg because he had no authority over territory west of the line between Wismar and Dömitz, telling Friedeburg he would have to discuss all issues of this sort with the Soviets. The talks seemed to have reached a dead end, but Montgomery made a counterproposal: "Will you surrender to me all German forces on my western and north-ern flanks, including all forces in Holland, Friesland with the Frisian Islands and Heligoland, Schleswig-Holstein, and Denmark? If you will do this, I will accept it as a tactical battlefield surrender of the enemy forces immediately opposing me, and those in support in Denmark." To back up his demands, the field marshal unrolled a map of the west-ern front that illustrated the futility of further German resistance. The German emissary asked for the opportunity to think things over. Montgomery would later write, "I sent them away to have lunch in a tent by themselves, with nobody else present except one of my officers. Von Friedeburg wept during lunch and the others did not say much."[78]

After that meal, the British commander issued an ultimatum. All German troops in the area in question would have to lay down their arms and unconditionally surrender, and all German materiel would have to be handed over, undamaged, to British forces. If the Germans refused, Montgomery made clear, the fighting would continue. Friede-burg objected that he was not authorized to agree to such demands and would have to obtain approval from Flensburg. That evening he and Friedel headed north, while Wagner and Kinzel stayed behind. Mont-gomery had set them a deadline of the following afternoon.[79]

MAY 4, 1945

At 9:00 a.m. on the morning of May 4, 1945, German military leaders convened at the naval academy in Flensburg for what would prove a decisive meeting. Hans-Georg von Friedeburg, who had returned that night, gave an extensive report about his negotiations with Montgomery to Dönitz, Krosigk, Wilhelm Keitel, Alfred Jodl, and Jodl's adjutant, Lieutenant Colonel Hermann Brudermüller. There were almost no objections to the Netherlands and Denmark being included in the surrender. German troops in those areas were not going to be able to hold out long anyway, and "a stubborn defense," as it was noted in the minutes, would only yield "further loss of face and considerable political liability."[1] Jodl voiced the only dissent, saying he did not want to give away the "trump card of Holland."[2] Dönitz, for his part, said he was concerned about surrendering the German fleet, which would make it impossible to keep transporting refugees and troops across the Baltic Sea. Friedeburg sought to dispel these concerns by pointing out that Montgomery had assured him that such activities could continue.[3]

More extensive discussion followed about Montgomery's demand for the surrender of all German military hardware, which Keitel and

Jodl considered incompatible with the "honor of German arms." They proposed immediately destroying all munitions and materiel. Krosigk, however, objected that this would violate the spirit of the surrender agreement and allow Montgomery to abrogate it and take punitive action. Dönitz was persuaded by this argument and ordered the Wehrmacht Supreme Command to tell its military commanders to hand over what was asked for, undamaged, to the enemy. Generally speaking, this order was carried out. The only exceptions were several submarines in North Sea and Baltic Sea ports. They were scuttled during the night of May 4.[4]

The minutes of the meeting concluded with the statement, "The grand admiral approves of the signatures of the conditions under the assumption of honorable treatment of prisoners of war and a dignified form of transition." At the same time, Friedeburg was assigned after the conclusion of the agreement with Montgomery to travel to Eisenhower's headquarters in Reims in order to arrange a "further partial surrender in the west."[5]

Meanwhile, Montgomery was already preparing a signing ceremony. Convinced that the Germans would accept his demands, he ordered a large tent to be erected atop the main hill in Timeloberg. "I had the surrender documents all ready. The arrangements in the tent were very simple, a trestle table covered with an army blanket, an ink-pot, an ordinary army pen that you could buy in a shop for twopence. There were two B.B.C. microphones on the table." At 5:00 in the afternoon, Montgomery held a press conference and invited journalists to witness the signing ceremony.

At 6:00 p.m., while the press conference was still under way, the two German emissaries returned from Flensburg. Montgomery invited Friedeburg into his caravan to assure himself the admiral was in fact authorized to agree to an unconditional surrender under the terms demanded. The German contingent was then escorted to the tent under the curious eyes of soldiers, war correspondents, and photographers. When Montgomery arrived, they all stood up. "The Germans were clearly nervous and one of them took out a cigarette; he wanted to smoke to calm his nerves," the field marshal recalled. "I looked at him, and he put the cigarette away."[6]

With little preamble, Montgomery read out the seven points in the articles of surrender and called on the four members of the German delegation to sign the document. By 6:30, the ceremony was over. The fighting would cease at 8:00 a.m. on May 5 in the Netherlands, Denmark, and northwestern Germany, including the Frisian Islands and Schleswig-Holstein.[7] The Wehrmacht reported, "The ceasefire after almost six years of honorable battles was agreed on the order of Grand Admiral Dönitz because fighting against the western powers no longer made sense and would only lead . . . to the loss of precious German blood. Resistance to the Soviets, however, will continue in order to protect as many German people as possible from Bolshevist terror."[8]

The BBC announced the German surrender in northwestern Europe on the evening of May 4, causing spontaneous celebrations in the Netherlands and Denmark. In Copenhagen, members of the underground resistance emerged in public wearing blue, white, and red armbands. The following morning the Reich plenipotentiary Werner Best asked the Danish foreign minister to guarantee his safety. He was initially allowed to remain under guard in his residence before being arrested on May 21 and imprisoned in Copenhagen's Kastellet citadel. A court in the city sentenced him to death in September 1948, but on appeal, his sentence was reduced to five years' imprisonment, with four years considered already served. Protests in Denmark against this court judgment were so fierce that the Danish minister of justice had no choice but to order a further appeal before Denmark's highest court. It sentenced Best to twelve years' imprisonment in March 1950. But only one-and-a-half years later, in August 1951, he was released and deported to West Germany.[9]

German capitulation in the "northern realm" was followed by

additional limited (but still unconditional) surrenders. Germany's Italian army had laid down its arms on May 2, making the positions of the adjacent Army Groups G and E (Southeast) untenable, and Field Marshal General Kesselring asked his superiors that same day for permission to negotiate a surrender for them as well. But he received Dönitz's authorization to conclude a ceasefire only for Army Group G, whose troops faced the 6th US Army under General Jacob L. Devers between the Böhmerwald forest and the Inn River in what is now the Czech Republic. As his negotiator, Kesselring nominated the supreme commander of the 1st Army, General Hermann Foertsch. Negotiations with the Americans were held on May 4 in Salzburg, and the following day, Foertsch signed the articles of surrender for Army Group G. The ceasefire began at 2:00 p.m. on May 6.[10]

Along with entire army groups, individual armies and divisions also tried to save themselves from Russian captivity by surrendering to the Americans or the British. Those that did so included the 12th Army under General Wenck and the remnants of the 9th Army under General Busse, who stood in the way of the advancing Red Army on the eastern bank of the Elbe. On May 3, Wenck sent an emissary, General Baron Maximilian von Edelsheim, across the river in an amphibious vehicle with an offer to surrender to the 102nd Infantry Division of the 9th US Army on the Elbe's western bank. Mindful of their duties to their Soviet Allies, the Americans refused to accept a formal surrender. But at negotiations in the town of Stendal on the morning of May 4, they did agree to accept individual soldiers from the 12th and 9th Armies as POWs, if they appeared on the western bank of the Elbe with raised hands or in boats flying white flags.

Chaotic scenes unfolded on the riverbank near the town of Tangermünde. A record keeper for the 102nd US Infantry Division described groups of German soldiers, panicked by their almost apocalyptic fear of the advancing Soviets, begging for permission to cross the river and doing so on driftwood, hastily built rafts, rubber tires, and washtubs.

An Associated Press correspondent with the division also described SS tank crews, once part of Germany's elite, paddling makeshift rafts or swimming across the river, having left their insignia-filled uniforms on the eastern bank. The reporter characterized these men, in the tens of thousands, as a fearful horde, worse than any defeated army, driven by a terror that could only have been caused by bad conscience.[11]

ON THE MORNING OF May 4, having taken Bad Reichenhall in south-eastern Germany, troops from the 3rd US Infantry Division and 1st US Airborne Landing Division marched quickly on Berchtesgaden with a French tank division under General Jacques-Philippe Leclerc in their wake. The previous day, the Nazi district leader, Bernhard Stredele, had handed over his authority to the regional councillor, Karl Theodor Jacob, and fled. Jacob went out to meet the Americans with a white flag and offered to surrender Berchtesgaden without a fight. A few hours later, Mayor Karl Sandrock officially handed over the city.[12]

The American troops' ultimate goal, however, was not the idyllic mountain town, but Hitler's Alpine retreat, the Berghof, located several hundred meters farther up the Obersalzberg. In the afternoon of May 4, a vanguard of the 3rd Infantry Division reached the complex, followed immediately by soldiers from the French armored division, among them actor Jean Gabin, Marlene Dietrich's lover. The commander of the SS contingent on Obersalzberg, Bernhard Frank, had also fled—but not before ordering his men to burn what was left of the Berghof, which had been bombed by the Allies ten days before.[13]

In the fall of 1928, Hitler had rented what was called Haus Wachenfeld for the first time and had bought it shortly after being named Reich chancellor in 1933, expanding the Alpine chalet into the imposing Berghof in 1935 and 1936. Martin Bormann, at that time staff director under the "Führer's deputy," Rudolf Hess, had played a key role in buying up the property around Hitler's residence. Anyone who did not sell voluntarily was subjected to massive pressure. Bormann replaced the old barns in the village with new buildings, including a complex of barracks in which SS security companies could be housed, a model farm, a greenhouse to keep the vegetarian Hitler supplied with fruit and vegetables year round, a small teahouse on the Mooslahnerkopf peak, and—at the greatest expense—a second, larger teahouse on the Kehlstein peak, some eight hundred meters above the Berghof.

In the early years of the Third Reich, Hitler admirers had been allowed to make pilgrimages to Obersalzberg to catch a glimpse of their idol. But in 1936, the mountain had been declared a "restricted Führer zone" accessible only to those with special identification.[14]

For Hitler, the Berghof had always been both a refuge from the public eye and an alternate center of government to the Reich chancellery in Berlin. While there, he received foreign guests of state, cooked up various diabolical plans, and made difficult decisions, such as his order in July 1940 to prepare for an attack on the Soviet Union. At the Berghof, he also assembled a clique of associates and intimates, a closed society that served as a kind of ersatz family. Rank within the Nazi hierarchy is not what determined whether people would be admitted to the Berghof circle but rather Hitler's personal feelings about them. And all regular visitors to Hitler's estate were expected to get along well with Eva Braun and accept her role as "lady of the manor." For that reason, among others, the most prominent members of Hitler's Alpine society were Albert Speer and his wife, Margarete.

Once the war began, the Berghof's function changed in that it became a "main Führer headquarters" whenever the supreme commander of the Wehrmacht spent time there. As the fighting dragged on, Hitler reconciled himself to the idea that Obersalzberg might be targeted by Allied bombers. Work began on a series of air-raid bunkers, with the first completed underground hideaway consisting of a 130-meter hollow shaft directly under the Berghof, which included living rooms and bedrooms for Hitler and Braun, space for personnel, a kitchen, well-stocked storerooms, and storage areas for the safekeeping of artworks, files, and books. But for years, no bombs fell on Obersalzberg.

That changed on April 25, 1945, when 359 RAF Lancaster bombers attempted to level the complex. The air raid was prompted by rumors that Hitler was about to withdraw to the mountains with his paladins and top figures within the Wehrmacht and the SS to prepare a final battle against the Allies. Although the talk of Hitler turning the Berghof into a gigantic "Alpine fortress" was baseless, it convinced the decision-makers at Allied main headquarters. The large-scale aerial bombardment was designed to seal off Hitler's path of retreat by destroying what was thought to be the heart of the control center for the supposed battle to the death.[15]

The British bombers hit their mark. "The Berghof was badly damaged," remembered Hitler's secretary Christa Schroeder, who had fled there only days before on one of the final planes to leave Berlin. "The walls were still standing—only one side had been breached. But the metal roof hung down jaggedly, and there were no more doors and windows. The floor of the house was covered in debris, and most of the furniture had been ruined. All of the side buildings were destroyed, the paths blocked and the trees stripped of leaves. No green could be seen. The picture was like a landscape of craters."[16] Göring's and Bormann's houses, the SS barracks, and the greenhouse were completely destroyed. The Kehlstein teahouse was one of only a few buildings to survive unscathed.[17]

The day after the bombing Hitler's longtime personal adjutant, Julius Schaub, arrived to destroy the dictator's private papers. During the night of April 25, he had flown from Berlin's Gatow airstrip to Munich and had emptied out the safe in Hitler's private apartment on Munich's Prinzregentenstrasse. With those materials placed in two trunks, he then drove to Obersalzberg, cleaned out the safe in Hitler's office, which had remained undamaged, and burned all of Hitler's papers on the Berghof terrace. "Schaub's act of destruction under open skies was a dismal sight," noted Schroeder, who in an unobserved moment was able to save a few documents, including a bundle of Hitler's architectural sketches.[18]

The administration of the "restricted Führer zone" dissolved after the April 25 bombing. Thousands of slave laborers pressed into service for the ongoing construction work were released and tried to make their way back to their home countries. Most of the service personnel fled. The area, which had previously been strictly cordoned off, became accessible to anyone, and some locals sensed an opportunity. "There was a flurry of activity on the mountain," reported Josef Geiss, who was in charge of overseeing construction companies on Obersalzberg. "The people rushed in, not infrequently with teams of horses, to empty the storerooms. They stared in amazement at the huge piles of food, material, clothing, shoes, tableware, soaps, et cetera, all of which immediately found new owners. Artworks were burned or stolen. In Bormann's cellar, the stocks of butter, sugar, flour, and other things came up to your calves."[19] Among the "thieves" were local suppliers and tradesmen who knew that their open bills would no longer be paid and thus balanced their accounts in this fashion.

On May 1, when the news of Hitler's death arrived at the Berghof, any remaining semblance of order disintegrated. Schroeder noticed that formerly servile personnel suddenly began acting as though they were the new masters of the house. Almost without exception, they grabbed whatever they could of value and left. Police who stayed behind tried to eradicate all traces of Eva Braun's existence. Porcelain bearing her initials was smashed, and her clothing was burned on the terrace.[20]

One of the first civilians to travel with the GIs up to Obersalzberg on the afternoon of May 4 was the American reporter Lee Miller. The thirty-eight-year-old former pupil of photographer Man Ray accompanied Allied troops from the Normandy invasion in June 1944 until the end of the Third Reich. Her photos of the liberation of the Buchenwald and Dachau concentration camps were seen the world over. When Hitler's death was announced on May 1, she was in the dictator's private Munich apartment. It was here that her friend David E. Scherman, a *Life* magazine photojournalist, took the famous image of Miller posing naked in Hitler's bathtub alongside a photo of the Führer.[21]

Miller photographed the ruins of the Berghof and recorded her impressions for a feature in *British Vogue*. She described a heavily bombarded landscape where buildings had been crushed like eggshells and craters covered the slope down to the valley. Hitler's house was still intact even while flames from the fire set by the retreating SS licked at its windows. Miller crawled over a mound of earth thrown up by the bombs and saw the ruins of Göring's house, with an empty flagpole where the Nazi flag had once flown. The SS had cut the swastika out of its middle and left the remaining red rectangle behind on the ground.[22]

The following morning Miller returned to Obersalzberg to inspect the underground shafts and rooms, where American and French soldiers were now souvenir hunting. She described them taking silverware and linens imprinted with eagles, swastikas, and the initials A. H. Books without an ex libris, a dedication, or a personal-looking cover were simply tossed aside. The scene was of a "very wild party," with champagne corks popped over the flagpole, while the house itself was beginning to collapse. Anticipating the perennially lucrative business of Hitler memorabilia, which continues today, Miller wrote, "There isn't even a piece left for a museum on the great war criminals, and scattered over the breadth of the world people are forever going to be shown a napkin ring or a pickle fork, supposedly used by Hitler."[23]

On May 8, the writer Klaus Mann traveled to Obersalzberg.[24] The oldest son of Thomas Mann had volunteered his services to the US Army and, after finally being granted American citizenship, had arrived in Casablanca on a troop transport in early January 1944. He was assigned to a unit in the Psychological Warfare Branch and supported Allied troops advancing through Italy, including by composing flyers dropped behind enemy lines calling on German soldiers to sur-

On May 1, 1945, American reporter Lee Miller posed in Hitler's bathtub
in his private Munich apartment. The image was taken by photographer
David E. Scherman.

render. In February 1945, he was transferred to the editorial offices of
Stars and Stripes in Rome. In early May, Mann wrote an obituary of
Hitler that remains one of the most incisive analyses ever published of
the German dictator and his world-historical criminality.[25] In a letter
to his father, Klaus Mann described his Obersalzberg visit: "For two
days, the 'Berghof' had been systematically plundered by our soldiers,
GIs and *poilus* [French soldiers]. It must have been an orgy of larceny
and triumph on a grandiosely rampant scale. . . . We found this famous
rural retreat guarded by military police—superfluously. After the terrible devastation wrought by the bombs, plunderers had diligently gone
about their work. Breached walls and charred beams, deep craters full
of debris and ash, broken furniture, shards and filth—it was a pile of
rubble with nothing else there."[26]

Until the spring of 1949, Germans were officially forbidden to
enter the former "restricted Führer zone." Once the prohibition was
lifted, the ruins on the Obersalzberg became a major tourist attraction.

In the summer of 1951, 136,560 people visited the site. "Many of them want to take home a bit of the Führer's fire," journalist Jürgen Neven-du Mont quoted a tour guide saying about the fireplace in the Berghof's Great Hall, which was gradually being dismantled by souvenir hunters. Neven-du Mont's report appeared in *Münchner Illustrierte* magazine with the headline "Propaganda Cell Obersalzberg" and created quite a stir. On November 1, 1951, the American occupation authorities granted a request by the Bavarian state government and released the site at Obersalzberg for public use, albeit on the condition that the remnants of Hitler's, Göring's, and Bormann's houses be completely removed. On April 30, 1952, seven years to the day after Hitler's suicide, what was left of the Berghof was demolished.[27]

"WHEN THE WAR ENDED, it was my dream to become the mayor of Cologne," the first West German chancellor, Konrad Adenauer, told his secretary while working on his memoirs in 1965.[28] Adenauer realized his dream even before the formal end of the war, when on May 4, 1945, the American military governor of Cologne installed the then sixty-nine-year-old in the post he had occupied from 1917 until Hitler's assumption of power. In March 1933, the Nazis had removed the popular mayor and prominent pro-democracy politician, whom they considered the embodiment of the hated "Weimar system," and subjected him to criminal investigation. Even though the inquiry ended with Adenauer's acquittal, he no longer had any political power and remained under constant Gestapo surveillance. Already a pensioner, Adenauer had withdrawn to his private home in the town of Rhöndorf and tried to survive the war years without being persecuted. Nonetheless, on August 23, 1944, he was arrested—not because of any proof he had been involved in the attempted anti-Hitler coup of July 20, 1944, but as part of the subsequent Aktion Gitter (Operation Prison Bars), ordered by Himmler, in which many former politicians from Weimar parties were taken into custody. Adenauer was brought to a concentration camp established on the Cologne trade fairgrounds, and, after a daring escape attempt was thwarted, he was brought to the Gestapo prison in Brauweiler. Thanks to some lucky circumstances, he was released in late November 1944. With his wife, Gussie, and five French POWs who had escaped a German camp, Adenauer followed the final stages of the war in the central Rhineland from the air-raid shelter in his Rhöndorf home south of Bonn. He moved back there after the Americans had succeeded in crossing the river over the nearby intact Remagen Bridge.[29]

By March 16, 1945, two US occupation officers had visited him and asked him on behalf of the regional US military governor, Lieutenant Colonel John K. Patterson, to reassume the office of mayor of Cologne. The name Konrad Adenauer topped the Americans' so-called white list of German leaders who had not compromised themselves between 1933 and 1945 and were considered fit for elevated administrative functions. But Adenauer hesitated, pointing out that three of his sons were still serving in the Wehrmacht and could face retaliation if their father were restored to his former post. Adenauer was no doubt wary given the fate of Franz Oppenhoff, whom the Allies had made mayor of Aachen but who had been murdered days later by the fanatic Nazi guerrilla movement Werewolf. In any case, Adenauer suggested that for the time being he should remain in the background as an "adviser"—a proposal Patterson accepted.[30]

Adenauer would never forget his first return to Cologne from Rhöndorf. "The bridges over the Rhine were destroyed, and meters-high rubble lay in the streets," he would write. "Gigantic heaps of debris rose from the bombed-out, bullet-ridden buildings. With its destroyed churches . . . its badly damaged cathedral, the ruins of its once so beautiful bridges protruding from the Rhine, and its endless sea of destroyed houses, Cologne looked like a ghost town."[31]

Adenauer doubted whether the city—which was down to about 32,000 inhabitants from its prewar population of 760,000—could

Aerial image of the destruction in Cologne, with its cathedral
in the background, taken immediately after US troops marched into
the city in early March 1945.

ever be rebuilt. Nonetheless, on May 3, when he attended a meeting
called by Patterson, he declared himself willing to take over the office
of mayor, although he insisted that he be allowed to quit at any time.
The following day, he officially started work.

Right from the start, Adenauer concentrated on not only the
administration of his home city but the future of Germany as a whole.
Appraising the situation, he assumed that the Soviets would gov-
ern their occupation zones as they saw fit and that Germany would
unavoidably be divided. "I view Germany's development with increasing concern," he wrote in early July 1945. "Russia is lowering an iron
curtain."[32] Adenauer thus concluded that the three western German
zones would have to join together and seek close economic and politi-

cal ties with Western Europe, particularly with France. These were the contours of a foreign-policy approach he would pursue rigorously when he became West German chancellor.

Although Adenauer occasionally complained to confidants about the incompetence of the American military administration, a trusting working relationship soon developed. That changed on June 21, 1945, when the Americans withdrew from Cologne and the British assumed command. In August, the Labour Party took over the British government, and the occupation authorities who supported the party regarded the Catholic Adenauer, who was seen to have conservative leanings, with mistrust.[33] By late September, a conflict arose when the British military administration demanded that Adenauer have the trees around the city, which he had planted before 1933, cut down to supply residents with firewood for their furnaces. Adenauer refused, demanding that the British release supplies of coal they had confiscated from city stockpiles.

On October 6, the commander of the North Rhine province, Brigadier General John Barraclough, summoned Adenauer and brusquely fired him. While he was aware of the difficulties the mayor faced, Barraclough claimed that Adenauer had failed to display the necessary energy in repairing buildings and removing rubble, thereby violating his duties to the populace of Cologne.[34] Adenauer would long resent being dismissed in this fashion, but in fact it turned out to be a stroke of luck: the prohibition on US-appointed mayors from engaging in political activity no longer applied to him, and he could now concentrate on the newly founded West German conservative party, the Christian Democratic Union. Rhöndorf became a center from which new networks were woven, and Adenauer's party colleagues began paying visits to what one of them jokingly called "Rhenish Obersalzberg."[35] By the spring of 1946, Adenauer had become the chairman of the CDU in the British occupation zone. It was a springboard to the biggest political stage. In early September 1948 Adenauer became the president of the parliamentary council charged with drafting a constitution—or Basic Law, as it was known—for the coalescing West German state. Finally, on September 15, 1949, at the age of seventy-three, Adenauer was elected the first chancellor of the Federal Republic. His margin of victory was one parliamentary vote—his own.

TWO DAYS AFTER THE surrender of Berlin, battle damage was still visible everywhere. "The streets are covered with wrecks from burned-out cars, tanks, motorcycles, artillery, and the like," noted Danish journalist Jacob Kronika on May 4. "Naturally until the present no one has had the time to bury all the bodies and cadavers, but now that is well under way. The Russians are taking care of Russian casualties, while the Germans have to bury their own dead."[36] The Soviet occupation authority's first daily orders were publicized on posters. A curfew was instituted for ordinary people from 10:00 p.m. to 8:00 a.m. Radio receivers, cameras, and weapons were to be handed over. And residents of Berlin were required to help with the cleanup efforts. In the early morning of May 4 in the Tiergarten district, more than a thousand people assembled along the Ost-West-Achse between the Brandenburg Gate and the Victory Column and began to cart away rubble and fill in the craters left behind by bombs and artillery shells. On this broad thoroughfare where Hitler had celebrated his fiftieth birthday with a massive military parade, the Red Army intended to stage a victory parade of its own.[37]

Berliners' main concern was food, and everywhere residents could be seen scrounging for something to eat. Most shops were closed and had been plundered. There was still no electricity, gas, or indoor running water, and long lines formed at Berlin's few water pumps. "Everyone waits patiently, moving forward one small step at a time," wrote musician Karla Höcker. "The moment when you arrive at the pump, and clear water splashes into your bucket—you always get a bit baptized in the process—is always magnificent."[38] But for many women, including the journalist Margret Boveri, making their way back with buckets full of water over long distances through rubble and debris was a dispiriting slog. "It all takes so much time," Boveri complained, "getting four to six buckets of water from far away and then carrying them up so many flights of stairs."[39]

To prepare their meager food rations, Berliners needed fuel for fires, so they picked through the ruins for wood, recovering shattered doors and window frames and painstakingly breaking them into small pieces. "We slave like coolies," wrote Ruth Andreas-Friedrich, unaccustomed to the work. "Building fires, collecting wood, chopping wood, sweeping away debris. And cleaning up, always cleaning up."[40]

Countless homes had been destroyed or badly damaged, and many Berliners lived in provisional accommodations, often in crowded basements, air-raid shelters, and allotment garden colonies. But others had no roofs whatsoever over their heads. "Too many people to count camp under open skies in Tiergarten park which is covered in destroyed military equipment," observed Kronika.[41]

But even those who had shelter of some kind were not safe from attacks. Red Army soldiers could forcibly enter people's homes at will. "Now and then there's a Russian visit," lamented Andreas-Friedrich on May 4. "They go from room to room, looking around and taking whatever pleases them. They stare straight through us as if we're not there. 'Watchi, watchi,' they say sometimes. And 'Schnapps and bike.'" Bicycles were particularly coveted. "Our bicycles are disappearing," Andreas-Friedrich added. "There's a paved street behind the cemetery. There the victors are learning how to ride. Like children. Diligently and with great stamina, without regard for what might get broken."[42]

But Russian soldiers were not the only ones looting and stealing. In the chaos of a society that had collapsed, suspending the limits of law and order, many Germans also had no scruples about helping themselves to others' belongings. "All notions of ownership have been completely demolished," Marta Hillers wrote. "Everyone steals from everyone else, because everyone has been stolen from and because we can make use of anything."[43] Eyewitnesses in many other large German cities recorded similar impressions. One of them was the pro-democracy Bremen politician Theodor Spitta, who was restored to his position as city senator after 1945: "Remarkable how people who want to rebuild their destroyed homes lose all measure of restraint and rob others' homes of everything they can use: roofing tiles, doors, windows, wood, et cetera."[44]

Public transportation had not resumed. There were no trams, buses, subways, or trains. When people had to go somewhere, they walked. Germans in Berlin and other destroyed cities were constantly on the go, beating paths through the rubble. "We have no way to move other than by using our legs," wrote Theo Findahl, a Norwegian correspondent in Berlin, about a trip from the outlying neighborhood of Dahlem to the centrally located Tiergarten park.[45]

On May 4, the actor Gustaf Gründgens, who had become the head of the Prussian State Theater in the Third Reich thanks to the patronage of Göring, decided to visit the actress Marianne Hoppe, to whom he had been married since 1936. He and his friend Karla Höcker set off from the downtown district of Charlottenburg toward Grunewald on the city's edge. "A strange route, terrible and beautiful," Höcker mused. "What's terrible are the savage traces of battle, the ruins of exhibition halls and railway bridges—the dead. What's beautiful are the wind and the fact that we're even able to walk, the lightness and ephemerality of this movement. Gründgens in his starched hat, topcoat, and suede gloves, the picture of the bon vivant. When I asked in amazement if he really intended to set off like that, his only response was, 'Anything else would be undignified.' "[46]

Germans found the lack of information almost as oppressive as the struggle for their daily bread, the insecurity of their lives, and the restrictions on movement. There were no newspapers, no telephones, no mail, and for many people no radio. "How often and in what ways

did we imagine the end of National Socialism," remarked the writer
Erik Reger on May 2. "And now we sit there, cut off from any possibility of learning anything from the outside world. No radio, no newspapers, nothing. . . . If only I could hear today's news with my own
ears." Reger, who had made a name for himself with a 1931 novel about
Rhineland industrial barons and who later cofounded and edited the
postwar *Berliner Tagesspiegel* newspaper, had moved with his wife in
August 1943 to Mahlow, a town of 2,500 people fifteen kilometers
south of Berlin. Looking back on the first days of May 1945, he would
write that he would "probably never recover" from the fact he "hadn't
experienced the essentials of world history over all these weeks."[47]
Boveri felt much the same: "We still don't know anything," she wrote
with disappointment on May 6, "and that's why we stayed in Berlin, to
experience everything at the center of events."[48]

At the same time, many Germans were too consumed by their
everyday problems to be particularly interested in what was happening beyond their narrow horizons. Fritz Klein, who would become
one of the most important historians in Communist East Germany,
spent the war as a POW in the Munsterlager camp in the Lüneburg
Heath. He would recall paying less attention to the "great events"
than to the "possibility of procuring a decent portion to eat or a place
to sleep protected from the rain." Klein added, "For this reason, I no
longer remember the hour when I learned of Hitler's suicide or the
German surrender."[49]

With reliable news available only in fragments, hearsay flourished.
"Gossip," remarked Hillers. "We feed on it."[50] The lines of people waiting for water pumps in particular became a market for half-truths and
falsehoods. After one such wait, an acquaintance of Andreas-Friedrich
reported what he had heard from another person in line. " 'There's
news!' he beamed while we schlepped our water back home in shifts.
Then he dropped his bombshells: Hitler was lying dead in the Reich
chancellery, and Goebbels had poisoned himself with his wife and chil-

dren. Himmler was fighting in Breslau, and Epp had engineered a coup d'etat in Munich."[51]

It was not until May 15, 1945, that a newspaper—the *Tägliche Rundschau*, which was approved by the Soviet authorities—was again published in Berlin. The front page of the first edition of this newly founded public organ carried a message from Stalin. Two days later, Höcker once again had running water in her apartment. "It's like something from a fairy tale!" she commented. On June 8, the power came back on: "We're like children, flipping the light switches on and off and looking forward to nightfall. We no longer have to stumble around in the dark. We can see each other when we converse!" Public transportation also slowly resumed operation. "Hordes of pedestrians in front of the few stops," wrote Höcker. "Often you have to wait for hours. But in many districts, things look better than in Charlottenburg."[52]

AS KONRAD ADENAUER was being restored as Cologne mayor, a young German officer who would also go on to become chancellor found himself in a POW camp in Belgium: Helmut Schmidt. He wrote in his diary around this time, "Many people are discovering that they were never Nazis. Some of them are merely opportunists, while others sense their own complicity in the catastrophe of the German people."[53]

Schmidt was born in 1918, the son of a Hamburg schoolteacher, and after completing his university-track high school diploma in 1937, he volunteered for the military. In November of that year, he began serving in an antiaircraft flak battery in Bremen's Vegesack district. "Thank God we were now in the only upstanding club," he would later write about his years as a soldier.[54] Schmidt's identification with the Wehrmacht, which always claimed to have kept itself free of the Nazis' ideological influence, was to last through the war and beyond.

Schmidt had viewed the beginning of the Second World War "like an event of nature." Although on the one hand he rejected National Socialism and expected a "terrible end to the war," on the other he had no qualms about "doing his duty as a soldier for Germany," as he subsequently admitted.[55] It is difficult to say how deep his antipathy for Nazism ran and whether he was truly convinced early on that Germany under Hitler was headed for a massive defeat. His superiors repeatedly noted his air of superiority but also attested to his "impeccable National Socialist attitude."[56]

After being promoted to reserve lieutenant, in the fall of 1940 Schmidt was transferred to the Supervisory Instruction Office IV of the General for Flak Weaponry on Berlin's Knesebeckstrasse. From there, he served at times as an instructor at the Flak Artillery School II in the town of Stolpmünde (Ustka in today's Poland). But Schmidt was itching to get to the front. "I was ashamed of not being able to wear any medals of bravery on my uniform through the streets of Berlin like the majority of soldiers because I hadn't taken part in any campaign," he recalled. "Thus it happened that, dissatisfied with the inglorious paper war in Berlin, I applied for a transfer to the fighting troops."[57]

By late August 1941, Schmidt got his wish and was flown in a Junkers Ju 52 to Army Group North on the eastern front. As a platoon leader, he commanded a light Luftwaffe flak company, which was part of the 1st Tank Division and helped lay siege to Leningrad. It was Hitler's wish that the city on the Neva River not be taken but starved to death. From the start of the siege until January 1944, when the Red Army finally succeeded in breaking the blockade, almost a million people would perish because of this policy of annihilation through attrition.[58]

Schmidt's unit also took part in the drive toward Moscow beginning in early October 1941. It ground to a halt two months later before the gates of the Soviet capital when a Red Army counteroffensive forced German troops to retreat. Operation Barbarossa, Nazi Germany's invasion of the Soviet Union, was expected to take a couple of months. It had already lasted longer than that, and now it had failed, signaling a decisive turning point in the war. As a POW, Schmidt would summarize his experiences on the eastern front in late 1941 as follows: "For the first time there was a breach in my personal faith in the Führer."[59] This can only mean that like the majority of Germans, Schmidt had previously trusted in Hitler and had exempted the dictator from criticism.

Schmidt's frontline tour of duty ended in January 1942. Having been promoted to the rank of first lieutenant on April 1, the twenty-three-year-old returned to his old post on Knesebeckstrasse, where again he worked as an instructor, writing guides for servicing and firing flak. Following an aerial bombardment in July 1943, his office was moved to the town of Bernau, and in early September 1944, Schmidt was ordered to attend a hearing in the trial of the conspirators behind the July 20 attempted assassination of Hitler before the notorious People's Court. This repulsive spectacle was a key moment in the life of the young officer. It was only then, as he told the historian Fritz Stern in 2010, that he realized the Nazis were criminals. "Too late," Schmidt added.[60]

Several weeks later, Schmidt was accused of "corroding defensive morale" for making a disrespectful remark about Göring. Schmidt's superior, Lieutenant General Heino von Rantzau, sympathized with him and made sure he was transferred to the western front, ensuring the accusations against him came to nothing. In January 1945, when Schmidt reported for his second tour of frontline duty, assuming command of a flak battery, the Ardennes offensive—Hitler's final attempt to turn the tide—had already failed, and German troops were retreating. In late March 1945, Schmidt's battery was destroyed by American forces. Small groups of survivors tried to skirt American lines and make it back to the German line. Schmidt and two comrades marched five hundred kilometers north for over three weeks before being surprised and taken prisoner by British soldiers while sleeping in a forest near Soltau on April 24.[61]

Initially, Schmidt was suspected of being a guard from the nearby Bergen-Belsen concentration camp, which the British had just liberated. After that misunderstanding was cleared up, he was taken to the Jabbeke POW camp near Bruges, which was designated for captured German officers. In the notes he made in his first days and weeks of incarceration, he tried to make sense of his situation. Like many members of his generation, Schmidt felt that what he had regarded as his devotion to "soldierly duty" had been misused by Hitler and his cohorts.[62] It would be many decades before he would acknowledge that he had served an organization, the Wehrmacht, that had committed the worst sort of crimes against humanity and without whose participation the genocide of the Jews in German-occupied Eastern Europe would not have been possible.[63]

Schmidt did not waste his time in captivity. Young officers in the camp felt they had a lot of catching up to do and tried to educate themselves, organizing a veritable "lecture series." Schmidt took a course in bookkeeping, among other things, and was able to freshen up his school English. "I'm among the best English speakers," he remarked with pride, "except for those who have spent a lot of time abroad."[64] And meeting fifty-four-year-old Lieutenant Colonel Hans Bohnenkamp proved a watershed moment in Schmidt's intellectual and personal life. He would later credit the former professor of pedagogy as the source of his "first positive fundamental ideas of democracy, the rule of law, and socialism." As a result, it was "almost unavoidable that I became a Social Democrat."[65]

At the start of his captivity, Schmidt had no hope of being set free anytime soon, writing, "I've . . . internally resigned myself to five years."[66] But on August 23, 1945, he was one of the first prisoners to be released from the camp. A week later he was back in his hometown of Hamburg. At the end of the year, he began a course in economics at the just-reopened Hamburg University, and in 1946, he joined the Social Democratic Party. It was the start of his meteoric postwar political career.

LIKE THE OTHER POWS in British camps, Schmidt had suffered from hunger and was emaciated by the time he returned home. But his experience was much better than that of German POWs held by the Americans. When US troops took the Rhineland and drove a wedge through the Ruhr Valley in the spring of 1945, they took huge groups of Wehrmacht soldiers prisoner. After Germany's final surrender on May 8, hundreds of thousands more were captured, and by mid-1945, the number of US-held POWs alone reached 3.4 million. The Americans were completely unprepared for the task of keeping them and had no choice but to accommodate prisoners in "temporary enclosures" in northern France and other places in Western Europe. Twenty such enclosures were set up between April and June 1945 along the Rhine. They became notorious as the "Rhine meadows camps."[67]

German soldiers who had voluntarily surrendered to the Americans in the belief that they would be treated in accordance with the Geneva Convention got a nasty surprise. The Rhine camps usually consisted of open fields surrounded by barbed wire in the vicinity of villages or towns. Adjacent farms and factories were used for administration, kitchens, or field hospitals. Every camp was divided into twenty "pens" packed with five thousand to ten thousand POWs each. Only women, generals, and the badly wounded were held in permanent structures. The masses of POWs had to make do with tarpaulins, dig holes in the ground for shelter, or camp out in the open. Spring 1945 was generally warm and sunny, but in late April and early May heavy rains transformed the camps into mud pits. "Countless thousands of feet dragged, limp and exhausted, through the softened fields, and the stubborn clay thudded and squeaked," one prisoner remembered.[68]

Initially, there was hardly any food, and while supplies increased gradually over the course of May, rations still could not satisfy even the most basic hunger. "Starvation is an infernal means of reducing human beings to the level of animals," wrote one inmate of the notorious POW camp in Bad Kreuznach. "Whereas once Iron Crosses and medals were most important, now crusts of bread are."[69] Under these conditions, the former bonds of comradeship and solidarity dissolved. It was every man for himself. Theft was rampant, and when sympathetic women from the surrounding areas threw food over camp fences, ugly fights often broke out for the scraps.

Responsibility for the POW camps in the Rhine meadows rested solely with the 106th US Infantry Division. Because it lacked the personnel to supervise so many prisoners, the 106th nominated German inmates to administer the camps internally. This group, from which camp police were also drawn, enjoyed numerous privileges, receiving more supplies and eliciting the hatred of the other captives.

From the very beginning, the hygienic conditions were disastrous. Water supplies were insufficient, and at the start there were only primitive latrines, if any at all. Most inmates arrived at their camp demoralized and weak. Malnutrition, poor hygiene, and inferior medical care meant disease spread rapidly. On top of that, feelings of shame and uncertainty about the duration of their captivity caused even psychologically stable people to go stir-crazy. "Six weeks of mud, rain and cold, six weeks of humiliation and privation, six weeks of being a nameless and insubstantial atom in a mob without will or function, only held together by the close confines of barbed wire compartments, have had their effect," wrote one inmate. "The physical and psychological attrition is increasing daily."[70]

Only two weeks after the end of the war, the Americans began releasing prisoners they considered politically harmless, and by the end of June, the first POW camps were dissolved. Afterward, though, releases were interrupted because the French government demanded a large contingent of German POWs for use as forced laborers in their reconstruction efforts. This relieved the Americans of the burden of the Rhine meadows camps, which were handed over to the French in the

German POWs at the Sinzig camp in the Rhine meadows in April 1945.

days leading up to July 10. The British had already assumed responsibility for the camps in their occupation zone. By the end of September, the final French and British camps were also dissolved. The lone exception was the Bad Kreuznach camp, which continued until 1948 as a transitional facility for German POWs returning from France.

There is no consensus as to how many of the millions of POWs in the meadows camps died.[71] There were no mass deaths of German POWs, to say nothing of consciously planned massacres. Reliable estimates of the number of German soldiers who died in Allied captivity range from 8,000 to 40,000.[72] Compared with the mortality rate in Soviet POW camps, these are relatively low figures. The most deadly POW camps were those run by the Germans: by the end of the war, 3 million of the 5.7 million Red Army soldiers unfortunate enough to fall into German hands had died. Most of them had been intentionally allowed to starve. Historian Ulrich Herbert is correct when he writes of this mass killing as "the greatest and most terrible German crime of the Second World War after the murder of European Jews."[73] American occupation authorities can by no means be accused of pursuing comparable policies, even if the treatment of their POWs did not conform at all times to the Geneva Convention.

LIEUTENANT WALTER STEIN of the 7th US Army could hardly believe his eyes when two other American soldiers and a German police captain entered the Haus Bergfrieden villa in Neuhaus am Schliersee on the afternoon of May 4 and discovered the former general gouverneur of occupied Poland, Hans Frank, having coffee with acquaintances. The much-feared "butcher of Poland" allowed himself to be taken prisoner without resistance. "After almost a quarter of a century, my march alongside Hitler had come to an end," he commented in the memoirs he wrote during the Nuremberg Trials.[74]

In fact, Frank's "march" had begun all the way back in 1919, when the nineteen-year-old law student in Munich joined the racist-nationalist Thule Society and, as a member of the paramilitary Freikorps Epp, helped put down the Munich Soviet Republic. In January 1920, as a follower of the German Workers Party, the precursor to the Nazi Party, he first heard Hitler at an event and was bowled over by his power as a speaker. "He spoke everything from his own soul and the souls of all of us as well," Frank wrote.[75] As a participant in the Beer Hall Putsch on November 9, 1923, Frank was a member of the exclusive circle of Hitler's "old-time streetfighters," and he enjoyed a close and trusting relationship with the Nazi leader, whom he advised in a number of court cases prior to 1933. After Hitler became chancellor, Frank was made Bavarian minister of justice and Reich commissar for the political realignment of the judicial system in the regional German states. From 1934 to the end of the Third Reich, he was also a Reich minister without portfolio.

In October 1939, Hitler rewarded the Nazi Party's top lawyer with the post of general gouverneur of those parts of western Poland not formally annexed by the Third Reich. From his offices in Wawel Castle in Kraków, the traditional residence of Polish kings, Frank established a regime of terror that left all previous forms of German occupation rule in its shadow. "Frank is behaving like a pasha who's succumbed to megalomania," noted the former German ambassador to Italy, Ulrich von Hassell, in late December 1939.[76]

Right from the start, the general gouverneur, who answered only to Hitler himself, issued a raft of edicts with no other purpose than to ruthlessly exploit Polish resources, degrade Poles to the status of slaves, and eradicate any chance of resistance. "My relationship to Poles is that between the ant and the aphid," Frank proclaimed in January 1940.[77] Those most vulnerable to being terrorized were the 1.7 million Polish Jews who had fallen under German control. Four days after Hitler had approved the murder of European Jews at a meeting of Reichs- and Gauleiters on December 16, 1941, Frank told the employees of the General Government, "The Jews—I want to tell you this openly—will have to be put an end to. . . . Gentlemen, I must ask you to gird yourself against any feelings of empathy. We must destroy the Jews, wherever we encounter them and wherever it is possible."[78] The three death camps that were part of the genocidal Operation Reinhard—Belzec, Sobibor, and Treblinka—were all located within the General Government zone. In 1942, more people were murdered in these camps than in Auschwitz, which became a central symbol of the Holocaust.[79]

Without any hesitation, Frank looted precious works of art and other valuables, and he and his wife rivaled even the corrupt Hermann Göring in their addiction to luxury and shameless self-enrichment.[80] In August 1944, with the Red Army having seized two-thirds of the area under the General Government, he arranged for his plunder to be transported to safety. Frank abandoned Wawel Castle on January 17, 1945, the day before Soviet troops seized Kraków. He fled via Breslau to Seichau in Upper Silesia and the castle of Baron Manfred von Rich-thofen, and then on January 23 to Alpine Bavaria. There, in the town of Neuhaus am Schliersee, Frank established an "outpost of the General Government," even though the administrative units he had once lorded over no longer existed, and in Haus Bergfrieden, he collected all his looted art, including works by da Vinci, Rembrandt, and Rubens.[81] When the Americans discovered him on May 4, they confiscated these stolen treasures. Members of the US Rainbow Division physically abused him as they took him into custody; haunted by visions of the horrific images from liberated Dachau, they vented their disgust and rage on their captive. Frank tried to commit suicide on several occasions and was brought to Mondorf-les-Bains in Luxembourg on May 20, where he was interned with other prominent representatives of the Nazi regime until late August 1945, when he was transferred to Nuremberg to stand trial.[82]

"TWO IN THE AFTERNOON—alarm—the Americans!" noted former Austrian chancellor Kurt Schuschnigg on May 4. "An American front-line company has seized the hotel and offered us protection. We are liberated!"[83] Along with his wife and small daughter, Schuschnigg was one of the 137 "special prisoners" from seventeen nations who had been transferred on Himmler's orders from various concentration camps to Dachau in the first weeks of April. What the SS leader's intentions were is not entirely clear. Perhaps he hoped to use the prisoners as leverage in his efforts to negotiate a separate ceasefire with the western Allies.[84] Among the foreign captives were former French prime minister Léon Blum; Captain Peter Churchill (who told the Germans, falsely, that he was Winston Churchill's nephew); British Secret Service agent Sigis-mund Payne Best, whom the SS had arrested following the November 8, 1939, assassination attempt on Hitler; Italian general Sante Garibaldi and his staff officers; former Dutch minister of war Jannes Johannes Cornelis van Dijk; Greek field marshal Alexandros Papagos and his general staff leaders; former Hungarian prime minister Miklós Kállay; and the son of the Hungarian Reich representative, Miklós Horthy Jr.

Notable Germans among the prisoners included industrialist Fritz Thyssen and his wife, who had left Germany in 1939 and been arrested in occupied France; former Reich economics minister and Reichsbank president Hjalmar Schacht and former army general chief of staff Franz Halder, both of whom had been arrested after the failed assassination of Hitler on July 20, 1944; Catholic Center politician and state secretary under Chancellor Heinrich Brüning, Hermann Pünder, who would succeed Adenauer as mayor of Cologne; and Pastor Martin Niemöller, who had been incarcerated since 1938 as a "personal prisoner" of Hitler, first in Sachsenhausen and later in Dachau. In addition, thirty-six people were detained as relatives of personae non grata, most of whom had been arrested after the July 20 assassination attempt, including relatives of Count Claus Schenk von Stauffenberg and Carl Friedrich Goerdeler.[85]

On the night of April 27, the prisoners were told to prepare to be moved from Dachau. At around 2:00 a.m., five busses set off south. None of the inmates knew where they were headed or what the next hours would bring. "The terrible question hanging over all our heads was: liberation or, in the last minute, 'liquidation'?" recalled Pünder.[86] News had spread among the prisoners that Admiral Wilhelm Canaris, General Hans Oster, and Pastor Dietrich Bonhoeffer had been executed in Flossenbürg Prison on April 9 and that would-be Hitler assassin Georg Elser had suffered the same fate in Dachau on that day as well.

The busses were guarded by a fifty-man SS commando unit under Obersturmbahnführer Edgar Stiller. The first stop was a special camp in Innsbruck.[87] Two days later they headed up the Brenner Pass. The further the convoy progressed, the more nervous the SS men became and the more confident their prisoners grew. "Our fear and respect of the SS melted away like snow in the sunshine," recalled cabaret performer Isa Vermehren, who had been detained in 1944 after her brother Erich Vermehren—an agent of the German military intelligence organization, the Abwehr, in Istanbul—had defected to the British. "By contrast, the SS were visibly losing the ground under their feet during these hours. The moment the fear we had of them was no longer reflected, they forfeited their sense of power, and their confidence and air of authority visibly drained away. They kept in the background all day, put on solicitous expressions when we encountered them, and acted as though what was happening was part of a plan that was going on unhindered, full steam ahead."[88] Apparently the SS guards had no idea what they were supposed to be doing with their important captives. They seem to have operated without any clear orders. "Often you saw them checking and exchanging dispatches and lists, whispering as a group," Pünder observed.[89]

On April 29, the convoy reached the town of Niederdorf in the southern Tyrol valley of Pustertal. While most of the SS departed, presumably to search for quarters, the prisoners waited in their busses. After several torturous hours of inaction, they decided to make their way into the village on their own. They encountered no resistance from the few guards who had remained behind and who apparently realized the game was up.[90] Amid the uncertainty, Colonel Bogislav von Bonin seized the initiative. The former head of the operations division in the Army High Command had been arrested at Hitler's instruction in January 1945 for ignoring a "Führer order" and was imprisoned in Dachau. Once in Niederdorf, he succeeded, unnoticed, in getting a telephone line to the chief of the general staff of Army Group C in Bozen, General Hans Röttiger, who promised to immediately send a company of soldiers under Captain Wichard von Alvensleben. On the afternoon of April 30, Bonin announced in the presence of the man in charge of the convoy, Stiller, that the prisoners were now protected under the authority of the Wehrmacht.[91] On May 1, the group was taken to the Pragser Wildsee winter sports hotel, located at an altitude of 1,500 meters. The SS guards were nowhere to be found.

On May 4, the day of their ultimate rescue, the "special prisoners" saw something completely different. "Countless military vehicles, small and large, drove into the courtyard," wrote Isa Vermehren. "All of them were painted green and bore the star of Allied forces. Soldiers teemed in the hotel's entrance and main reception hall—it was an American vanguard troupe of the 5th Army." Vermehren was struck by how relaxed the GIs seemed: "The soldiers stood around or lounged on chairs with their feet up on the tables or their legs stretched out. All of them carried their hands deep in their pockets. Some had cigarettes in their mouths, and with others you could see the slow up-and-down motions of their lower jaws, as they chewed gum."[92]

But the captives' glee at having been rescued from SS custody did not last long. Two days later an American general told them he had orders to take them to southern Italy. In a convoy of forty jeeps, the crossed the snowbound Alps toward Verona, where five planes were waiting to fly the group to Naples. From there they were taken to Capri, where the German prisoners were quartered in the Hotel Paradiso and extensively interrogated. A further four weeks elapsed before Isa Vermehren returned to Frankfurt am Main. "The first fourteen days in Frankfurt were the most difficult and arduous part of our return home," she would recall. "The thick curtain drawn across this country in the past twelve years had finally come down, openly revealing all the terrible things that had gone on behind it."[93]

MAY 5, 1945

On May 5, 1945, Grand Admiral Dönitz summoned his closest associates, Schwerin von Krosigk—now Germany's foreign minister—and Hitler's former armaments minister Albert Speer, for a meeting. The main item of discussion was "the formation of a government and a cabinet."[1] Originally the admiral was unsure about whether it made sense to form a government that would be so powerless. But Krosigk had convinced him it was necessary, arguing that staffing the vacant ministries was the only way to tackle urgent problems, including easing the suffering of refugees, ensuring the populace was supplied with food, and restoring public transportation and the economy. They decided to nominate a "caretaker Reich government" to be headed by Krosigk, who refused Dönitz's offer of the title of chancellor. Instead, Krosigk preferred to be called the "directing minister." To underscore the provisional character of the new government, its ministers were not officially appointed but rather charged with "directing business."[2]

The decisive factor in the choice of ministers was supposed to be expertise, but actually Krosigk was content to call on the ministers and state secretaries who had retreated to the "northern realm," including those who were politically compromised. In addition to remaining foreign minister, Krosigk renewed his own appointment as finance minister, which he had held without interruption since 1932. He was flanked by two state secretaries: Friedrich Wilhelm Kritzinger, who had already served the head of the Reich chancellery as a state secretary, and Gustav Adolf Steengracht von Moyland, who had succeeded Ernst von Weizsäcker as state secretary in the foreign ministry in 1943. The latter owed his career to Joachim von Ribbentrop, who had brought him along in 1936 to Germany's London embassy and had appointed him legation secretary in 1938 after being named foreign minister.[3]

The tasks of the ministries of the interior and culture were given to Wilhelm Stuckart. An interior ministry state secretary under Wilhelm Frick, Stuckart was a doctor of law and had played a central role in the formulation of the 1935 Nuremberg Laws and their subsequent supplementary ordinances. He had drafted the "Law on the Reunification of Austria with the German Reich" and the edict establishing the Reich Protectorate of Bohemia and Moravia. He also attended the Wannsee Conference of January 20, 1942, at which the head of the Reich Main Security Office, Reinhard Heydrich, enlisted top German administrators for the "final solution to the Jewish question." An unscrupulous functionary, Stuckart had also served as the right hand of Himmler, when the latter had succeeded Frick as interior minister in August 1943. In return, Stuckart had been rewarded with the rank of SS Obergruppenführer.[4]

Herbert Backe, whom Krosigk confirmed as minister of food, agriculture, and forestry, boasted a career of similar moral decrepitude. Backe, who had a degree in agriculture, had been a state secretary in the ministry under Walter Darré as of October 1933, and in that position he had helped preside over the 1941 "starvation plan" for the Soviet Union, which would have included the deaths of thirty million people in German-occupied territories if carried out. "There is hardly anyone else in Germany who has so constantly acted in the interests of the Führer," Backe wrote of himself at the time to his wife.[5] When

Darré was fired in May 1942, Backe took over as a deputy before officially being made the head of the ministry in April 1944. In his testament, Hitler confirmed him in this post.[6]

Assisting Backe in the Dönitz government was Hans-Joachim Riecke, another technical specialist with an agricultural degree and another early member of the Nazi Party. As the head of the Main Group for Food and Agriculture in Göring's Economic Staff East, he was also involved in the homicidal plans for exploiting occupied Soviet territories. After Darré's dismissal he became a state secretary under Backe. The fact that he was tapped in Flensburg to continue in this capacity shows how much old connections still mattered.[7]

In a similar vein, the seventy-five-year-old Julius Heinrich Dorpmüller, whom Krosigk wanted to retain as transportation minister and also named as Reich postal minister, was by no means the apolitical technocrat depicted by his supporters after 1945. A former director general of the national rail company, the Reichsbahn, Dorpmüller had pledged his unconditional loyalty to the "national government" in a 1933 appeal to railway employees and was named transportation minister in Hitler's cabinet in 1938. He had been complicit in the transportation of Jews from across Europe to the death camps in the east. Even more compromised was his state secretary Albert Ganzenmüller. In a letter dated August 13, 1942, SS Obergruppenführer Karl Wolff thanked Ganzenmüller for his assistance in the mass murder of Jews: "With particular joy, I received your news that for the past 14 days, a daily train full of 5,000 members of the Chosen People travels to Treblinka, so that we are now able to carry out this movement of population at an accelerated tempo."[8]

The record of Franz Seldte, who continued in the position of labor minister and was given additional responsibility as social affairs minister under Krosigk, was likewise appalling. Seldte had volunteered for the First World War in 1914 and lost an arm at the Battle of Somme in 1916. In 1918, he founded the Stahlhelm association for former frontline soldiers, which was dedicated to destroying the Weimar Republic. Together with media mogul Alfred Hugenberg, the head of the jingoistic German National People's Party (Deutschnationale Volkspartei, or DNVP), and the chairman of the NSDAP, Adolf Hitler, he had led a 1929 campaign against the Young Plan, which finally set the level of German reparations for the First World War and had helped unite the antidemocratic right in the "Harzburg Front" movement in October 1931. Along with Franz von Papen and Hugenberg, Seldte had played a major role in the intrigues that led to Hitler being named chancellor in January 1933. In return, he was named labor minister in Hitler's "government of national concentration"—an office he held until the end of the war. As recent studies have shown, his ministry was much more deeply implicated in the crimes of the Nazi regime, particularly in the procurement of slave laborers in occupied Europe, than previously assumed.[9]

It was considered a given that Speer would be part of the new government. Hitler's former protégé had made his way to the Dönitz government's headquarters on April 30 and, ever mindful of the need to carve out a postwar career for himself, had not left the admiral's side since. Now Speer was up for the post of economics and production minister. His exalted status was underscored by the fact that after a few days he left the government's common quarters on the passenger ship SS *Patria* and moved into the waterside estate of Glücksberg a few kilometers away, which the Duke of Mecklenburg had put at his disposal. Supported by his adjutants Manfred von Poser and Karl Cliever and his secretaries Annemarie Kempf and Edith Maguira, he quickly made himself comfortable. Speer arranged to be chauffeured to the cabinet meetings in Flensburg every morning.[10]

Otto Ohlendorf, however, was the man who was actually supposed to run the economics ministry. As the other members of the Dönitz regime surely knew, Ohlendorf was an SS Gruppenführer at the start of Operation Barbarossa, from June 1941 to June 1942, commanding

Einsatzgruppe D in the southern Soviet Union, which was responsible for murdering at least ninety thousand people. In other words, he was the worst sort of war criminal.[11] Since 1943, along with his work in the Reich Main Security Office, where he oversaw the secret Security Service reports on the public mood in Germany, Ohlendorf had been a ministerial director and deputy state secretary in the economics ministry under Walther Funk. In this capacity, his duties included planning the postwar economy, which no doubt qualified him in Speer's eyes for his new job in Flensburg.

Ohlendorf was not content to offer his services as an economics expert, and he proposed to Dönitz that personnel from the Reich Main Security Office that had moved with him to the "northern realm" could serve as the basis for a new German intelligence body. The "intelligence office," established by edict only a few days later, would be responsible for the collection and analysis of all domestic and foreign political, economic, and military intelligence, as well as publishing and disseminating government statements, proclamations, and orders. In contrast to the thinly staffed economics ministry, the "intelligence office" comprised 59 officials and full officers as well as some 170 subordinate officers, auxiliaries, and employees. In other words, the personnel of the "caretaker government" consisted primarily of men from the Reich Main Security Office.[12]

The Dönitz government provided anything but a fresh start. On the contrary, almost without exception, Nazi elites remained in positions of power. It was inconceivable that the Allies would ever accept the new regime in Flensburg as a serious negotiating partner.

AT 6:00 A.M. ON THE morning of May 5, a speaker on Czech radio opened the daily broadcast by announcing the time of day in the usual mix of Czech and German. As the day progressed, the hours were given in Czech only—in contravention of longstanding instructions from the German station director that all broadcasts were to be bilingual. This was the start of the Prague uprising that would end German rule in the Protectorate of Bohemia and Moravia.[13]

Since the summer of 1944, when it became clear that Hitler's Germany was headed for defeat, anti-German resistance had been growing among Czechs, with partisan attacks on railway lines and other important sites increasing. In response, State Minister Karl Hermann Frank, who was also the supreme SS and police minister in the protectorate, turned to even more brutal countermeasures. Exemplary punishments and draconian threats were supposed to scare Czechs and prevent them from rebelling. "Every attempt to call forth unrest domestically . . . will be nipped in the bud," Frank proclaimed on April 8, 1945. "Calm and order will prevail within the protectorate. The leadership is intact and possesses nerves of steel and an iron will not to surrender or give up a thing, nothing whatsoever."[14]

Nonetheless, by later in the month, unrest was spreading to nearly all parts of Bohemia and Moravia. The Red Army's encirclement of Berlin and the rapid advances of Allied troops in the west were unmistakable signs that the end of the war was near. On the evening of April 30, Frank addressed "Czech citizens" on Prague radio. The Czech people, he said, were being prompted "with all means of seduction" by enemy radio broadcasts and flyers to "stab the Reich in the back." Acting in accordance with enemy slogans would lead to chaos and civil war, he cautioned, once more warning against speculation that the German occupation was weakening. "German weapons are loaded with live ammunition and will deal a devastating blow to fomenters of unrest," he threatened.[15] Frank, however, had no illusions about the explosiveness of the situation. During a brief trip to Flensburg on May 3, he reported that the protectorate was "on the eve of revolution" and could not be "held either militarily or politically."[16] During the night of May 4, the state minister returned to Prague, where he would be proven right more quickly than even he had expected.

Electrified by the radio broadcast on the morning of May 5, Prague's populace took to the streets. The German language was removed from plaques and signs, and Czech flags were raised above public buildings. Czechs seized control of government offices, arresting their German overlords. Bitter fighting erupted around the radio station at about noon. At 12:33 p.m., the radio announcer once again took to the airwaves, this time to issue a plea for help: "Everyone to the Czech radio station! Czechs are being shot down here! Come as quickly as possible! Come to our aid!"[17] This was the signal for a planned revolt. By shortly after 6:00 p.m., the Czech radio station was in the hands of the insurgents, and the Czech National Council—an organization of various resistance groups that had formed in late February 1945—issued a general proclamation. From that day forward, the council said, it was taking control of the government of the Czechoslovakian Republic "as the representative of the revolutionary movement of the Czech people." The protectorate ceased to exist.[18] At 11:00 p.m., the people of Prague were called on to erect barricades throughout the city to repulse the expected German counterattack. The call to arms attracted an overwhelming response. When the morning of May 6 dawned, some 1,600 barricades had been put up in the part of the city controlled by the insurgents.[19]

The uprising caught SS and Wehrmacht units stationed in the city off guard, and initially they did nothing more than hold their positions. Still, from the very start, the Waffen SS commander in Bohemia and Moravia, Gruppenführer Count Carl Friedrich von Pückler-Burghaus, left no doubt that he was prepared to put down the rebellion with force. By the evening of May 5, he had already sent a radio message to the main headquarters of the supreme commander of Army Group Center, Field Marshal General Ferdinand Schörner, calling for Prague's historic city center to be bombed. "Great number of incendiary bombs," he demanded. "This whole rats' nest must burn."[20]

The following morning, Waffen-SS troops—among them Tank

One of the many barricades erected the night of May 5, 1945,
during the Prague uprising.

Grenadier Regiment 4, which had been responsible for the massacre
in the French village of Oradour-sur-Glane in June 1944, one of the
most infamous acts of mass murder in Western Europe—moved into
Prague's outer districts, committing atrocities as they advanced. As they
used civilians as human shields, German planes dropped leaflets telling city residents they had a choice between "fighting, destruction, and
senseless bloodshed, on the one hand, and calm, order, and preservation
of public welfare until a new order can be established, on the other."[21]

News of the uprising in Prague reached Flensburg at 10:00 a.m.
on May 6, and Dönitz immediately ordered Army Group Center to
"withdraw as far west as possible as quickly as possible to save the greatest number of German soldiers."[22] Only the day before, Schörner had
admonished his soldiers "not to lose your nerve and become cowardly in
these most difficult days of our Reich," adding that "our discipline and

the weapons in our hands are our guarantee that we will emerge from this war in upstanding, courageous fashion."[23] Yet now he hastened to carry out the order to retreat. To do so, he pressed the SS units advancing into Prague to reseize the means of transport necessary for German troops to flee. Brutal fighting took place in the streets leading to the city center. The situation of the insurgents was grave. They pinned their hopes on the 3rd US Army under General George Patton, who that day had taken the western Bohemian city of Pilsen (Plzeň), only about a hundred kilometers from Prague. The Czechs, however, had no way of knowing that the Americans had already reached an agreement with the Soviet leadership on a demarcation line seventy kilometers west of the Czech capital and that the supreme commander of the Allied forces, General Eisenhower, insisted it be strictly maintained.[24]

Assistance for the insurgents came from an unanticipated source. In November 1944, the German occupiers of the Czech half of Czechoslovakia had raised a unit of largely anti-Communist Russian expatriate volunteers, called the Vlasov Army after its commander Andrej Vlasov, to help the Wehrmacht battle the Soviet Union. In mid-April 1945, the 1st Vlasov Division, numbering twenty thousand men, under Sergei Kuzmich Bunyachenko, had been dispatched to the protectorate. On May 6, these troops decided to change sides and support the Czech partisans. "We Russian soldiers who are leading the fight for the liberation of our national Russia from further bondage by Bolshevism cannot stand on the sidelines of this battle of the Czech nation," read one flyer.[25] But Bunyachenko's motives were anything but selfless. He thought that by supporting the insurgency he would make it less likely that he and his men would be taken captive by the Red Army. He, too, did not yet know the Americans would halt their advances in western Bohemia and leave Soviet troops to liberate Prague. At noon on May 6, Bunyachenko's division entered the city in three columns of tanks and artillery. It succeeded in halting the attack by the Waffen-SS and in pushing the Germans back from several city districts.

The Vlasov Army's intervention was not universally welcomed within the Czech National Council. Communist council members saw the army as consisting of traitors to the Soviet Union and Stalin. Owing to the urgency of the situation, they finally agreed to accept the support but insisted that a message be broadcast on Prague radio on the morning of May 7, explaining that "the actions of General Vlasov against German forces" were "his units' own business" and that the Czech National Council had "not reached any political agreements with them."[26] Bunyachenko was annoyed by this, and when news arrived that night that the Americans had stopped their advance, he ordered his division to move west. Only several hundred of his men remained behind in Prague and continued fighting alongside the Czechs.

The battle in Prague continued into the morning of May 8, when at 11:00 a.m., the Wehrmacht's liaison at the State Ministry for Bohemia and Moravia, General Rudolf Toussaint, and representatives of the Czech National Council began negotiating a ceasefire. After a difficult back-and-forth, an agreement was reached at 4:00 p.m. All German forces, including Waffen-SS and police, would be allowed to withdraw freely from Prague and the surrounding area. Moreover, German women and children, "insofar as they don't withdraw with these units from Prague" would be protected by the International Red Cross.[27] During the night of May 8, State Minister Frank and his family left his offices in Czernin Palace and surrendered to the Americans. In early August 1945, Frank was sent back to Prague, where in May 1946, after a trial, he was hanged in the city's Pankrác Prison.[28]

On the morning of May 9, 1945, the Red Army entered the already liberated city. "Great celebrations in the streets," wrote one Prague resident in his diary. "There were cries of 'Long live . . .' and 'Gloria'! Hundreds of people waved their hands in the air. . . . A tempest of jubilation went up as every one of the giant tanks rolled in."[29] It was the polar opposite of the popular reaction on March 15, 1939, when the Wehrmacht marched into the Czech capital.

Once Germany's general unconditional surrender went into force at midnight on May 8, most of the men in Army Group Center became Soviet POWs. Its last supreme commander, Field Marshal General Schörner, who had demanded extreme discipline from his men to the very last, fled for the Austrian Alps in a Fieseler Storch light aircraft. Several days later, he surrendered to the Americans, who deported him to the Soviet Union. In February 1952, he was sentenced by the Supreme Soviet Military Court in Moscow to twenty-five years imprisonment, but he was released in December 1954.[30]

General Bunyachenko's fate was considerably harsher. He, too, was extradited by the United States to the Soviet Union and taken to Moscow. But along with General Vlasov and seven other commanders of the "Russian Liberation Army," he was executed in early August 1946. After the Soviets' initial arrival in the city in May 1945, two hundred wounded members of the Vlasov Army fell into the hands of the Red Army in Prague and were immediately liquidated.[31]

FOR GERMANS WHO REMAINED in Prague, the end of the war was the beginning of a nightmare. The hatred that had built up in the six years of German occupation exploded in a bloody spree of revenge targeting the guilty and the innocent in equal measure. Peter Demetz, who was born in Prague in 1922 and who later became one of the leading experts in the United States on German literature, recalled day after day of terror: "An old woman was pushed out a window, a musician who was a member of a touring German orchestra was beaten to death on the street because he couldn't speak Czech, and others who were not all members of the Gestapo were strung up, doused in gasoline, and set ablaze like human torches. An enraged mob searched hospitals for victims who were still alive. . . . In dozens of places in Prague—cinemas, schools, sports stadia, and garages—Germans were rounded up and transported to holding camps nearby. By July, some 30,000 had been removed from the city. Postwar Czech Communist paramilitaries—

the Revolutionary Guards, whom many skeptical citizens referred to as the 'robber guards'—made no distinctions between 'Reich Germans' who had arrived with the occupation and Prague Germans who had lived in the city for generations."[32]

What began in Prague expanded between May and July to the former protectorate and the Sudetenland. Everywhere, regular Czech soldiers, Revolutionary Guards, and civilians hounded Germans; beatings, murder, and plunder were daily occurrences. Politicians stoked people's desire for revenge. Three days after the Soviets marched into Prague, Czech prime minister Edvard Beneš returned from British exile and declared, "The German people stopped being human and humanly tolerable during this war and now appear to us to be a single huge inhuman monstrosity. . . . We have told ourselves that we must liquidate the German problem in the republic."[33] Although Sudeten Germans had not by any means all been Nazi supporters, they were now held collectively responsible for the occupiers' crimes. The decrees issued by Beneš in the weeks that followed were aimed solely at removing as much of the German population as possible. The idea was to make the German question a fait accompli before the victorious powers met for the Potsdam Conference in mid-July. A period of "wild expulsions" began, although these acts were less spontaneous than that phrase suggests. As a rule, the Czechs who drove Germans from their homes acted on the express orders or at least with the tacit approval of Czech authorities.[34]

The nadir was reached on May 30 with what Germans call the "Brünn death march." While Czech onlookers applauded and church bells rang, some 26,000 Germans, primarily women, children, and old men, were forced to leave the city of Brünn (Brno). During their march to Austria, hundreds died of exhaustion.[35] All told, around eight hundred thousand Sudeten Germans were affected by the first wave of expulsions from May to July 1945. By July 3, the council of the Moravian regional committee was able to report that most parts of southern

Moravia had been "cleansed of Germans." A week later, Social Democratic vice–prime minister Zdeněk Fierlinger informed a meeting of his party in Prague that "cities like Litoměřice and Ústí nad Labem, to say nothing of Brno, Jihlava, and Znojmo, are Czech once more."[36] The removal of Germans from various parts of eastern and central Europe would continue for decades, but they would never be accompanied by the sort of extreme violence that marked the immediate aftermath of the German occupation.

ON MAY 5, ALLIED SUPREME commander Dwight Eisenhower took to the radio to address the many foreigners who found themselves in Germany. He told these so-called displaced persons not to leave the areas they were in and to wait for additional instructions. He also encouraged them to form small groups based on nationality and to elect representatives who could negotiate on their behalf with American authorities. The address was translated into a number of languages.[37]

According to a November 1944 memo from the Supreme Headquarters Allied Expeditionary Force, displaced persons (DPs) were understood to include "civilians outside the boundaries of their country by reasons of war . . . desirous but unable to return home or find homes without assistance."[38] The definition covered civilian workers, POWs from countries around the world, and foreign prisoners liberated from concentration camps. In total, there were about 11 million people overall who fell into this broad category at the end of the war, with 6.3 million in the three western occupation zones and 7 million in Germany as a whole.[39]

The largest subgroup consisted of "foreign workers," young men and women who had been taken mostly from Poland and the Soviet Union to Germany during the war. By September 1944, the number of foreign slave laborers in Germany had swelled to 7.6 million: 5.7 million civilians and just under 2 million POWs. Every fourth person working in German industry and agriculture was foreign. The massive exploitation of forced labor allowed the Nazi leadership to continue to wage war for more than two years after the debacle at Stalingrad.[40]

The huge populations of slave laborers became a feature of German society in the final years of the war. Every large city had a network of camps and barrack facilities, and every day residents saw "foreign workers" being herded toward their places of labor or made to clear rubble left by aerial attacks. Poles and "Eastern workers," those people forcibly brought from the Soviet Union, came in for the worst treatment. Special edicts subjected them to comprehensive discrimination and surveillance. Among other things, they were required to wear special badges giving their identity as "P" (Polish) or "Ost" (East), they were housed in enclosed barrack facilities surrounded by barbed wire, and the men were subject to the death penalty if caught having intimate relations with German women.[41]

As the end of the war approached, unrest among the "foreign workers" increased, and the punishments meted out to them became more draconian. The presence of millions of slave laborers from formerly occupied parts of Europe, who had every reason to want revenge for the suffering inflicted on them, sowed fear among the German populace. Nazi authorities increasingly reacted to the sense of threat with extreme violence. In the final days of the war, hundreds of foreigners, especially "Eastern workers," were murdered by Gestapo commandos in the industrial Ruhr Valley.[42]

After the Allied invasions of Germany, slave laborers often took revenge. An American military official noted that the thirst for vengeance was the greatest among those forcibly taken from the Soviet Union.[43] Former slave laborers did not lash out blindly, but specifically targeted foremen, camp directors, and, in the coal mines of the Ruhr, pit bosses they felt had treated them particularly badly. Along with attacks on hated superiors, there was also a wave of "theft." Reporting from Frankfurt in early April 1945, American journalist Marguerite Higgins described foreign workers who had been starved and physically abused by Germans for years engaging in plunder after being liberated.[44] Some liberated DPs formed gangs and prowled the area around their camps in search of compensation for their years of hardship. A report by the 9th US Army told of displaced persons moving from farm to farm in groups of thirty to forty, demanding provisions, clothing, and sometimes jewelry and other personal items.[45] The liberation of the Sandbostel POW camp in late April 1945 made for some uneasy days for the residents of nearby Bremervörde. "What a sight in the city!" complained one eyewitness on May 3. "The streets almost blocked by tanks and soldiers. Between them, foreigners going from one of the destroyed buildings to the next, plundering and thieving."[46]

The threat from displaced persons was a prominent worry for Germans in the early days of May 1945. A stereotype arose of DPs as an asocial, out-of-control "horde," seamlessly extending negative images used to justify slave labor under Nazi rule in the first place. For many Germans, reports of unrest among DPs were somewhat welcome since they assuaged bad consciences about the brutal treatment of the "Eastern workers" and Soviet POWs. The truth was that "crime" rates among DPs were not significantly higher than those among Germans, which had soared dramatically after the war. But no matter where crimes were perpetrated, the first suspects were always DPs.[47]

In mid-April 1945, the Allies had set themselves the goal of providing for the DPs after their liberation and repatriating them as quickly as possible to their home countries. In the general chaos of the Third Reich's demise, with Allied troops continuing to march forward, some slave laborers in western Germany decided to set off for home on their own. In early April, the *London News Chronicle* had described vagabond laborers making their way along roads and streets, alone or in small groups of up to twelve, some in rags and others wearing shabby uniforms from a dozen different armies.[48] On May 3, Norwegian correspondent Theo Findahl wrote, "In long processions, the foreign workers left Berlin on foot, pushing handcarts with all their worldly possessions from which little Danish, French, Dutch, and Belgian flags flapped in the wind. Onward to the West! Onward to the West!"[49]

Eisenhower's May 5 radio address was aimed at dissuading people from trying to get home without American assistance and oversight. The majority of DPs were accommodated in so-called assembly centers, often former military barracks or POW and slave-labor camps. Here and there, German people's dwellings were requisitioned, invariably causing outrage. It was an exception when all residents of the town of Haren were forced to leave their homes in May 1945 to make room for Polish slave laborers and POWs.[50] Because the military administrations in the three western occupation zones were overwhelmed trying to house and feed DPs, they enlisted the United Nations Relief and Rehabilitation Administration (UNRRA), an international aid organization, to supervise the camps.

The condition of DPs when the Allied forces found them varied greatly. Slave laborers who had worked in agriculture were usually in better health than those in the armaments industry, and the latter were in superior condition compared with concentration-camp inmates. With surprising speed, the Allies succeeded in providing for many millions of DPs and improving their physical health.[51] Military authorities were also impressively successful in their repatriation efforts. Between May and September, an average of 33,000 people per day were returned to their home countries from the three western occupation zones. All told, the number of DPs dropped by around 5 million in these months, so that only about 1.2 million remained in Germany by the fall of 1945.[52] DPs from Western Europe, who were eager to go home, were the least problematic. By contrast, many former slave laborers from Eastern Europe—those from Poland, in particular—had no desire to return, in some cases because they rejected the new Communist governments and in others because, with Eastern Europe's redrawn boundaries, their hometowns were now located in the Soviet Union.[53]

There were also difficulties in repatriating some Soviet DPs. At the Yalta Conference in February, the western Allies and the Kremlin agreed that all Soviet citizens would be collected in special camps without regard to an individual's own feelings—as was subsequently finalized in the practical guidelines that April.[54] By October 1, 1945, a total of 4.1 million Soviet citizens were repatriated: 1.85 million from the operational area of the Red Army and 2.25 million who were handed over by the western Allies to Soviet authorities—often against those people's own wishes. A not insubstantial number of Soviet DPs were suspected of having colluded with the Nazis. Some DPs had obviously colluded: for instance, the former "volunteers" and members of the Vlasov Army. But for Red Army soldiers, the mere fact that one had surrendered was enough to be potentially branded a "traitor." Soviet slave laborers who had worked in the Nazi armaments industry were also greeted with similar mistrust.

Word quickly got around of the punishments that awaited DPs back home, which led many to resist repatriation. In a camp in Mannheim in early September 1945, six hundred Ukrainian DPs rebelled against the plan to return them to the Soviet Union. After American officers had granted them a four-day reprieve, UNRRA observers found that the Ukrainians were so overjoyed and grateful at this postponement that they kissed officers' and UNRRA workers' boots, prayed loudly, and expressed their feelings in the most emphatic ways imaginable.[55]

Dramatic scenes also played out in January 1946 in Dachau, where two barracks in the former concentration camp were used to house Soviet DPs. American GIs tried to convince them, in vain, to board a waiting train. When the soldiers eventually stormed two barracks, using tear gas, some of the DPs attempted to commit suicide. A US soldier described the mayhem to *Stars and Stripes*: "It just wasn't human. There were no men in that barrack when we reached it. They were animals. The GIs quickly cut down most of those who had hanged themselves from the rafters. Those still conscious were screaming in Russian,

Soviet women forced into slave labor greet their liberators in Berlin
in early May 1945.

pointing first at the guns of the guards and then at themselves, begging us to shoot."[56]

For some of the Soviet DPs who were successfully repatriated, their suffering was anything but over, as they were interned in "filter camps" and subjected to intensive interrogation. Those deemed to have collaborated were sent to work battalions and penal camps. Even those who escaped such punishments could be targets of discrimination. Their involuntary time in Germany was a lasting stigma, leaving them second-rate citizens. It was only with the demise of the Soviet Union in the early 1990s that the treatment of "Eastern workers" became a topic of public discussion, in large measure thanks to the Moscow human-rights organization Memorial. In numerous interviews, former slave laborers for the first time spoke publicly of their experiences.[57] More time would have to pass before the SPD-Green German government under Chancellor Gerhard Schröder convinced German industry to pay into a fund to compensate onetime slave laborers.[58]

THE RELATIVELY SMALL NUMBER of Jewish DPs presented a special challenge for Allied authorities. Only around fifty thousand to seventy thousand Jews had survived the concentration camps in the western occupation zones. Many were near death and badly traumatized when they were liberated, and some had lost their entire families and had no homes to return to. More than any other group of DPs, they required help and care. But the Allied military administration did not grasp the special situation of Jewish former concentration-camp inmates. Initially they were not regarded as a discrete group and were forced to live in overcrowded DP camps with non-Jews, which awakened memories of their past suffering. US State Department envoy Earl G. Harrison, who inspected the DP camps in the American occupation zone, reached a devastating conclusion in his final report to Harry S. Truman on August 24: "As matters now stand, we appear to be treating the Jews as the Nazis treated them except that we do not exterminate them. They are in concentration camps in large numbers under our military guard instead of SS troops. One is led to wonder whether the German people, seeing this, are not supposing that we are following or at least condoning Nazi policy."[59]

Owing in no small part to Harrison's report, US authorities recognized their grievous mistake, immediately setting up camps exclusively for Jews and to be self-administered by the residents. The daily allocation of calories per person was raised, and Jewish DPs were given priority when new places to live were assigned. On August 31, 1945, Truman wrote to Eisenhower about the "special responsibility" Americans had to those in their occupation zone who had been victims of persecution and tyranny. There was no better opportunity, Truman added, to demonstrate that the United States was living up to this responsibility than in the way the nation treated Holocaust survivors in Germany.[60]

The heightened attention Jewish DPs received only strengthened the German populace's antipathy toward them. Fourteen-year-old

Ruth Klüger, who had survived the concentration camps in Theresienstadt, Auschwitz-Birkenau, and Christianstadt, a satellite of Gross-Rosen, and had found a place to live in the Bavarian town of Straubing, would recall these times years later, after she had become a well-known literature scholar and writer in the United States: "Jew-hatred had gone underground in Germany, but it was still simmering just as a ragout continues to stew and remains warm in a good cooking pot, even if the flame on the stove has been turned off for a while. How could it have been any different? By their mere presence, the survivors recall what had gone before and the crimes that had been committed."[61]

In the course of 1946, the situation of Jewish DPs fundamentally changed as their numbers rose considerably, owing to the constant influx of Jews from Eastern Europe. They were fleeing anti-Semitic violence that began soon after the end of the war and reached its zenith with the pogrom in Kielce, Poland, in July 1946. By November, 111,139 Jews from Poland and other Eastern European countries had sought refuge in the US occupation zone. They were recognized as DPs even though they did not meet the original criteria. "With that the paradox arose that only a short time after the war the perpetrator of the Jewish tragedy, Germany, became the largest and safest place for Jewish refugees, who now waited in DP camps for permission to travel on," write historians Angelika Königseder and Juliane Wetzel.[62]

A large majority of Eastern European Jewish survivors were only passing through the DP camps in Germany. They wanted to emigrate to Palestine and hoped the United States would support them in this ambition. But the dream of emigration would not be swiftly fulfilled for most. The British government feared that increased Jewish immigration would worsen problems with the Arab population in Palestine, so policies concerning Jewish arrivals remained restrictive. After Israeli independence in May 1948, which was received enthusiastically in the DP camps, the waiting was over for many would-be émigrés. In January 1949, 64,000 Jews still lived in 48 different camps in the American occupation zone. By November of that year, those numbers had decreased to 15,000 in nine camps. One by one, the Jewish DP camps were closed, with the last, the Föhrenwald camp in Alpine Bavaria, shuttered in February 1957.[63]

AT NOON ON MAY 5, 1945, the first American armored reconnaissance vehicles under Sergeant Albert J. Kosiek reached the Mauthausen concentration camp in Alpine Austria. The SS had abandoned the camp a few days previously, handing over responsibility to the Vienna Fire Safety Police and members of the Volkssturm, who allowed themselves to be disarmed without resistance. As a US patrol appeared on the roll-call grounds, the inmates reacted with jubilation. Prisoner number 127371, Simon Wiesenthal, would later relate that he and everyone else in the camp ran toward the American tanks rolling in, although he was so exhausted that he had to crawl back on his hands and knees.[64]

Mauthausen was the final stop on an odyssey of suffering that had taken Wiesenthal through a number of camps. He was born in 1908 in the eastern Galician town of Butschatsch, which had originally been in the Habsburg Empire but became part of Poland after 1919. His father was a representative for a sugar refinery who gave his life for his country in the First World War. After completing high school, Wiesenthal studied architecture in Prague before transferring to Lwów (today's Lviv), where he graduated with a degree in engineering. In late June 1941, when German troops marched into Lwów, it was home to between 160,000 and 170,000 Jews. Only 3,400 of them would survive the war, including, miraculously, Wiesenthal. He had been arrested only a few days after the Germans took the city and had been deployed as a slave laborer in a repair facility of the eastern German railway, the Ostbahn. In September 1943, he successfully escaped from the Janowska slave-labor camp. He hid underground until June 1944, when he was arrested again and transported to the west in one of the last trains that departed Lwów.[65]

Via the Plaszow, Gross-Rosen, and Buchenwald concentration camps, Wiesenthal arrived at Mauthausen in mid-February 1945. As in Dachau, because of prisoners being evacuated from the east, the camp's living quarters were hopelessly overcrowded. Sanitary conditions deteriorated week by week, and mortality rates were extremely high.[66] In the two-and-a-half months Wiesenthal spent in the infirmary because of a frozen foot, his life, too, hung by a thread. Wiesenthal later described the terrible race between death and liberation, saying that the concentration-camp guards eventually refused to enter the barracks housing prisoners because they were afraid of infectious diseases and nauseated by the stench. He added that the Russians in the camp were given only bowls of viscous liquid described as "soup" to eat.[67] Thousands of people in fact died from the lingering effects of their incarceration in the days after Mauthausen was liberated.

Wiesenthal, however, recovered surprisingly quickly. His path back to normal life took him to Linz, the Danube River city where Hitler had spent his youth. Only a few weeks after being liberated, Wiesenthal launched into the task that would become his life's work: hunting down and bringing to justice those who were responsible for the monstrous crimes of Nazism. In late May 1945, he handed the US camp commander in Mauthausen an eight-page list with the names of nearly 150 Nazi perpetrators. Soon thereafter, he began interviewing Jewish Holocaust survivors for the US military administration. The information they gave him about perpetrators and places crimes had been committed would form the basis of the documentation center he founded in Linz in 1947 and would later continue in Vienna. By chance, Wiesenthal learned that his wife, Cyla, whom he had married in 1936, had survived as a slave laborer in the German town of Solingen thanks to a fake passport. When the two reunited in 1945 and drew up a list of all their family members murdered in the Holocaust, it encompassed 89 names.[68]

Wiesenthal achieved some spectacular successes in his hunt for Nazi criminals. As early as 1953, he informed Israeli authorities that Adolf Eichmann, one of the main organizers of the Holocaust, was living under an assumed name in Argentina: this was seven years before Mossad agents arrested Eichmann in Buenos Aires and took him to Israel, where he was put on trial and executed in early 1962. Wiesenthal's part in this coup made him a household name around the world. In 1963, he located other well-known criminals, including Austrian SS Oberscharführer Karl Josef Silberbauer, the man who had arrested Anne Frank and her family in Amsterdam in 1944. After the war, Silberbauer returned to Vienna, becoming a police officer in the 1950s. In 1964 charges against him were dismissed—one of the many disappointments Wiesenthal was forced to swallow. In 1967, Wiesenthal succeeded in tracking down the commandant of the Treblinka death camp, Josef Stangl, in São Paulo, Brazil. Stangl was extradited to West Germany and sentenced to life imprisonment by a regional court in Düsseldorf in December 1970. Six months later he died in prison.[69]

Wiesenthal had his detractors, including many people who wanted to put fascism behind them and so referred to him dismissively as a self-promoting "Nazi hunter." Some of Wiesenthal's methods may have been questionable, and he certainly loved being the center of attention. But those traits do not diminish the magnitude of his achievements. Without his courage and determination, more Nazi criminals would have escaped punishment after 1945. Wiesenthal's biographer, Tom Segev, praised him for keeping the memories of the dead alive while fighting Holocaust denial—just as Wiesenthal himself had fought death and revered life.[70]

MAY 6, 1945

On the morning of May 6, 1945, General Eberhard Kinzel arrived in Flensburg to report on the status of negotiations with Eisenhower. Kinzel was one member of a small delegation charged by Admiral General Hans-Georg von Friedeburg, after the conclusion of German talks with Montgomery on May 4, with traveling to Allied headquarters in Reims to hammer out a German surrender to the Americans.[1] That very day, Eisenhower had received word that the German delegation would be paying him a visit, but the American commander made clear from the outset he would not agree to any further partial surrender of German troops. The secret talks about the capitulation of German Army Group C in Italy in March and April 1945 had already caused a crisis in the anti-Hitler alliance and awakened Stalin's mistrust of the western Allies.[2] "Any suggestion that the Allies would accept from the German Government a surrender only of their western forces would instantly create complete misunderstanding with the Russians and bring about a situation in which the Russians could justifiably accuse us of bad faith," Eisenhower wrote in his memoirs.[3]

To avoid further tension, Eisenhower hastened to inform the Soviet leadership by telegram that German envoys were on their way and offered reassurances that he would welcome only a complete surrender and that a partial capitulation of the Wehrmacht in the west would be rejected. At the same time, he asked for a Red Army officer to be sent to his headquarters to represent the Soviet Union during the negotiations. The Soviet Supreme Command nominated General Ivan Alexeyevich Susloparov, the head of the Soviet military mission in France.[4]

Eisenhower appointed his chief of staff, General Walter Bedell Smith, and his assistant chief of staff for intelligence, British general Kenneth W. D. Strong, to lead the negotiations. Eisenhower himself wished to have no contact with the German emissaries. Since April 12, when he visited the liberated Ohrdruf concentration camp, a satellite of Buchenwald near Gotha, his antipathy toward the Germans had become even more pronounced. "I have never felt able to describe my emotional reactions when I first came face to face with indisputable evidence of Nazi brutality and ruthless disregard for every shred of decency," he would write. "I have never at any other time experienced an equal sense of shock."[5]

When Friedeburg arrived at Eisenhower's headquarters in a Reims school building (today's Lycée Polyvalent Franklin Roosevelt) on the afternoon of May 5, he quickly sensed the frosty atmosphere. Smith had prepared a map showing German and American troop positions. Two large red arrows on the map indicated supposedly planned US Army operations. The idea was to convince the Germans the situation was hopeless. With no preamble, Smith confronted Friedeburg with Allied demands for Germany's unconditional surrender in all theaters of war. German troops were to remain in their current positions and lay down their arms. Warships, warplanes, and other weaponry were to be handed over undamaged. The Wehrmacht Supreme Command would have to guarantee that these conditions were met. Friedeburg explained that he was not authorized to accept a total capitulation on all fronts and would have to contact Dönitz and ask for new directives.[6]

Friedeburg's message, which Kinzel reported at 9:00 a.m. on May

6, caused outrage in Flensburg. Eisenhower's conditions were "unacceptable," according to Dönitz, Krosigk, Keitel, Jodl, and the director of the civilian cabinet, Gauleiter Paul Wegener, because "the armies in the east cannot be delivered up to the Russians." The conditions were also "impossible to implement since no soldier on the eastern front would follow an order to lay down his arms and remain standing where he was." Yet, as the minutes of this meeting made clear, Dönitz and his advisers knew only too well that "the hopeless military situation, the threat of further losses in the west to aerial bombardments and acts of war, and the certain unavoidable military collapse of the armies still intact" demanded that a solution be found. Thus, the German leadership decided to make another attempt "to explain to Eisenhower with utter openness why a complete surrender is impossible but a capitulation in the west would be immediately accepted."[7]

Jodl, a staunch opponent of total surrender, was given this task. After consulting with Krosigk, Dönitz sent him on his journey with clear instructions: "Try to explain one more time the reasons why we strive for a partial capitulation to American forces. If you fail to convince Eisenhower, as Friedeburg did, ask for the following procedures for a total surrender. Two dates are to be arranged. On the first one, fighting will be suspended, but German troops will be allowed to move. That freedom of movement will end on the second date. Try to get the greatest possible span of time between the two dates."[8] Dönitz hoped this unusual plan for a two-stage surrender would give him time to bring as many German soldiers and refugees as possible behind the advancing American lines. In accordance with these instructions, Jodl was granted authority to sign a general surrender agreement for all fronts, although he was required to secure Dönitz's explicit permission by telegram first.

Jodl flew to Reims on the afternoon of May 6, arriving about 5:30 p.m. He, too, had no luck convincing the Americans to change their minds. Again, Smith insisted that a one-sided ceasefire in the west was out of the question and that the only acceptable option was a general capitulation to all of the Allies. Jodl responded by suggesting that the general articles of surrender be signed not by himself but by the supreme commanders of the three parts of the Wehrmacht: the army, the Luftwaffe, and the navy. They would need until May 8 to arrive in Reims, Jodl said, and the German side would require forty-eight hours to inform its troops; so a general ceasefire would first take effect on May 10.

The Americans knew all too well that the Germans were playing for time, and Eisenhower rejected Jodl's suggestion out of hand, issuing an ultimatum that the signing must take place without any further delay. Jodl was given a half-hour to consider the terms. If he refused, Eisenhower threatened, the bombing campaigns would resume and American lines would be closed to all Germans coming from the east.[9] The Americans would, however, grant the Germans two days between the signing of the articles of surrender and their coming into force.

At 9:45 p.m. on May 6, Jodl sent a radio message to Keitel: "General Eisenhower insists that we sign today; otherwise Allied front will be closed to all those trying to surrender, and negotiations will be discontinued. I see no choice other than chaos or signing. Please send wireless confirmation that I have the authority to sign the surrender. The capitulation can then take effect. Hostilities will end at midnight on May 9, 1945, German summer time."[10] It was after midnight, in the early morning of May 7, before the radio message was received in Flensburg.

DURING THE AFTERNOON of May 6, Dönitz decided to take the long overdue step of relieving Himmler of all his offices. Initially the Reichsführer SS, interior minister, and commander of the replacement army, who had fallen from Hitler's graces because of his contacts with the western powers and whom the dictator had ignored in his final testament, had aspired to play the role of number two in Dönitz's government. The admiral had strung him along, believing that a break would be inadvisable as long as Himmler controlled the police, the Gestapo, and the SS.[11] On the night of May 2, when Dönitz moved his government to Flensburg, Himmler had followed, bringing a horde of ranking SS concentration-camp leaders, including the former commandant of Auschwitz, Rudolf Höss, to northern Germany. In his memoirs, written while he was in Polish custody in 1946 and 1947 before he was executed, Höss described Himmler as "beaming and in the best of moods" during their final encounter on May 4.[12] Indeed, Himmler seems to have assumed that he and the SS would be deemed indispensable as a "factor of order" in the fight against Bolshevism.[13] He repeatedly turned up unexpectedly at cabinet meetings and left an impression of confidence. Although Dönitz chose not to give him a position in the new government, on May 4 he did agree to a statement that clarified somewhat Himmler's nebulous status: "While maintaining the leadership of the Waffen-SS, Reichsführer SS Heinrich Himmler has taken over the task of preserving calm and order as the head of the German police."[14]

Dönitz likely soon realized that he had given Himmler too much leeway. The very next day, the admiral changed the wording of his statement: "The Reichsführer SS Heinrich Himmler has placed himself at the disposal of the grand admiral." Himmler was dissatisfied with this version and also refused to agree to a compromise proposal by Krosigk: "The Reichsführer SS Heinrich Himmler has placed himself at the disposal of the grand admiral for preserving calm and order."[15]

Himmler's power was unraveling, and once the partial capitulation in the north came into force and a new regime had been formed, Dönitz no longer felt any need to mollify him. At 5:00 p.m. on May 6, he summoned Himmler and told him that he was forgoing his services and that he considered "all ties between him and the current government dissolved."[16]

In Dönitz's name, Keitel told the Reichsführer SS to refrain from visiting the admiral's headquarters in the future.[17] An eyewitness recalled

Himmler saying before he went underground that he felt "very certain he wouldn't be discovered and would wait away from the public eye for developments to turn his way, as they surely would in short order."[18]

On May 11, Himmler left Flensburg with a fake military paybook identifying him as "Sergeant Heinrich Hitzinger." He was accompanied by members of his staff, including his adjutant, SS Obersturmbahnführer Werner Grothmann, and Sturmbahnführer Heinz Macher. A few days later they crossed the Elbe in a fishing boat near the village of Friedrichskoog. Himmler seemed to have planned to escape through the Harz Mountains to the Alps, but a British patrol apprehended him, Grothmann, and Macher on May 21. The three men were taken to the British interrogation camp of Bad Nenndorf near the city of Lüneburg, where Himmler admitted his true identity. Interrogators initially had difficulty believing that the unassuming man in torn civilian clothes was one of the most wanted criminals from the Nazi leadership. He was taken to the main headquarters of the 2nd British Army in Lüneburg proper. In the process of giving Himmler a thorough physical examination on May 23, the attending doctor discovered a pointed blue object in the prisoner's mouth, but before he could remove it, Himmler bit down on the cyanide capsule and thus escaped being called to account for his crimes, just as Hitler, Goebbels, and Bormann had done before him.[19]

ON MAY 6, SOLDIERS of the Second Regiment of the 5th US Infantry Division marched into the town of Volary in southern Bohemia in what is now the Czech Republic. In a factory shed, they discovered 118 Jewish women in terrible physical condition. The medical officer who was assigned to take the women to a field hospital, Major Aaron S. Cahan, reported four days later, "My first glance at these individuals was one of extreme shock not ever believing that a human being can be degraded, can be starved, can be so skinny and even live under such circumstances. . . . One thing that surprised me when I entered this

barn is that I thought that we had a group of old men lying [down]. . . .
I was surprised and shocked when I asked one of these girls how old
she was and she said seventeen, when to me she appeared to be no less
than fifty."[20]

These women were survivors of a death march that had begun
three weeks previously at the Helmbrechts concentration camp, a satellite of Flossenbürg, which had been established in the summer of
1944 approximately fifteen kilometers southwest of the Bavarian city
of Hof. In February 1945, some 600 gentile women, primarily from
Poland and the Soviet Union, had been interned at Helmbrechts and
forced to work twelve-hour shifts for the Neumeyer armament company. On March 6, 621 Jewish women arrived in the camp. They had
already been put through two cruel evacuation marches from the satellite camps of the Gross-Rosen concentration camp and were extremely
weak, with many suffering from dysentery and frostbite. They were
jammed into two barracks, separate from the others, in conditions far
worse than the non-Jewish women. They received no medical treatment and were usually fed only a half-liter of diluted soup per day. They
were no longer used for labor, and the female camp guards did all they
could to rob them of the last shreds of human dignity. In the five weeks
they spent in Helmbrechts, 44 of them died.[21]

On April 13, with American troops only fifty kilometers away, the
camp commandant, SS Unterscharführer Alois Franz Dörr, decided
to evacuate Helmbrechts. That afternoon 1,171 female inmates, 580
of them Jewish, were forced to begin marching. The gentile women
received a bit to eat and some clothes and blankets. Arranged in three
columns, the inmates were accompanied by armed SS troops and female
guards equipped with wooden batons. Many of the Jewish women were
so weak they could hardly stand and had to be supported by their fellow prisoners. The guards would immediately shoot anyone who was
unable to keep up, and the female guards mercilessly beat the women,
driving them forward.

The march seems to have had no fixed destination. The route initially led southeast through Schwarzenbach an der Saale and Neuhausen. There, on the second day, a message arrived from Himmler to Dörr that "no more executions be carried out since negotiations with the Americans are commencing and are not to be disturbed."[22] That did little to alleviate the women's misery. From then on, the guards could do as they wanted with them with no fear of punishment from their superiors.

In Neuhausen, Dörr learned that US troops were only fifteen kilometers away and ordered all records from Helmbrechts destroyed. The march continued that night. In the confusion of a hasty departure, fifty of the gentile women were able to escape, and several female guards also took the chance to flee. On April 17, the march ended for the non-Jewish women at the Zwodau (Svateva) women's camp, but the Jewish women remained under Dörr's authority.[23] The route was now more southerly, passing through the Sudetenland territory Germany had annexed back in 1938. "It is difficult to convey the misery of these women as they dragged themselves, often shoeless, along frozen roads, one pain-filled step promising but another, one pain-filled day yielding seemingly inevitably but another," writes Daniel Goldhagen in *Hitler's Willing Executioners*, the book that sparked fierce debate about the complicity of ordinary Germans in the Holocaust. "The women had no known destination, no end point in sight. Every step required the marshaling of their energies, for they were at best listless, in their emaciated and diseased conditions. Every dawn saw them awake with gnawing hunger, swollen and pus-filled feet, limbs that no longer functioned, and open wounds that would not heal. They knew that an entire day's march stood before them, during which they would be given few opportunities by their tormentors to rest. Perhaps, when evening finally came, they would consume a few morsels of food. They would then end the day in shivering, pain-filled half-sleep, only to awaken to another day's and night's cycle of horrors. Such was a 'normal' day."[24]

For days, the women were given nothing to eat, and they often had to sleep in the open. Many died of exhaustion in the night. Those too sick or weak to carry on marching were loaded onto horse-drawn carts. In this fashion, the march dragged itself through the heavily forested hills of Böhmerwald until it reached Volary on May 3. Dörr decided to leave the women who were unable to continue behind and press on for the town of Prachatice on the border between Bohemia and Moravia. On their arrival, the survivors were finally set free. Dörr and his fellow perpetrators went underground. In March 1969, a jury at a court in Hof sentenced Dörr to life imprisonment for his role in leading the march, but he was pardoned in 1979.[25]

Of the 625 Jewish women who left the Zwodau camp on April 19, at least 278 died. Another 129 perished while marching or succumbed to cold or hunger at night. A further 49 were murdered by guards because they no longer had strength to go on or tried to flee. The causes of death of the others remain unknown.[26]

THE HORRIFIC TREK FROM Helmbrechts was only one of many death marches in the final days of Nazi rule. In addition to Jews, victims were slave laborers, POWs, and political prisoners of various nationalities, including Russian, Polish, Czech, French, Belgian, Hungarian, and German.[27] In the last weeks of the Third Reich it was common to see thousands of concentration-camp inmates, often little more than skin and bones, dragging themselves along country roads and through villages. Of the 714,000 concentration-camp prisoners still alive at the start of 1945, an estimated 250,000—more than a third—perished during these forced marches.[28]

Such horrors can only be understood against the backdrop of the chaos of the Nazi regime's collapse. The evacuation of the large camps in Eastern Europe—Auschwitz, Gross-Rosen, and Stutthof—before the advancing Red Army bore all the hallmarks of haste and improvisation. Inmates were forced to march in the icy cold without sufficient supplies or protective clothing. Refugees and quickly retreating Wehrmacht soldiers clogged roads, and in the general confusion, guards became increasingly willing to rid themselves of their prisoners. During the night of January 31, a terrible massacre was carried out on the shores of the Baltic Sea in Palmnicken, when SS troops used machine pistols to gun down three thousand prisoners, mostly Jewish women from Stutthof and its satellite camps. Days later, their bodies remained lying where they had fallen.[29]

The concentration camps in Germany proper and in annexed territories were completely unprepared to handle tens of thousands of completely exhausted prisoners coming from the east and so housed them in conditions that were in most cases even more catastrophic than in the camps from which they came. By April 1945, when the western camps—Buchenwald, Sachsenhausen, Flossenbürg, Neuengamme, Ravensbrück, and others—were in turn evacuated, these inmates were in considerably worse physical shape than the others and had a commensurately lower chance of surviving until they were liberated.

In the administrative turmoil of the final days of the war, there were no clear orders about how the prisoners were to be treated in transit or even where they were supposed to be taken. Consequently, many columns of marchers were herded back and forth in the ever-smaller corridor of German territory not under Allied control, and it was largely left up to guards to decide whether to shoot the unfortunate people who had no strength to continue on. The difference between life and death depended on the guards' whims and the particular, local situations in which the prisoners found themselves, before US, British, or Russian troops arrived.

The death marches took place in plain sight of the German populace. Many inhabitants of rural areas witnessed massacres from their front doors or watched as guards beat the emaciated people and shot them to death. Reactions varied. Some ordinary people, mostly women, touched by the prisoners' plight, showed sympathy and left them food

Prisoners from the Dachau concentration camp are driven through
Starnberg on April 28 on a death march toward Bad Tölz.
This photo was taken secretly.

or handed out scraps. A particularly courageous few actively helped
prisoners escape from their guards. But passivity and denial were more
common. Many people viewed the marchers with indifference or
fear—not just of the SS, who sometimes responded brutally to those
who tried to help, but also of the prisoners, whose desperate condition
was seen as living proof that they must be "anti-socials," "parasites on
the people," or dangerous criminals.[30]

Not infrequently, ordinary Germans helped carry out murders. An especially horrific crime occurred in early April in the city of Celle. Hundreds of prisoners from a satellite of the Neuengamme concentration camp had taken advantage of the aerial bombardment of the city's train station to flee from their train cars and hide in a nearby forest. The following night, SS camp guards, aided by local Sturmabteilung (SA) men, police, and a group of civilians, including fourteen- to sixteen-year-old Hitler Youths, hunted them down. More than 170 inmates were killed.[31]

Terrible scenes also unfolded in the town of Gardelegen to the east, where 1,100 survivors of a death march from two satellite camps of Mittelbau-Dora arrived on April 13. They were locked in a barn on the edge of town, and the building was set on fire. Those who sought to escape the flames were cut down by machine-gun fire. The man most responsible was the fanatic Nazi district director Gerhard Thiele, who feared that Americans would enter the town within hours and that the liberated prisoners would take revenge. Rumors about atrocities carried out by vagabond prisoners were circulated to fuel a general sense of panic. In this atmosphere, Thiele had no trouble recruiting people, especially members of the Volkssturm militia, to assist him in his murderous enterprise. When American troops arrived on April 15 and inspected the scene of this inhuman crime, they found a thousand charred bodies.[32]

The massacres in Celle and Gardelegen illustrate that the murder of concentration-camp inmates during the death marches at the end of the war was not ordered "from above" or centrally directed. On the contrary, it developed in an uncoordinated, dynamic process "from below," in which SS guards, local party functionaries, and members of the police, Volkssturm, and Hitler Youth joined with ordinary citizens in criminal mobs. The resulting mass killings are incontrovertible evidence of how much the virus of uninhibited violence had infected parts of German society.

"MAY 6, MORNING—A REFRESHING silence prevails," noted Horst Gleiss, a fourteen-year-old Breslau schoolboy and member of the Volkssturm, in his diary. "Pale people crawl out of dark basement holes and fill their lungs with May air. The universal opinion is: An end must be put to this murderous war. If we in Breslau continue, none of us will survive."[33] In fact, since that morning, the guns in the Silesian capital had gone silent, and two German officers and an interpreter were making their way across no man's land to Russian lines with an offer of surrender. At around 6:00 p.m., General Hermann Niehoff, the final commandant of Breslau, signed a surrender agreement in Villa Colonia on the southern edge of the city. Afterward General Vladimir A. Gluzdovsky invited him to dinner. "Candles illuminated mountains of cold food, fish dishes, meat pies, *zakuskis* [hors d'oeuvres], and of course everywhere in between bottles of vodka," Niehoff recalled. "The victor wanted to celebrate his triumph. And I was politely asked to join him."[34]

In the fall of 1944, Hitler had declared Breslau a "fortress," meaning it would not be allowed to surrender and had to be defended at all costs.[35] At the time the city faced no immediate threat. The Red Army was three hundred kilometers away in central Poland, and because Breslau was so far east, it had been spared attacks by British and American bombers. But on January 12, 1945, the long-feared Soviet winter offensive began along the entire eastern front, and after a few days, it became obvious that the Red Army had achieved a major breakthrough. Its unexpectedly rapid advances created a wave of refugees. Hundreds of thousands of people fled the eastern German provinces in frigid weather in horse-drawn carts or on foot, heading west or trying to reach Germany's Baltic ports to the north. Groups of refugees were arriving in Breslau every day.

On January 19, Karl Hanke, the Gauleiter and Reich defense commissar of Lower Silesia, ordered Breslau's civilians to evacuate—too late for a city of almost one million people. The streets were blocked by refugees and retreating German troops, and the Reichsbahn did not have nearly enough trains to handle the massive demand. "A veritable panic has seized the masses, who have completely lost their heads," wrote Pastor Paul Peikert in his diary. "For days, the train stations have been so overcrowded that there's no getting through the throngs of people. Everyone is pushing to get on trains that have only limited capacity. The majority has to stay behind and try again."[36]

The following day, Hanke took to loudspeakers to order Breslau's women and children to leave the city on foot. "Small hand baggage can be taken along," he instructed. "Women with small children should arrange for spirit cookers; the NSV [Nazi relief organization] will set up spots for cooking and distributing milk."[37] Hundreds of thousands of people left the city in temperatures of −20°C and joined the columns of refugees from the east. With a knapsack containing the absolute necessities, a pair of sturdy boots, and a bag full of food for the coming days, Elisabeth Erbrich was one of those who set out from Breslau. "Like a caravan, the refugees left on foot, taking their remaining belongings on small carts and baby carriages, or cars and horse-drawn wagons, in the gleaming white snow. Hundreds of thousands of people were on the move, including columns from villages on the left bank of the Oder River who had been on the road for days. Because of the terrible cold and the constant marching, they had many dead bodies on their wagons, whom they simply stretched out along the side of the road because they couldn't be buried in the ground, which was frozen as hard as rock."[38]

Right from the start, Hanke left no doubt that he intended to defend the city to the last, and he announced as much on January 22.[39] He gave his friend Albert Speer, who visited him that day, a tour of the Old Upper Presidium, which had been built by the architect Carl Gotthard Langhans and had been recently renovated. Speer later recorded in his memoirs that Hanke exclaimed, "The Russians will never get their hands on this. I'd rather burn it down."[40]

On January 24, after a phone call with all the Gauleiters in Germany's eastern territories, Goebbels noted that "of them, Hanke makes the best impression. His statements were determined and firm. He described the improvised measures he had taken to defend Breslau. I was very pleased when he told me that what he had learned from the Berlin School and with me was very much coming in handy in his crucial work in critical situations. He shows exceptional determination. . . . In any case, Hanke is set on defending Breslau by all possible means."[41]

In the days that followed, Goebbels remained full of praise for his former state secretary in the propaganda ministry. On January 28, Hanke had a Volkssturm commando execute Breslau deputy mayor Wolfgang Spielhagen for allegedly preparing to flee and then announced Spielhagen's punishment on posters—measures that drew Goebbels's unreserved applause. Hitler, too, approved of the murder. "In a fortress under siege, you can't act according to legal paragraphs," the dictator pronounced. "You have to do what seems effective and necessary."[42]

By February 15, Breslau was completely encircled. Two hundred thousand civilians, including tens of thousands of slave laborers, POWs, and concentration-camp inmates, were still in the city—together with 45,000 troops, commanded by General Hans von Ahlfen and later Niehoff, defending the "fortress." They were cobbled together into formations of Waffen-SS, Wehrmacht reserves, and Volkssturm troops and Hitler Youth, who faced Gluzdovsky's 6th Army of 130,000 battle-hardened men.[43] The Soviets attacked from the south, overrunning the suburbs and reaching the Hindenburgplatz, only four kilometers from the city center, on February 24. But their advance halted as the makeshift German forces put up fierce resistance, and the result was bitter house-to-house combat reminiscent of the battle of Stalingrad.[44]

Significant parts of the city were reduced to rubble, with its defenders responsible for more devastation than the Soviet artillery barrages. The Germans burned down buildings and blew up ruins to create clear paths to fire at the enemy. Without regard for the consequences, command posts, artillery batteries, and munition depots were set up in churches and other historic buildings, which then became targets for Soviet dive bombers.

Symbolic of the German-led destruction was the creation of a 1.3-kilometer-long, 300-meter-wide airstrip in the heart of the city to ensure it could be supplied by air should Gandau Airport fall into enemy hands. Various buildings in the university district, including the Silesian State Archive and two churches, were razed. An estimated three thousand people assigned to these tasks—many of them slave laborers but also Breslau civilians, including women and children—were killed by Soviet artillery and dive bombers. "We sleep like rabbits—with eyes open—and wait for death," remarked one worker. "Warplanes strafe the landing strip. Again lots and lots of dead. . . . Whenever bombs come up short nearby, the women scream terribly."[45]

On March 3, Hanke addressed the German people on national radio, calling on them to follow Breslau's example and to join the ranks of those "who work and slave for victory." He concluded with a promise: "We in the fortress of Breslau pledge to stand unshakably in our faith in the Reich and the Führer, never to waver in the face of the hard days to come, and fight as long as there is still a spark of strength within us."[46] Goebbels found the speech "poignant and forceful" and thought it displayed "a dignity and level of political morale that deserves admiration." As he put it, "If all our Gauleiters in the east were like this and worked like Hanke, we'd be in a better situation than we are. Hanke is the exceptional figure." Hitler had listened to the speech and was also full of "the highest praise," as Goebbels noted with satisfaction.[47]

On March 7, Hanke and Niehoff instituted mandatory labor for all Breslau residents, male and female, including boys aged ten and above and girls twelve and above. Anyone who failed to report and take possession of a labor identity card faced a court martial. "Just as the soldier who deserts his post is punished by death as a traitor to his country, the same punishment must be meted to anyone who evades his labor duty to the fortress," the two men declared.[48] Courts martial convicted hundreds of soldiers, civilians, and slave laborers of "evasion of duty," "plundering," and "sabotage." Lists of those executed were published in the only daily newspaper that still existed in the city, the *Frontzeitung der Festung Breslau* (Front Newspaper of the Fortress of Breslau), to deter further rebellion and recalcitrance.[49]

In late March, Gluzdovsky threatened for the first time to subject Breslau to massive bombardment if the city refused to surrender; but Niehoff rejected any notion of capitulation, and Hanke assured Goebbels by phone that Breslau could be held "for the foreseeable future."[50] On Easter Sunday and Monday, April 1 and 2, the Soviet air force dropped thousands of bombs on Breslau, creating a firestorm in the old city center. "From the Kaiserbrücke we could see the indescribably sad sight of the burning city of Breslau—an unforgettable, horrifying spectacle," wrote Peikert. "Flames licked from the helm roofs of the cathedral. The entire roof was a sea of fire, and St. Michael, the Sand Church, St. Vincent, St. Adalbert, St. Mauritius, St. Bernhardin, the Christopher Church, and all the streets in between were ablaze. . . . Breslau in flames on Easter Monday evening and night was a monstrously horrific sight, the demise of the most beautiful part of the city."[51]

By mid-April, the Red Army had in fact taken Gandau Airport and was advancing to the western edge of the old town. As parts of the civilian populace grew more desperate and angrier at the senseless continuation of the fighting, neither Hanke nor Niehoff budged. In his daily orders on Hitler's birthday, April 20, the city commandant invoked the mythology of the Führer: "Our trust in him will be all the stronger, the longer we hold on, for Adolf Hitler is on the side of the brave, and his strength will become our capacity for resistance."[52] Speer congratulated Hanke on his "achievements as the defender of Breslau," telling him that his "example . . . will later be of the same inestimably high value for our people as very few of the heroes of German history."[53]

Goebbels and Hitler shared Speer's enthusiasm. The dictator awarded Hanke the prestigious German Order in Gold and named him, in his April 29 testament, to succeed Himmler as Reichsführer SS and head of the German police.[54]

Even after the news broke of Hitler's suicide and Berlin's surrender, the battle in Breslau went on. On May 4, the *Frontzeitung* proclaimed, "Every artillery shot and every bomb Ivan has dropped on us should make it clear to even the simplest people that the only motto able to combat such a murderous enemy as Bolshevism is 'Stick together and fight!' "[55]

At noon that day, a delegation from both major Christian faiths met with Niehoff to urge him to stop the fighting. Pastor Ernst Hornig described the terrible rise in civilian deaths. Every day, hundreds of people were dying, some by their own hands out of desperation amid the hopeless situation. Trust in the Nazi Party and the military leadership had cratered. "Under these circumstances," he asked Niehoff, "how can you justify before God to keep on defending the city?" Niehoff brushed the clergyman off, saying, "I share your concerns."[56] But he had already secretly decided to start negotiating a surrender. On the afternoon of May 5, he summoned his officers to his command post in the basement of Breslau University's library for a "final roll call," declaring that "Adolf Hitler is dead, Berlin has fallen, and the Allies have joined hands in the heart of Germany. With that, the conditions for defending Breslau are no longer present. Every further sacrifice is a crime. I have decided to end the fighting and to offer to hand over the city to the enemy and allow him to occupy it honorably. The final bullet has been fired. We have done our duty as the law demanded."[57]

Gauleiter Hanke, the man who had ordered that anyone trying to escape the city be executed, did not for a moment intend to die a hero's death himself. During the night of May 5, he flew out of Breslau in a Fieseler Storch, from the very runway he had built at such a terrible cost. There are different versions of his ultimate fate; most likely,

Breslau surrendered on May 6, 1945. It was one of the last German cities
to do so. This photograph offers a view from the Rathaus of the
devastated inner city.

he was stopped by Czech militia while fleeing through Sudetenland
and beaten to death.[58] General Niehoff was condemned to death by a
Soviet military court, a sentence later commuted to twenty-five years
in prison. He returned to West Germany in 1955. Together with his
predecessor, General Ahlfen, he published a book, *So kämpfte Breslau*
(How Breslau Fought), which glorified the senseless violence and death
in the city in its last moments as a "fortress" of the Third Reich.[59] At
least six thousand German and eight thousand Soviet soldiers lost their
lives in the battle. Far higher was the number of civilian casualties: estimates range from ten thousand to eighty thousand deaths.[60]

Only two days after Breslau surrendered, a vanguard group of
Polish administrators and civil servants arrived to document Poland's
claim to the city in line with the agreements at the Potsdam Conference, which shifted Polish borders west to compensate for the eastern

Polish provinces annexed by the Soviet Union. Wrocław, as the city is now known, became part of the new Polish state. Between 1945 and 1947, its ethnic makeup completely changed. Germans were systematically driven out and replaced by Polish "repatriates" from the Soviet-controlled east. In late December 1945, only 33,297 Poles were registered in the city compared with five times as many Germans. Only nine months later, the proportions were reversed. And by March 1947 Wrocław was home to 196,814 Poles and only 17,496 Germans among its 214,310 inhabitants.[61]

As was the case in Prague, Germans who stayed behind now felt the full brunt of the hatred that had built up during the years of Nazi occupation. They were often forced from their homes by newly arrived Poles and were required to wear white armbands emblazoned with the letter N for "Niemiec" (German). Defenseless against attacks, many were sent west in sealed freight-train cars by the city's new masters.[62] The writer Hugo Hartung, who had come to Breslau in 1940 as a theater dramaturge and had served as a member of the Volkssturm during the Soviet siege, described the dramatic transformation of the city in his diary in early July: "Another type of march pushes its way in the opposite direction as ours, with carts and baby carriages, trudging tiredly, miserable and infinitely long: Poles from the Lemberg (Lwów) district of the General Government. They have yet to settle down in this city we are no longer allowed to call home. Like marionettes driven by incomprehensible destiny, the two marches pass one another without a word."[63]

WHILE DESPERATE FIGHTING was still going on in such cities as Prague and Breslau, in other places new political life was beginning to grow. On May 6, 130 Social Democrats convened in the auditorium of the Hanover Police Presidium to reconstitute the local chapter of the SPD. Their impresario was forty-nine-year-old Kurt Schumacher. Born a merchant's son in 1895 in the West Prussian town of Culm,

Schumacher completed a university-track high-school degree before volunteering for the military after the start of the First World War. He was badly wounded, losing an arm, after which he was discharged and went on to study law and economics. His dissertation was entitled "The Battle for the Idea of State in the German Social Democratic Movement." In January 1918, in the waning days of Wilhelmine Germany, he joined the SPD. His political career began in earnest in 1920, when he became the editor of the party newspaper *Schwäbische Tagwacht* in Stuttgart. In 1924, he was elected to the Württemberg regional parliament and six years later to the Reichstag. He earned the hatred of the Nazi Party with a speech on February 23, 1932, in which he castigated Nazi rabble-rousing as "a constant appeal to people's bastard within." Responding to remarks by Goebbels, Schumacher countered, "If we recognize anything in National Socialism, it is the fact that for the first time in German politics, human stupidity has been completely mobilized."

The Nazis would not forget these words. In July 1933, Schumacher was arrested, marking the start of a series of internments in various concentration camps until he was finally released from Dachau, extremely ill, in the spring of 1943. He lived out the final two years of the Third Reich with his sister in Hanover, under Gestapo surveillance. Following the assassination attempt on Hitler on July 20, 1944, the regime launched Aktion Gitter (Operation Prison Bars) against the former representatives and functionaries of the political parties in the Weimar Republic, and he was arrested again, spending a month in captivity in the Neuengamme concentration camp.[64]

On April 10, 1945, American troops arrived in what was left of Hanover, and only nine days later Schumacher and some like-minded Germans decided to rebuild the Social Democratic Party. At the founding meeting of the local Hanover chapter on May 6, Schumacher was elected its chairman. Visibly scarred by his imprisonment in the camps, he gave a foundational speech in which he summed up the experience of twelve years of Nazi rule and sketched out his vision of a democratic new beginning, epitomized by the phrase "We do not despair." His speech has been called, correctly, "the first postwar document of the German Social Democratic movement."[65]

Schumacher began with the idea that Marxism was not a rigid dogma but rather a "method for us to examine facts," citing Ferdinand Lasalle's dictum "Say what is." Schumacher proceeded to analyze the fateful development of German history that had led to National Social-ism, directing blame, very much in historicist Marxist fashion, at the "alliance of heavy industries and the arms industry, indeed of finance capital as a whole, with the forces of Prussian-German militarism." This had resulted in the particularly aggressive character of "German imperialism," which had elevated "the worship of violence to a guiding principle" and had provoked the catastrophe of the First World War. In their refusal to accept Germany's defeat in 1918, reactionary forces had planted the seeds of a new global war. Following this line of reasoning, Schumacher saw National Socialists as "pawns of large-scale capital-ism," whose rise had inevitably caused a complete "moral corrosion and degrading" of the German people. Schumacher recalled his Reichstag speech of February 1932, lamenting the fact that his and other early warnings about the consequences of Hitler coming to power had not been heeded.

The leader of the nascent postwar SPD emphatically distanced himself from the idea of collective German guilt. "We Democratic Socialists, who were the actual rivals of National Socialism and made great sacrifices battling it, are especially grateful to be put into the same pot," he remarked acidly. He had only contempt for the "all too many" Germans who had turned out be "stupid followers of Hitlerism and crass worshipers of power and success." Their ex post facto claims to have known nothing about the regime's crimes lacked credibility. "It may be that they didn't know everything, but they knew enough," Schumacher said. "In any case, they knew enough about the concentration camps to be deathly afraid of them, and this fear was one of the main pillars of the system. They gladly accepted everything their sons, fathers, and husbands [looted and] brought back with them from the occupied territories. Above all, they witnessed with their own eyes the bestial cruelty with which Jews were tortured, robbed, and driven away. Not only did they stay silent. They would have preferred it, had Germany won the Second World War, leaving them in peace and with a bit of profit." The "complicity of large parts of the people in the bloody reign of Nazis," Schumacher added, could only be "mitigated but never removed . . . through the honest insight that Germany should never again be ruled by a regime given free rein, without any oversight."

Schumacher insisted that the "men behind the scenes" who had helped the Nazis seize power—including "the most infernal German after Hitler, Mr. von Papen"—must be held to account. Punishing them, he argued, was more important than "going after a lot of often arbitrary party members who had been forced to join." Nonetheless, Schumacher called for a clear stance on former fascist "party comrades," demanding that the SPD not become a "refuge for politically homeless Nazis."

The Social Democrats' new leader devoted a section of his speech to the SPD's future relationship with the Communists. He conceded that the desire for both parties to work together after the fierce quarrels of the years before 1933 was understandable. But he rejected the idea of a "unified workers' party," arguing that whereas "the Communists are bound to a single one of the greater victorious powers and are dependent on Russia as a state and its foreign-policy aims . . . we cannot and don't want to become the autocratically wielded instrument of some foreign imperial interest." At the same time, Schumacher encouraged factions that had broken off from the SPD before 1933 to return to the fold. The Social Democratic movement had to act as a magnet for splinter groups, he said, cautioning that "the future has room for only one party of democratic socialists in its party system."

As Schumacher saw it, the SPD was the only party in Germany that had held the "line of democracy and freedom, which has proven the correct one." For that reason, the SPD had a claim to a leading role in the postwar era. Schumacher concluded with pathos: "For our goals, the indivisible triad of peace, freedom, and socialism, we aim to work with progressive forces around the world. . . . We won't fall short in this task, and if we can help our people in this spirit, we will be of use to all of humanity."[66]

Twenty-five-year-old Annemarie Renger—in the town of Vissel-hövede in northwestern Germany, where she and her young son had fled to escape the air raids on Berlin—read excerpts of Schumacher's speech in the *Hannoverscher Kurier* newspaper and was electrified. "This was what I had been waiting for: for people in our country to be snatched from their lethargy and hopelessness and begin to tackle problems themselves," she recalled. "I wanted to join in the work there, in Hanover, where this Kurt Schumacher had refounded the German Social Democratic Party, the party I had grown up in."[67]

After discussing the situation with her father, a former function-ary in the working-class fitness and athletics movement, which had its own network of sports clubs, Renger wrote to Schumacher asking if he could use her help. An invitation to Hanover quickly arrived. "The man across from me was tall and thin," she wrote on meeting Schumacher. "Deep lines crossed his face, which was dominated by his bluish-green, penetrating eyes. He was different than I had imagined him. He was just shy of his fiftieth birthday, but he looked a lot older. . . . Without any ado, he asked me if I knew stenography and could type perfectly. He was very demanding, he said. Confidently, I answered that I was quite good at both and had won prizes in my stenography club."[68] On October 15, 1945, Renger became Schumacher's private secretary. It was the springboard for a career that would see her become one of the best-known SPD politicians and serve as president and vice president of the West German parliament, the Bundestag, between 1972 and 1990.

Schumacher's speech on May 6 reinforced his position at the top of the local SPD chapter in Hanover and allowed him to play a leading role in the American and British occupation zones. He had seized the opportunity instead of waiting for permission from the military governments for Germans to form new political parties, and he had made Hanover the center of the reconstituted SPD. Over the course of a few months he had established "Dr. Schumacher's office" at Jacobstrasse 10 in the traditionally left-wing district of Linden as a "new center of power and factory of ideas."[69]

In late July 1945, Schumacher was able to report to his old party ally and the former Prussian interior minister Carl Severing, based in Bielefeld, that "despite all the obstacles, we have built up a relatively large party and have already reached agreements on policy and personnel with our comrades in Braunschweig, Hamburg, Württemberg, Baden, Hessen, and Hessen-Nassau."[70] On August 20, fourteen of the nineteen reestablished regional SPD organizations in the British and American zones gave their okay and authorized Schumacher to start preparing a joint conference.[71]

On August 28, 1945, Schumacher sent out invitations for the reconstituted party's first conference in the town of Wennigsen, near Hanover, in early October. Enclosed with the invitations were "political guidelines" intended to serve as a basis for discussion. These guidelines defined socialism and democracy as two sides of the same coin: "Socialism is per se democratic. It is a battle for the intellectual, political, and economic liberation of the working masses, and as such it is a battle for the rule of law and freedom from exploitation and servitude." At the same time, Schumacher stressed Germans' right to "national self-determination . . . in a state of their own." For that reason, the SPD was "the most committed and determined enemy of all separatist movements." This was the beginning of the conflict with his main rival, Konrad Adenauer, who as chancellor doggedly pursued the Federal Republic's integration into the West at the expense of national unity. Once again, Schumacher made it clear in the conference guidelines that while he did not want an "anti-Communist or even less an anti-Russian thrust to our politics," he strictly rejected merging with the Communists to form a unified party since the KPD was indissolubly bound to the Soviet Union and its foreign-policy aims.[72]

Among the attendees at the conference on October 5 and 6 were three members of the SPD executive committee in exile from London—Erich Ollenhauer, Fritz Heine, and Erwin Schoettle—who were flown in on a British military airplane. They were shocked by the view from the air of Germany's destruction: "On the flight from the coast to Germany, we could already see the evidence of the terrible war everywhere," Schoettle reported. "When we flew over Osnabrück, the horror that had passed over the country became visible. A field of ruins and empty window frames that peered out, sinister and dark, into the late-afternoon sun announced what we were about to experience up close in Hanover: a destroyed German city such as was the norm at the end of the Second World War."[73] Schumacher and the London émigrés quickly reached agreement on every important question. Ollenhauer succumbed to Schumacher's charm and put aside his own ambitions to lead the SPD. "The party is returning to work with a truly elemental force," he said on returning to London.[74]

The situation was different for socialists in the Soviet occupation zone. In June 1945, a group of former Social Democrats under the leadership of Otto Grotewohl, Max Fechner, and Erich Gniffke in Berlin formed an SPD "central committee," which promoted solidarity among various working-class organizations and welcomed unification with the Communist KPD. This ran contrary to Schumacher's intentions, of course, and he spent most of the time at the Wennigsen conference trying to ward off the Berlin SPD's claim to leadership and reject any merger of SPD and KPD. "We cannot make the Social Democratic Party and its supporters dependent on the conditions and assumptions of a single occupation zone," he fumed.[75] To this end, an agreement was reached with Grotewohl that as long as "Reich unity" was not restored, the "central committee" in Berlin would only be responsible for leading the SPD in the Soviet zone, while Schumacher would function in the three western zones as the "politically authorized" leader. In a letter to Severing in which he summed up the most important outcome of the conference, Schumacher wrote, "Practically, things are such that the political dangers that could have resulted from the ambitions of our Berlin comrades have been deflected."[76]

The fate of the SPD in Berlin was a foregone conclusion. As the KPD in the Soviet zone increased pressure on Grotewohl and the "central committee" to merge with them, resistance grew among the Berlin Social Democrats. On March 31, 1946, more than 86 percent of members in the three western sectors of the city voted against any compulsory fusion of SPD and KPD. A fortnight later, a "unification party conference" convened in the Admiralspalast theater in the eastern sector, and the Socialist Unity Party (SED) was founded.

A little more than a month after that, on May 9, 1946, delegates from the three western zones of what was rapidly becoming a formally divided Germany came together for another conference in Hanover and nearly unanimously elected Kurt Schumacher as the first chair of the postwar SPD. His rise to the status of unchallenged party leader was complete, and at the end of the conference, he confidently proclaimed that "the Social Democratic Party will be the decisive [political] factor in Germany, or nothing will come of Germany, and Europe will become a hot spot of unrest and decay."[77]

ON MAY 6, UNITS OF the 1st Polish Tank Division under Colonel Franciszek Skibiński rumbled into the northeastern German town of Jever. The division had been formed in 1942 in Scotland as part of the Polish government-in-exile's army. It had played a role in the Normandy landing and fought with British and Canadian troops across northern France and Belgium and into the Weser-Ems region. While

British forces quickly advanced to the Elbe, their Polish comrades headed north to take Jever and Wilhelmshaven. "In the villages and town districts we pass through [there are] white flags and celebrating crowds of liberated POWs and slave laborers lining the streets," Skibiński reported. "At the hotel where our brigade was to set up its headquarters, a gigantic Polish flag was already flying." Before entering the hotel, the Polish colonel was received by the regional councillor, the mayor, and the hotel owner. "If anyone in the city feels like hurling a stick at a Polish soldier or throwing a stone at anywhere Poles are quartered, you three will be hanged, and the city will go up in smoke," Skibiński was said to have threatened.[78]

Three days earlier, in the late afternoon of May 3, something unusual had occurred in Jever. More than two thousand people had gathered in the city's largest square, Der Alte Markt, to protest the plan to defend the city against approaching Allied troops. The senior city administrator, Hermann Ott, tried to pacify the crowd and was hauled down from the podium. The head of the Nazi Party in the Friesland district, Hans Flügel, did not have better luck. His exhortations to hold out were drowned out by cries of "String him up from a streetlight, this golden pheasant!" Two men grabbed Flügel and stripped him of his pistols, as courageous citizens raised a white flag from the tower of Jever Castle. They were arrested by a company of naval soldiers on the evening of May 4 and taken to Wilhelmshaven. They likely only escaped with their lives because the partial capitulation of German troops in the northwest of the country was announced shortly thereafter.

Many of Jever's residents were aware of what their fellow Germans had done in Poland and feared the worst when the Polish forces arrived. But their terror proved unfounded. "Originally, we were afraid of the Poles, but they behaved beyond reproach," remembered one eyewitness.[79] Polish troops withdrew from Jever and Wilhelmshaven on May 20 and 21 and were replaced by British and Canadian units.

MAY 7, 1945

In the first hour of May 7, 1945, at fifteen minutes after midnight, Jodl's radio message from Eisenhower's headquarters, in which he asked for authorization to sign an unconditional surrender, arrived in Flensburg. Grand Admiral Dönitz immediately summoned his closest associates for consultations. They all agreed that Eisenhower's demands represented "absolute blackmail." Particularly upsetting was the American commander's threat, in the event his demands were rejected, "to deliver all Germans still east of his lines up to the Russians." Nonetheless, the group was under no illusions that Jodl, who had just that morning argued against complete surrender, must have had further "telling reasons" if he saw no other way out. At least the provision that the ceasefire would take effect at one minute after midnight on May 9 had secured forty-eight hours that could be used to "save a majority of the eastern troops." At 1:00 on the morning of May 7, Dönitz sent a telegram authorizing Jodl to sign an unconditional surrender.[1]

Preparations were already under way at Eisenhower's headquarters in Reims for the signing ceremony. In the building's map room, cameras and microphones had been set up to capture the historic moment. At 2:41 a.m., Jodl signed the articles of surrender in the presence of

Admiral General Friedeburg and Major Wilhelm Oxenius. Putting his name to the document for the Allied expeditionary force was General Walter Bedell Smith; for the Soviet Supreme Command, General Ivan Susloparov; and as a witness, from France, Major General François Sevez. Eisenhower's chief of staff described the Germans' "stone-like" demeanor during the ceremony, and there was no sign of elation from the Allied officers either over the end of many long years of war. "It was a moment of solemn gratitude," Smith recalled.[2] In a short declaration, Jodl appealed to the victors' generosity, saying that with his signature he had delivered up the Wehrmacht and the German people "to mercy or not." He continued, "Both have achieved and endured more in this war than perhaps any people on earth. I can at this hour only articulate the request that the victors treat them with mercy."[3] Afterward Jodl and his two companions were taken to Eisenhower, who had thus far avoided meeting the Dönitz government's emissaries. The supreme commander of the Allied expeditionary force asked the Germans whether they had understood all the provisions in the articles of surrender and whether they were prepared to carry them out to the best of their abilities. Jodl and the others answered in the affirmative, saluted, and left the room.[4]

In article 1, Germany declared that it would "surrender unconditionally to the Supreme Commander, Allied Expeditionary Force and simultaneously to the Soviet High Command all forces on land, sea, and in the air." Article 2 required the German High Command to "issue orders to all German military, naval, and air authorities and to all forces under German control at 2301 hours Central European time on 8 May"—one minute past midnight on May 9 in German summer time—"and to remain in the positions occupied at that time."[5] At 10:55 a.m. on May 7 the Dönitz government received the exact wording of the capitulation agreement, which was then passed along via radio and telephone to Wehrmacht units. In addition, couriers were sent in Dönitz's name to the commanders of the army groups to explain the absolute necessity of the total surrender and to convince them to follow their orders loyally.[6]

At 12:45 p.m., the "directing minister" of the "caretaker government," Krosigk, announced on the radio the unconditional surrender of all German troops, calling it a "tragic moment" in German history. As he told listeners, "After six years of heroic fighting of unique severity, Germany's strength has been exhausted by the overwhelming power of our enemies. Continuing the war would have only meant the senseless shedding of blood and useless destruction. A government that possesses a sense of responsibility for the future of our people must draw the logical conclusions from the collapse of all our physical and material strength and beseech the enemy to discontinue hostilities." No one should have any doubt, Krosigk warned, that hard times lay ahead and would require great sacrifices, but Germans should not despair or become paralyzed by hopelessness. To this end, Krosigk invoked the "idea of a community of the people," which during the war had found its "most beautiful expression . . . in the comradeship at the front abroad and the mutual readiness to help others through all emergencies at home."

While Krosigk was invoking one of the main propaganda themes of National Socialism, he also drew a line for the first time between the present moment and Hitler's regime of injustice and violence: "We must make the law a basis of our life as a people. . . . We must also, as a matter of inner conviction, acknowledge and respect the law as the basis of relations between peoples. Respect for contracts concluded should be sacred to us, so, too, the feeling of belonging to the European family of peoples, as a member of which we want to offer all our human, moral, and material strength to heal the terrible wounds the war has inflicted."[7]

At 4:00 p.m., Jodl arrived back in Flensburg and reported about the deal struck in Reims. Once again, he complained about Eisenhower's inflexibility and extreme gruffness. Not only had the American

Early in the morning of May 7, 1945, Colonel General Alfred Jodl
signed Germany's unconditional surrender in Allied headquarters in
Reims. (Left to right: Major Wilhelm Oxenius, Jodl, and
Admiral General Hans-Georg von Friedeburg.)

commander threatened to seal off American lines to fleeing Wehrmacht units and leave them at the mercy of the Red Army, but he had also announced his willingness to bomb cities in nonoccupied Schleswig—with the justification that the partial surrender the Germans had negotiated with Montgomery three days previously did not apply to American air forces. After intense discussion, the German leadership in Flensburg concluded that total unconditional surrender had been the only alternative. "There was no other option," the minutes taken at the time noted.[8]

ON THE MORNING OF MAY 7, British first lieutenant Arnold Horwell, the man who had just been put in charge of the Bergen-Belsen camp, received an unexpected visit. A woman dressed in GI fatigues, wearing a helmet and combat boots, entered his office and introduced herself as Captain Dietrich. She had heard her sister Liesel was interned there, she said, and asked to see her. After overcoming his initial surprise, Horwel recognized the woman as Hollywood star Marlene Dietrich.[9]

British troops had liberated Bergen-Belsen three weeks before. In no other camp did more prisoners die of disease and privation in the final months of the war. In March 1945 alone, 18,168 of an estimated 45,000 inmates died, including the sisters Margot and Anne Frank, who had been transported to the camp from Auschwitz in late October 1944. When the SS commandant Josef Kramer surrendered the facility, British soldiers witnessed a horrific sight. More than 13,000 bodies lay strewn all over the grounds. Thousands more died after being liberated.[10]

Dietrich had come to Munich to entertain troops under General Omar Bradley, and on May 6 she was informed that a woman named

Following the liberation of the Bergen-Belsen concentration camp
on April 15, 1945, British soldiers made former guards and
German civilians collect the bodies of people murdered there.

Elisabeth Will in Bergen-Belsen was claiming to be her sister. Dietrich had not heard from Liesel in six years and suspected that the Nazis had interned her in a concentration camp as payback for Marlene's service to the US Army. On the morning of May 7, she flew in Bradley's plane to Fassberg Air Base in the Lüneburg Heath in northern Germany and was then driven the thirty kilometers to Bergen-Belsen in a Jeep. But when Horwell summoned Elisabeth Will, Dietrich was stunned to learn that she was not an inmate but rather had, with her husband, Georg Will, run a movie theater near the camp for the entertainment of the Wehrmacht soldiers and SS members who worked there.

Dietrich feared, not without reason, that her embarrassing relatives would cast a shadow on her exemplary contribution to the fight against Hitler's Germany. Thus, while she promised her sister material support, Elisabeth Will had to pledge in return to keep a low profile, not to give interviews, and to conceal the fact that she was closely related to a Hollywood star.[11]

Marie Magdalene "Marlene" Dietrich was born in 1901 in Berlin's Schöneberg district and grew up with her sister, two years her senior, in an affluent household. Her father, Louis Erich Otto Dietrich, was a police lieutenant, and her mother, Josephine, was the daughter of a jeweler who owned a luxury shop on Unter den Linden boulevard. The two sisters could not have been more different. Elisabeth was small in stature, somewhat overweight, and shy and retiring. Marlene was charming and vivacious and attracted attention from an early age. After their father's death in 1908, their mother married a Prussian officer named Eduard von Losch, who died in 1916 from a wound sustained in the First World War. Josephine raised her daughters in a strict household, emphasizing the "Prussian virtues" of diligence, honor, and discipline. Whereas Elisabeth obeyed, earning the scornful sobriquet "terrible tubby of virtue" from her sister, Marlene rebelled.

After attending the Victoria-Luisen-Schule in the Wilmersdorf district, which Marlene left in 1918 before receiving a degree, the two sisters went their separate ways. Having failed at her childhood dream of becoming a concert violinist, Marlene began doing the rounds as a chorus girl in nightclubs, getting her first experience on stage, and also playing bit parts in silent movies. During the shooting of the film *Tragödie der Liebe* (Tragedy of Love), she met Rudolf Sieber, a production manager, whom she married in May 1923. In December of the following year, their only child, a daughter named Maria, was born.[12]

In 1929, the director Josef von Sternberg handed the still little-known actress the role of Lola Lola in *The Blue Angel*, an adaptation of Heinrich Mann's best-selling novel *Man of Straw*. The role of the brash nightclub hostess fit Dietrich perfectly. She completely overshadowed the male lead, Emil Jannings, and was on her way to becoming a global star. Immediately after the premiere in Berlin's massive Gloria film auditorium, she followed Sternberg to America, where she was given a lucrative seven-year contract by Paramount Pictures. In her first Hollywood film with Sternberg, *Morocco* (1930), she acted alongside Gary Cooper, and in quick succession she appeared in further films by the director, including *Shanghai Express* (1932), *Blonde Venus* (1932), *The Scarlet Empress* (1934), and *The Devil Is a Woman* (1935). Her transformation from a bratty young Berliner into a Hollywood diva was complete.[13]

By contrast, her sister Elisabeth's life was anything but glamorous. In 1926, Elisabeth married theater manager Georg Will, giving up her career as a schoolteacher and devoting herself to her family after the birth of their son Hans-Georg in June 1928. In 1933, although her husband had joined the Nazi Party, he was effectively prohibited from working because he had run the Tingel-Tangel Theater alongside the Jewish composer Friedrich Hollaender. In August 1936, Georg Will wrote to Hans Hinkel, the director of the Reich Culture Chamber, asking for help "finding a job again soon, either in the press or theater." He stressed that he had always felt fully affiliated with the "national cause," and by way of example mentioned that in 1919, as a member of the "Oberland" paramilitary militia, he had helped "liberate" Munich and Upper Silesia from revolutionary, left-wing governments.[14]

At this point, Goebbels had not yet given up hope of luring Marlene Dietrich back to Germany. In April 1936, he saw *Desire*, her second film with Gary Cooper, and wrote in his diary that the two were "very great actors . . . above all Dietrich whom we unfortunately no longer have in Germany."[15] In February 1937, when he saw Dietrich's first American color film, *The Garden of Allah*, costarring Charles Boyer, Goebbels found it "stupid and verbose." But he still remarked that "Dietrich performed marvelously."[16]

Goebbels enlisted Dietrich's brother-in-law in his efforts to bring her "back home to the Reich," and although she resisted the siren calls from Berlin—Dietrich applied for US citizenship in 1937—Georg Will was rewarded for his services. The Propaganda Ministry put the unemployed vaudeville manager in charge of three movie theaters on military exercise grounds: in Wildflecken in the Rhön region, in Oerbke near Fallingborstel, and in Bergen-Belsen. Will hired others to run Wildflecken and Oerbke, but he personally oversaw daily operations at the Bergen-Belsen cinema, which could seat almost two thousand soldiers. Shortly before the start of the Second World War, his wife and son joined him, moving into a spacious apartment above the theater. There are no written records regarding Elisabeth Will from the war years, but she can hardly have been unaware of the horrors at the concentration camp a mere two kilometers away.[17]

In June 1939, Marlene Dietrich became an American citizen, and a few weeks later, she began shooting *Destry Rides Again*, in which she played the saloon singer Frenchy, a part harkening back to her roles in the late 1920s. Her song "The Boys in the Back Room" became almost as popular as "Falling in Love Again (Can't Help It)" from *The Blue Angel*. The war in Europe still seemed very far away, but after Japan attacked Pearl Harbor in December 1941 and the United States was drawn into the conflict, Dietrich crisscrossed the country drum-

Captain Marlene Dietrich with American soldiers in Germany
in the spring of 1945.

ming up support for war bonds, cooked for soldiers in the "Hollywood Canteen" with other movie stars, and visited the wounded in hospital wards. She felt it was important to take an active part in the war against Nazi Germany. "I felt responsible for the war caused by Hitler," she would write in her 1978 memoir. "I wanted to help to bring this war to an end as quickly as possible."[18]

In 1944, she applied to the USO to entertain troops overseas. Wearing a uniform and holding the rank of captain, she flew to Algiers, where she performed her first concert for GIs. Soon her repertoire included a song that had been equally popular in pre–Nazi Germany and in America: "Lily Marlene." From North Africa, she traveled on to Italy, where she and her unit followed the Allied advance. In June 1944, a few days before the Normandy landing, she entered Rome with American GIs. In an August 1944 interview with the *New York Herald*

Tribune, she described the Romans not believing their eyes when they first saw her in a Jeep: "They must have thought Americans are wonderful. We bring them freedom, bread—even movie stars."[19]

After a short furlough in New York, Dietrich set off in September 1944 for her second USO tour. From Paris, she joined the advancing troops of General George S. Patton. During the Ardennes Offensive of December 1944, Hitler's final attempt to turn the tide of the war, her unit was temporarily surrounded and only narrowly escaped being captured.

Dietrich's first encounter with Germans after crossing the German-Belgian border turned out to be far less stressful than she had feared. "We arrived in Germany, and to our great surprise there was no threat, nothing to be afraid of," she wrote in her memoir. "The people on the street would have loved to hug me. They asked the Americans for small favors. They couldn't have been nicer."[20] In mid-April she followed American troops into southern Germany as they headed for Bohemia. In Plzeň, American and Soviet soldiers celebrated their victory together, and for the first time Dietrich sang for Red Army troops. A few days later, in Munich, she received word about the woman in Bergen-Belsen claiming to be her sister.[21]

"Thank you for coming all that way," Elisabeth Will wrote two weeks after her reunion with her younger sister. "I'm convinced you'll find Mom as well."[22] Josephine von Losch had in fact survived the war in Berlin, and in September 1945, Dietrich flew in a military plane to Tempelhof Airport, where she was reunited with her mother. Dietrich could hardly find her way around the city she had left fifteen years previously. "The Kaiser Wilhelm Memorial Church is destroyed as well as Zoo Train Station, Tauentzienstrasse, Joachimsthaler—all of it in ruins," she wrote to Sieber, to whom she had remained married despite her numerous affairs. The house where her mother had lived had been destroyed by fire. "The balcony sagged. Mom had searched the rubble for days, and on top of one pile of it . . . was the bronze mask of my face, undamaged. She sat there for a long while, crying."[23] Twice a day, Dietrich performed for GIs. In October 1945, she traveled back to Paris. In November 1945, Josephine von Losch died at the age of sixty-three. That same month, Dietrich made another brief stop in Bergen-Belsen and saw her sister, although she took precautions to keep her visit secret.

Like many Germans who went along with the Nazi regime, Georg Will had quickly changed sides after the war. He was allowed to continue to run the movie theater, which now catered to British soldiers. When that commission expired in 1950, he opened the Metropol-Lichtspiele cinema in Hanover, leaving his wife behind in Bergen-Belsen. There she lived in seclusion but free from any material concerns, as Dietrich sent her most of her royalties from her German music sales and repeatedly gave her large monetary gifts. Elisabeth kept her side of the bargain and never let on in public that she was Dietrich's sister.[24]

After the war Dietrich went back to making movies, including Billy Wilder's *A Foreign Affair* (1948), in which she played a seductive nightclub singer with a dark past. In 1953, she started a second career, primarily as a singer at the Sahara in Las Vegas and the Café de Paris in London. Soon, she was touring the world, and in 1960 she passed through Germany, where she was by no means welcomed everywhere with open arms. In the eyes of many Germans, this courageous opponent of the Nazis was a "traitor to the fatherland." By contrast, in the United States in 1947, she had been awarded the Medal of Freedom, one of the highest American civilian honors.[25]

Occasionally Dietrich invited her sister to her concerts, after which the two would secretly meet. On May 7, 1973, twenty-eight years after Dietrich's first visit to Bergen-Belsen, Elisabeth Will died in a fire in her home.[26]

Dietrich survived her sister by almost two decades. In 1961, she made her last major picture, *Judgment at Nuremberg*. Alongside Spencer Tracy as Judge Dan Haywood, Dietrich played the widow of a

Wehrmacht general who had been hanged as a war criminal and who, like most Germans after 1945, claimed to have known nothing about the Nazi crimes against humanity. After breaking her leg in a fall while onstage in Sydney in September 1975, Dietrich quit performing as a singer, withdrawing entirely from the public eye. She died on May 6, 1992, in her Parisian apartment on Avenue Montaigne, not far from the Champs-Élysées. She had been interviewed there by the actor and director Maximilian Schell in the fall of 1982. Asked whether she had any siblings, she simply said, "No."[27]

ON MAY 7, 1945, the Reich commissar for the occupied Dutch territories, Arthur Seyss-Inquart, was arrested in Hamburg. That same day, thousands of people gathered on the Dam, the main central square in Amsterdam. The mood was celebratory because the liberators that the city's residents had long been waiting for were due to enter the city around noon, in the form of the 1st Canadian Army. The crowd was patient as the hours passed. Suddenly, at approximately 3:00 p.m., shots rang out over the square. Members of a German naval unit had barricaded themselves in the second story of a building and were firing into the mass of people below them. In a panic, those in the crowd tried to flee or threw themselves to the ground. "It was a final drama before the people of Amsterdam were finally free and felt safe from the hated occupiers," the historian and journalist Barbara Beuys wrote in her epic account of Amsterdam under German occupation. "On this festive day on the Dam, twenty-two residents of Amsterdam paid with their lives. Sixty were wounded. People left the city center and headed home, shocked and horrified."[28]

The "drama" of that day had roots stretching back to the morning of May 10, 1940, when Wehrmacht soldiers crossed the German-Dutch border. The government of the Netherlands had given its people a false sense of security, assuring them that Hitler would respect Dutch neutrality. So the Dutch were doubly dismayed to find themselves, like

Britain, France, and Belgium, at war with their aggressive neighbor to the east. On May 13, Queen Wilhelmina and the government's ministers fled to London, and two days later the Netherlands surrendered. German troops moved into Amsterdam that very day. On May 26, Seyss-Inquart arrived in the Hague and assumed his position as the highest authority in the country. At first, he seemed to take a gentle approach. With manifest relief, the Amsterdam history teacher Hendrik Jan Smeding wrote in his diary on June 5, "We are awakening somewhat from a bad dream. There has been no persecution of Jews, no raids, and no cleansing at universities."[29]

At the start of the war, almost 80,000 of the Netherlands' 140,000 Jews lived in Amsterdam. Among them were nearly 7,000 émigré German Jews, including the four members of the Frank family—Otto Frank; his wife, Edith; and his daughters, Margot and Anne—who had moved from Frankfurt am Main to the Dutch capital in 1933 and lived in an apartment on Amsterdam's south side, at Merwedeplein 37. Initially, as was true for the rest of Amsterdam's residents, their lives did not change very much. But soon enough, demonstrations in favor of the House of Orange-Nassau were prohibited, film censorship was introduced, and all political parties save the National Socialist Movement under Anton Adriaan Mussert were banned. In October 1940, all of Amsterdam's approximately 25,000 state employees—from porters to professors—were required to sign a declaration of their Aryan heritage. Jewish civil servants and public employees were subsequently fired.

In January 1941, Seyss-Inquart ordered people of "entire or partial Jewish blood" to register themselves with the Nazi occupiers. This tactic had two purposes: to collect data on Jews in the Netherlands and simultaneously isolate them socially. Soon, signs reading "Jews unwanted" hung in cafés, restaurants, and hotels. Meanwhile, gangs of Dutch National Socialist thugs began terrorizing Jews on Amsterdam's streets. Whenever Jews resisted, Hanns Albin Rauter, the head of the SS and the German police in the Netherlands, used it as a pretense to intensify the violence. During a raid on Jewish homes in Amsterdam on February 22 and 23, 1941, more than four hundred men were rounded up and deported to the Buchenwald concentration camp. In solidarity with the deportees, the people of Amsterdam staged a public transport strike on February 25 and turned out in the tens of thousands to protest the occupiers' actions. Revenge came swiftly. Four Communist workers and fifteen members of small anti-Nazi groups were executed in the dunes near Scheveningen. On March 12, 1941, Seyss-Inquart announced in Amsterdam's famous Concertgebouw concert hall, "We will strike the Jews wherever we encounter them, and anyone who sides with them will suffer the consequences."[30]

Anti-Jewish repression became more and more severe. Jews were banned from shops, cinemas, theaters, and swimming pools and were required to hand over their radios. Jewish doctors and lawyers were prohibited from accepting any Aryan patients and clients, and Jewish children were barred from public schools. For Anne Frank and her older sister, this meant that as of October 1941 they had to make the long trek to the city's Jewish Lyceum every day. As of May 3, 1942, eight months after the introduction of a similar rule in Germany, all Jews aged sixteen or older in the Netherlands were required to wear a six-pointed yellow star bearing the inscription "Jood." The underground Dutch newspaper *Het Parool* condemned this policy, calling it not just "an insult to Jews but a slap in the face of the entire Dutch people."[31]

On June 12, 1942, Anne Frank celebrated her thirteenth birthday at Merwedeplein 37. Her father gave her a diary with a checkered cloth binding and a clasp lock. "I hope I will be able to confide everything to you, as I have never been able to confide in anyone," she wrote in her first entry. "And I hope you will be a great source of comfort and support."[32] Eight days later, she remarked self-critically that "it seems to me that later on neither I nor anyone else will be interested in the musings of a thirteen-year-old schoolgirl."[33] She could not have been more wrong. Anne Frank's diary, in which she continued to write until her arrest on August 1, 1944, would become one of the most extraordinary and profoundly moving testimonials of the fate of Jews under Nazi domination in Europe and would make her a household name around the world.

In mid-April 1942, while visiting Amsterdam, Adolf Eichmann told the director of the Central Office for Jewish Emigration, Ferdinand aus der Fünten, that the deportation of Jews to the death camps "in the east" would begin that summer. On July 5, 1942, the first notifications were issued that Jews would be sent to a "labor detail" in Germany. That same day, Margot Frank received a letter telling her to report to the city's Central Office. This prompted her father to move his family into a carefully prepared secret annex in the attic of the rear building at Prinsengracht 263, where he had formerly had his office. After a few days, they were joined by Hermann and Auguste van Pels and their son Peter, and later by a dentist named Fritz Pfeffer. "So much has happened, it's as if the whole world had suddenly turned upside down," Anne Frank wrote on July 8, when the family's perilous move was complete.[34]

During the night of July 14, the first train of deportees rolled out of Amsterdam's main station. After a stop at the Westerbork transit camp, the train continued to Auschwitz-Birkenau. By the end of the year, forty thousand Amsterdam Jews had been forced to make the journey "to the east." The eight people hiding out on Prinsengracht were under no illusions about the fate of the deportees. "Nothing but dismal and depressing news to report," Anne Frank wrote on October 9. "Our many Jewish friends and acquaintances are being taken away in droves. The Gestapo is treating them very roughly and transporting them in cattle cars to Westerbork." Miep Gies, a former employee of Anne's father who risked her life to keep the group supplied with food, reported to them about the horrific conditions in the transit camp. "It must be terrible in Westerbork," Frank wrote in her diary. "The people get almost nothing to eat, much less to drink, as water is available only one hour a day, and there's only one toilet and sink for several thousand people. Men and women sleep in the same room, and women and children often have their heads shaved. Escape is almost impossible; many people look Jewish, and they're branded by their shorn heads. If it's that bad in Holland, what must it be like in those faraway and uncivilized places where the Germans are sending them? We assume that most of them are being murdered. The English radio says they're being gassed. Perhaps that's the quickest way to die."[35]

Assisting the German police and the SS in rounding up Jews was the so-called Henneicke Column, composed of fifty-four Dutch collaborators under the command of Willem Christiaan Henneicke. In March and April 1943 alone, they seized almost six thousand people; for each person apprehended the Central Office paid a bounty of seven-and-a-half guilders (three dollars, or approximately forty-five of today's US dollars). In early October 1943, the German occupiers declared Amsterdam officially "Jew-free." The hunt for Jews who had gone underground continued, but the period of major organized raids was over.[36]

The Franks and the others held out in the secret annex, constantly fearful of being discovered. On June 6, 1944, they experienced a moment of hope when news arrived that the Allies had landed in Normandy. "A huge commotion in the Annex!" wrote Anne Frank. "Is this really the beginning of the long-awaited liberation? The liberation we've all talked so much about, which still seems too good, too much of a fairy tale ever to come true? Will this year, 1944, bring us victory? We don't know yet. But where there's hope, there's life. It fills us with fresh courage and makes us strong again."[37]

But a mere eight weeks later, a four-man Gestapo squad led by SS Oberscharführer Karl Josef Silberbauer raided the rear building on Prinsengracht and took the Franks, the van Pelses, and Pfeffer into custody. It has never been determined who betrayed them. Miep Gies, who found the annex empty a short time later, collected some paper effects scattered on the floor, including Anne Frank's diary. The captives were interned in a prison in Weteringschans and then, after four days, taken to Westerbork. On September 3, one last train left the transit camp. Among the nearly 1,000 people on it—498 men, 422 women, and 79 children—were Edith and Otto Frank, their daughters, the Van Pelses and their son, and Fritz Pfeffer. The train arrived in Auschwitz on September 5.

Anne and Margot Frank were sent by train in late October to Bergen-Belsen, where both died of typhus sometime in February or March 1945. Edith died on January 6, 1945, in Auschwitz. Hermann van Pels died in the gas chambers in October. His wife, Auguste, was taken from the death camp via Bergen-Belsen and Buchenwald to Theresienstadt. It is not known precisely when she died. Peter van Pels was forced on a death march to Mauthausen, where he died on May 5, 1945, the day US soldiers liberated the camp. Fritz Pfeffer died in Neuengamme on December 20, 1944. Otto Frank, who remained in Auschwitz, was the only member of the group to survive, and he returned to Amsterdam on June 3, 1945. Miep Gies gave him the diary she had found, saying, "Here is what your daughter Anne left for you."[38]

September 5, 1944, the day the final deportation train from Westerbork arrived in Auschwitz, would go down in Dutch history as "dolle Dinsdag" or "Crazy Tuesday." The previous day, Seyss-Inquart had declared a state of emergency in Amsterdam following reports of swift Allied advances to the south. "The armies of liberation have crossed the border!" announced *Het Parool* on its front page. "Breda, Tilburg, Roosendaal, and Maastricht are already free! The glorious German Wehrmacht has been defeated and has taken flight."[39]

Thousands of German occupying soldiers and bureaucrats fled the Dutch capital on the evening of September 4. Among them were Dutch collaborators who feared their compatriots would exact retribution. On September 5, the people of Amsterdam took to the streets.

The color orange, traditionally a symbol of the Dutch royal family, was everywhere, and images of Queen Wilhelmina adorned countless windows. But the jubilant mood would soon end. The liberators failed to arrive. "The English didn't come," noted painter Max Beckmann drily in his diary. He had emigrated to Amsterdam in 1937 and lived there through the entire German occupation.[40] The Wehrmacht had by no means given up, and an attempt by British paratroopers to take the strategically important bridge at Arnheim ended in disaster.

Only a few days after "Crazy Tuesday," the German occupation was reinstated, with German police once more patrolling the streets of Amsterdam. The city's residents were made to suffer as never before. Every act of resistance was met with arbitrary arrests and public executions. In late September 1944, after Dutch rail workers went on a national strike to aid the Allied war cause, Seyss-Inquart declared an embargo that cut off most food supplies to Amsterdam. In the harsh winter of 1944–45, many people became malnourished. And in the spring, when it was clear to everyone that Hitler's Germany was headed toward imminent defeat, the occupiers stepped up their terrorizing of the Dutch. In early March, in an act of retribution for the attempted assassination of Rauter, 263 Dutch people were murdered.[41]

By April 1945, the front was getting ever closer, and on the twelfth of that month, Canadian soldiers liberated the Westerbork transit camp. On May 3, Queen Wilhelmina arrived in the Hague. Two days later, Germany's surrender in northwestern Europe took effect, and on May 6, the supreme commander of the Wehrmacht in the Netherlands, General Johannes Blaskowitz, signed the articles of surrender in Wageningen. The German occupation was finally over. "Drank half a glass of vermouth," wrote eighteen-year-old Carry Ulreich, a young Jewish woman who had survived with her parents and older sister by going into hiding in Rotterdam. "Went to bed at 12:30, but at 2:30 we still hadn't fallen asleep. How we talked, and how loudly! We're allowed to do that now. Joy, happiness, gratitude that we escaped with our lives."[42]

In Amsterdam, people still anxiously awaited the arrival of the Canadians, who did not appear in time to stop the German naval unit from firing into the crowd on the Dam. On May 8, soldiers of the Seaforth Highlanders of Canada finally entered the Dutch capital, where they received an enthusiastic welcome. That day, Seyss-Inquart, whom the British had arrested in Hamburg, was taken in a military plane to the Netherlands and handed over to a Canadian military police unit at Hengelo Airport.[43] He would be hanged in Nuremberg.

MAY 8, 1945

The ink on the articles of surrender signed in Reims was hardly dry when Eisenhower received an angry telegram from the Soviet deputy chief of staff Aleksei Antonov. It declared that the Russian High Command refused to recognize Germany's surrender because the text of the articles sent by Walter Bedell Smith did not conform to the wording prepared by the European Advisory Commission on behalf of the governments in Washington, London, and Moscow. Eisenhower hastened to respond with reassurances that he had taken great care to abide by his responsibility not to conclude a separate ceasefire agreement. He also pointed out that General Susloparov, a Soviet representative, had been present in Reims and had cosigned the document.[1]

Stalin, however, insisted that the ceremony be repeated in Red Army–occupied Berlin. The Soviet Union had, after all, borne the greatest burden in the war, so it seemed to him only right and proper to force the leaders of the three branches of the Wehrmacht to capitulate in front of all three of the main Allies. Eisenhower initially agreed to travel to Berlin but then canceled after consulting with his staff and with Churchill, who argued that the Germans had already surrendered unconditionally in Reims and that the new ceremony in Berlin was

Soviet business alone and aimed solely at satisfying Stalin's personal need for acclaim.[2]

In the end, the western Allies sent British air marshal Arthur Tedder, US general Carl Spaatz, and French general Jean de Lattre de Tassigny to Berlin. The German side was represented by Wilhelm Keitel as Wehrmacht supreme commander, Hans-Georg von Friedeburg for the navy, and Colonel General Hans-Jürgen Stumpff in place of the wounded Luftwaffe high commander Robert Ritter von Greim, whom Hitler had named to succeed Göring on April 26, 1945. Around noon on May 8, three passenger planes carrying the British delegation landed at Tempelhof Airport. They were received by a Soviet group led by Marshal Zhukov's deputy, General Sokolovsky, and including a guard of honor three rows deep. A brass band played the national anthems. While the Americans and British inspected the Soviet honor guards, the Germans were taken directly to cars waiting to bring them to Zhukov's headquarters in Karlshorst. "At the front is Keitel in a long overcoat and large, high-peaked general's cap," observed Soviet war correspondent Konstantin Simonov. "He consciously avoids looking right or left and walks in long, expansive strides."[3]

Zhukov had ordered the officer's mess in the Pionierschule building in Karlshorst repurposed for the ceremony, and Red Army soldiers requisitioned the necessary furnishings, carpets, glasses, silverware, and flowers. The streets leading to the building were cleared of rubble and lined with the flags of the victorious Allied powers.[4] One of those who helped with the preparations was Erich Honecker, later Walter Ulbricht's successor as the chairman of the Socialist Unity Party and the leader of Communist East Germany, who had spent almost ten years in prison during the Third Reich. On April 27, 1945, after being liberated by the Soviets, he had set off on his own from the Brandenburg-Görden Prison for Berlin, some ninety kilometers to the east. On May 4, he arrived at the apartment of the woman who would become his first wife, police officer Charlotte Schanuel, on Landsberger

Strasse 37. Before joining the Ulbricht Group, he received orders to raise the flags of the Allies along Landsberger Strasse. Many years later, he still remembered with pride having gathered flags (and having new ones sewn) so that the Allied motorcades would be greeted by a sea of their national banners as they drove to Karlshorst.[5]

The German delegation was put in a small villa next to the Pionierschule, where they waited as the surrender ceremony, originally planned for 2:00 p.m., was delayed while the victors' representatives bickered about seating arrangements and the order of the signatures. Agreeing to the precise wording of the terms of surrender also took hours. For the western Allies, it was another harbinger of the difficult negotiations to come with their Soviet partners. Finally, consensus was reached on a document that differed little from the articles of surrender of May 7, merely replacing the words "Soviet High Command" with "Red Army High Command" and explicitly stating in article 6 that the Russian and English versions of the agreement, not the German version, were the definitive ones.[6]

The German contingent had been treated to a cold buffet while they waited, and every now and then a curious reporter would appear and make recordings of the scene. When Keitel remarked to a Russian officer that on his drive through Berlin he had been appalled by the extent of the destruction, the officer answered, "Mr. Field-Marshal, were you not appalled when the Germans, on your orders, wiped off the face of the earth thousands of Soviet towns and villages, leaving millions of our people, including many thousands of children, buried under the ruins?"[7]

At 11:45 p.m., Zhukov invited Tedder, Spaatz, and Lattre de Tassigny into his office next to the officers' mess to go over the final details. At the stroke of midnight, the deadline that had been set for the May 7 surrender agreement to take effect, they entered the mess hall and sat down at a long table in front of flags of the Soviet Union, the United States, Britain, and France. A dozen Soviet generals, a row of ranking

Allied officers, a number of orderlies, and more than a hundred journalists and photographers were present. Zhukov said a few introductory words and then ordered that the German delegation be brought in. Everyone fell silent. The only sound was the whirring of the cameras as a side door opened and Keitel, followed by Friedeburg and Stumpff, came into the room. The Wehrmacht supreme commander stood straight as an arrow and raised his marshal's staff in greeting. Not a few of those in attendance found, as Harry C. Butcher, US naval aide to General Eisenhower, put it, that Keitel's demeanor was one of "arrogance and defiance," the epitome of "the living Prussian-ism of which I had heard so much."[8] Zhukov had a different impression: "Before me was another man, no longer that haughty Keitel who accepted the surrender of defeated France. Now he had a beaten look, although he tried to present at least some of his outward assurance."[9]

The Germans were instructed to sit at a small table near the door, whereupon Zhukov asked Keitel whether he had read the articles of surrender and was authorized to sign them. Keitel answered in the affirmative and called for the documents, but Zhukov told the German delegation to approach the presidium table: "Keitel quickly rose from his seat and turned his eyes on us. He then lowered his gaze and, slowly picking up his field marshal's baton, walked unsteadily to our table. His monocle dropped and dangled by its cord. Keitel's face was covered with red blotches."[10] The field marshal sat down, put his cap and staff aside, took off one of his gloves, put the monocle back in front of his left eye, and, as the photographers' flashbulbs popped, signed five copies of the articles of surrender. It was sixteen minutes after midnight. After Keitel returned to the small table, Friedeburg and Stumpff also signed the documents. Zhukov and Tedder then added their signatures as representatives of the Allies, while Spaatz and Lattre de Tassigny signed as witnesses. At 12:43 a.m. on the morning of May 9, the ceremony was over, and Zhukov told the German delegation to

The surrender ceremony repeated at Stalin's insistence: shortly after midnight, on May 9, 1945, Field Marshal General Wilhelm Keitel agreed to Germany's unconditional capitulation in Berlin-Karlshorst.

leave. Keitel, Friedeburg, and Stumpff stood up, bowed, and departed, followed by their staff officers.[11]

"Suddenly, the pent-up tension was released from the room," wrote Simonov. "It dissipated, as though everyone had been holding their breath and now exhaled. A collective sigh of relief and exhaustion was let out."[12] In the name of the Soviet High Command, Zhukov congratulated all of those present on their victory. Soviet officers shook hands with their allies from the west. At the subsequent banquet, the victors toasted their comrades in arms and promised to deepen friendly relations among the members of the anti-Hitler coalition—a bit of wishful thinking that would soon be contradicted by Cold War reality. The night of May 8 was one of rare harmony. Vodka and champagne flowed freely, and buoyed by the joyous atmosphere, Zhukov even performed a Russian folk dance on the parquet floor of the officers' mess.[13]

The German delegation, who spent the night in their small villa, would never forget it either. Zhukov's head quartermaster had prepared an opulent meal for them, disingenuously excusing himself for what he said was its modesty. "I couldn't help but answering that we were unaccustomed to such luxury and such a richly set table," Keitel recalled from his prison cell in Nuremberg. "For dessert there were frozen fresh strawberries, which I tasted for the first time in my life. Apparently, a Berlin gourmet restaurant had delivered this feast, since the wines, too, were of German origin."[14] Later that morning, the Germans flew from Tempelhof back to Flensburg, landing at 10:00 a.m.

WHILE GERMAN REPRESENTATIVES were surrendering for a second time in Berlin, Dönitz summoned his advisers to discuss whether, after the capitulation of the Wehrmacht, to continue the government or whether the time had come for him and his cabinet to resign. The most forceful advocate of standing down was Speer, who argued that Dönitz's mission of ending the war had been accomplished. The Allies occupied the entire Reich, with the exception of their Flensburg enclave, so that in practical terms the government no longer had the freedom to act, leaving no alternative but a "dignified departure."[15]

Speer apparently believed that the Americans would have little choice but to reach a deal with him so that they could use his expertise in arms production, and only a week later, on May 15, the first Americans appeared at Glücksberg Castle and interviewed him extensively. There, he gave a performance that was convincing to some of his former enemies—and not only to them: Speer portrayed himself as the apolitical technocrat who had been enthralled for a time by Hitler's demonic powers of seduction but who had courageously resisted the Führer's destructive rage at the end of the war.[16]

The most vigorous supporter of prolonging the government was

Krosigk, who argued that Dönitz and the "caretaker government" were the "visible embodiment of the sovereignty and unity of the Reich." Total, unconditional surrender, Krosigk reasoned, applied only to the Wehrmacht. To his thinking, the German state continued to exist, and even if his capacity for action was limited, Dönitz was still the head of state of the German Reich. Moreover, Krosigk added, the government had a duty to share the fate of the German people instead of evading responsibility. Dönitz ultimately sided with Krosigk. The minutes of the meeting read, "Resigning is an irrevocable decision and cannot be made prematurely."[17]

At 12:30 p.m., Dönitz took to the microphone of Flensburg's radio station to explain himself to the nation: "With the occupation of Germany, power resides with the occupiers. It is in their hands whether the government I convened and whether I myself can be active or not. If I can serve and help my fatherland, I will stay in office until the will of the German people expresses itself in their choice of a head of state or the occupying powers make it impossible for me to continue my duties." It was only his "love of Germany and sense of duty" that kept him in his post, the admiral assured his listeners, adding that he would remain in his position as long as it was "compatible with his honor." He owed that to the Reich, he concluded, as its "highest representative."[18] The Allies allowed the Dönitz government to continue only for fifteen more days.

THE NEWS OF GERMANY's unconditional surrender came as a "complete surprise" to a large portion of the populace, according to the Dönitz government's intelligence service. Many Germans did not understand why the Wehrmacht could not keep fighting against the Red Army. German refugees in particular lamented that the last hope they had clung to—that the western powers would turn against the Soviet Union—had now disappeared. As they saw it, Germany's eastern territories had been "lost forever."[19]

At 8:00 p.m. on May 8, the Wehrmacht Supreme Command announced on national radio, "At midnight on May 9, all hostilities against our former enemies are to be suspended in all theaters of war and by all parts of the Wehrmacht, all armed organizations and individuals. Any destruction of or damage to weapons and munition, aircraft, equipment, and hardware of any kind as well as damage to or sinking of ships runs contrary to the terms accepted and signed by the Wehrmacht Supreme Command and is to be prevented at any cost in the name of the German people."[20] The last fighting against the Red Army in Czechoslovakia, Austria, and the Baltics ended on May 9. In Courland 180,000 German soldiers and in East Prussia 150,000 allowed the Soviets to take them prisoner,[21] but only after destroying most of their military hardware in contravention of the articles of surrender. "It's lunacy in Michelswalde forest," one German private wrote in his diary on May 9, after escaping on one of the last ships across the Baltic Sea. "Vehicles rest next to other vehicles, passenger cars, and trucks. Tanks and all-terrain vehicles are constantly being blown up. . . . Materiel of all sorts is lying around. Horses and other animals roam in large numbers. It's a picture like that in Dunkirk in 1940."[22] The following day, German garrisons in the "Atlantic fortresses" of Lorient, Saint-Nazaire, and La Rochelle also surrendered. The commandant of Lorient dutifully reported by radio to his superiors: "I am signing off in the name of my determined and unbeaten men. Our gravely tested homeland is in our thoughts. Long live Germany."[23]

Dönitz's primary goal had been to delay total surrender for as long as possible by agreeing to partial capitulations so that German civilians and soldiers could be brought behind American and British lines. Even though Eisenhower had rejected German wishes and insisted on an immediate unconditional surrender on all fronts, Dönitz did succeed, before the surrender went into effect, in removing 1,850,000 soldiers on the eastern front from the grasp of the Red Army. By contrast, after May 8, 1,490,000 men became POWs of the Soviets and their Yugoslav allies. In total, more than half of German troops on the eastern front were able to surrender to the western Allies.[24]

In its last report, on May 9, the Wehrmacht Supreme Command took leave of its defeated soldiers with a hugely dishonest statement: "Since midnight, the weapons have fallen silent on all fronts. On the command of the grand admiral, the Wehrmacht has ceased the fighting that had become hopeless. With that, almost six years of honorable battle have concluded. It brought us great victories but also heavy defeats. In the end, the Wehrmacht has been honorably bested by an overwhelming force. . . . The subsequent judgments of history will ultimately honor these unique achievements on the front and the home front."[25] Dönitz sounded the same notes in a speech to officers in Flensburg on May 9. "We have nothing to be ashamed of. What the German Wehrmacht achieved in battle and the people in persistence during these six years is unique in history and in the world. It is unprecedented heroism. We stand here as soldiers with no blemishes on our honor."[26] Thus was born the legend of the "unbesmirched Wehrmacht," which would endure until being thoroughly discredited by two historical exhibitions by the Hamburg Institute for Social Research in 1995 and 2001.

AT NOON ON MAY 8, 1945, Major Ralph E. Pearson, a regimental commander of the 80th American Infantry Division, left the Alpine Austrian town of Schwanenstadt with two Jeeps and a truck full of infantrymen. His destination was Altaussee, a town in the Salzkammergut region north of the Alps. The day before, he had received a sensational report from an Austrian officer, whose name was not recorded, that artworks of inestimable value had been stored in the region's salt mine. After a four-hour drive, at around 3:30 p.m., Pearson and his men arrived in Altaussee, which was teeming with German soldiers. None of them had any intention of putting up further resistance. The first action Pearson took was to dismiss the mayor and install a new one. Then he drove to the salt mine, where he was met by a mineralogist named Hermann Michel, who led him to the mine entrances, which had been sealed off. Michel told him that within the mine were art treasures looted at Hitler's behest from all over Europe. Before returning to his home base, Pearson had the mine secured and ordered Michel to hand over all the files and documentation he could get his hands on.[27]

Hitler's art collection had made a long journey before it ended up in Altaussee. On April 8, 1938, only a few weeks after the annexation of Austria into the Reich, the dictator had visited Linz and sketched out some ideas for a megalomaniacal remaking of the city he considered his hometown. The core of his plan was a gigantic "Führer museum" that would hold works by famous painters from Germany and all of Europe. On his state visit to Italy in May 1938, Hitler spent a great deal of time in the museums of Rome and Florence. The Galleria degli Uffizi, in particular, influenced his plans for the Linz museum.[28]

To lead the project, Hitler chose the head of the Dresden Gemäldegalerie Alte Meister (Old Master Painting Gallery), Hans Posse, an internationally renowned art historian, curator, and museum manager. This decision raised eyebrows among Nazi functionaries in the Saxon city, because Posse had been fired on the suspicion that he had promoted "degenerate art." Nonetheless, after Hitler visited the gallery in June 1938, he ordered Posse rehired, and one year later, the dictator summoned him to Berghof and outlined his plans. The Linz museum was to contain "only the very best from all periods" and to overshadow the collections of Vienna. In a special order from the Führer on June 26, 1939, Posse was appointed the director of the "Linz Special Project," and all party functionaries and offices were required to "assist him in carrying out his tasks."[29]

Posse had access to nearly limitless funds to buy paintings, but he did not just purchase masterworks. He also confiscated them, using a so-called special Führer privilege that allowed Hitler to personally decide what to do with seized artworks. The right of intervention was first formulated in June 1938 in connection with Jewish-owned art collections appropriated during the amalgamation of Austria into the Reich. In October 1940, the special Führer privilege was extended to the entire Reich and, the following month, to all occupied and yet-to-be-occupied territories.[30] Posse was thereby given blanket permission to select among artworks looted from all over Europe those pieces he considered particularly suitable for the Linz museum. In December 1941 and April 1942, he sent Hitler albums with photographs of the works—almost a thousand in number—procured as part of the "Special Project." To house the holdings of the future Führer Museum, a central depot was established in a Benedictine monastery in Kremsmünster in Alpine Austria.[31]

On December 7, 1942, Posse died of lung cancer. Hitler gave him a state funeral, with Goebbels delivering the eulogy. This was the first time the public learned about the planned Linz museum. The following February, Hitler named Hermann Voss, the director of the Painting Gallery of the Nassau Regional Museum in Wiesbaden, as Posse's successor. Together with his most important associate, Hildebrand Gurlitt, Voss continued to acquire looted art while cataloging the artworks already procured.[32]

With the Reich increasingly subject to Allied bombing, Hitler feared for the safety of his priceless masterpieces, fretting about whether the aboveground depot in the Kremsmünster monastery was adequately fortified. In December 1943, the specialist in charge of storage for the Linz project, Gottfried Reimer, proposed the Altaussee salt mine as a new location. Hitler agreed, and once the storage spaces had been constructed, the first artworks began arriving there in May 1944. Gradually all the art earmarked for Linz ended up in the salt mine. These included such treasures as Vermeer's *The Art of Painting* and *The Astronomer*. Some works that were not slated to be part of Hitler's collection, such as Michelangelo's *Madonna of Bruges* and Jan and Hubert van Eyck's *Ghent Altarpiece*, were also stored in Altaussee.[33]

Hitler's pet project was immensely important to him. In the final months of the war, he would sit for hours in front of the gigantic model of Linz the architect Hermann Giesler had set up in the New Reich Chancellery building in February 1945.[34] Meanwhile, an apocalyptic despair was taking hold in parts of the Nazi leadership. One of Hitler's most fanatic followers, the Gauleiter of Upper Danube, August Eigruber, was determined to follow the dictator to the death and thought that if Nazi Germany's demise was inevitable, it should fall in a spectacularly destructive fashion. For Eigruber, this meant that the artworks in the salt mine could not be allowed to fall into Allied hands but must be destroyed. To that end, on April 10, 1945, he had eight five-hundred-kilo aerial bombs taken to the mine in wooden crates marked "Caution: Marble, Do Not Drop."

On April 13, a personal assistant of Martin Bormann visiting Altaussee, Helmut von Hummel, learned of Eigruber's wishes and informed the mine director, Emmerich Pöchmüller, and the onsite art experts, the director of the Vienna Institute for the Preservation of Monuments, Herbert Seiberl, and Berlin master restorer Karl Sieber. They discussed how to dissuade Eigruber from his monstrous plan. Hummel called Bormann and beseeched him to present the situation to Hitler and secure a "Führer decision." The answer from Berlin came promptly, with Hitler forbidding the destruction of the artworks. Instead, controlled detonations were to seal off the entrances to the mine if and when the enemy approached.[35]

As destructive as the dictator's whims were, he wanted the collection to be preserved for posterity. In one of his two testaments of April 29, 1945, Hitler declared that he had "never" claimed the works for "private purposes," but rather solely for the establishment of the museum in Linz. "It is my fondest wish that this legacy become reality," Hitler wrote.[36] On May 1, the day after Hitler's death, Hummel sent Sieber a letter once again stressing Hitler's decision: "In recent weeks, in response to renewed inquiry, [it is Hitler's will] that the artworks kept in the Upper Danube mine not be allowed to fall into enemy hands but by no means should be destroyed forever. On the contrary, steps are to be taken to protect the artworks for a long time from the possibility of foreign access."[37] Eigruber was in no mind to fulfill this final wish of the Führer and posted military guards armed with machine pistols and hand grenades at the entrances to the mine, as rumors swirled that detonation teams would arrive on May 3 or 4 and set off the bombs. But then the mine workers themselves intervened. They were concerned less with saving the artworks than with preserving their jobs, because the detonation of the bombs would have surely destroyed most of the mine itself. On May 3, the regional mining councillor Otto Högler informed the miners about the bombs before their shift. Immediately, men volunteered to guard the crates containing the bombs and bring them out of the mine if necessary. One of them, Alois Rauschdaschl, hit upon the idea of contacting the head of the Reich Main Security Office, Ernst Kaltenbrunner, who like several Nazi henchmen, including Adolf Eichmann, were in the area. Kaltenbrunner gave the miners approval to remove the bombs from the mine and gave Eigruber such a dressing down in a midnight telephone call that the latter meekly relented. On the morning of May 4, the bombs were taken from the mine shafts into a nearby forest. Afterward the entrances to the mine were sealed, as Hitler had instructed.[38]

On May 11, three days after he had the mine secured, Major Pearson asked for the assistance of the "Monuments Men," a division of the US Army formed in 1943 to save European artworks. In the meantime, the press had gotten word of the find, and news of the fabulous art treasures traveled around the world. On May 13, Captain Robert K. Posey, a member of the Monuments Men group, appeared in Salzkammergut and was briefed in detail by Pearson. By May 27, the sealed-off entrances to the mines were cleared, and Captain Posey and his assistants were able to inspect the interior of the mine and determine that the artworks had indeed not been damaged. On June 17, the first trucks carrying the precious cargo pulled out of Altaussee. The Americans had set up their "central collecting point" in the Administrative Building and the Führer Building in Munich, both of which had largely escaped damage during the war. By the end of the year, all of the art had been transported from the mine. Four Monuments Men and more than a hundred German assistants now had their hands full photographing and cataloging the works and trying to locate their rightful owners. The process of restitution continues today.[39]

SHORTLY BEFORE MIDNIGHT on May 8, 1945, the day after Dönitz had dismissed him from his post and dissolved his office, Josef Terboven, the Reich commissar for the occupied Norwegian territories, committed suicide.[40]

At a May 3 meeting in Flensburg, Terboven had declared the military and political situation in Norway and Denmark stable and argued against the surrender of German troops in his area of authority. On the contrary, with the support of the Wehrmacht commanders in Norway, Franz Böhme and Georg Lindemann, he had demanded that a "final honorable battle" be waged. But such exhortations had fallen on deaf ears among Dönitz and his advisers.[41]

On May 5, the capitulation in northern Germany, the Netherlands, and Denmark came into force. That day, Terboven returned to Oslo. In front of his underlings, he still played the role of the tough leader, telling them that Norway would be held for as long as possible for use as a bargaining chip in negotiations with the Allies. Everything depended on continuing to work with discipline and refusing to show any signs of weakness. But Terboven was dismissed two days later. He summoned his administrative director, Hans-Reinhard Koch, and charged him with handing over responsibility for the Reich commissariat to Böhme. Back in his residence in Skaugum Estate, the traditional home of the Norwegian crown prince just outside the gates of Oslo, Terboven destroyed files and withdrew to his private chambers.

One of the Monuments Men (wearing an "N" on his uniform) and German experts inspect a portion of the Ghent Altarpiece recovered from the Altaussee salt mine.

He had previously ordered his lead guard to pack a small bunker on the estate grounds with explosives. Terboven went to the bunker at 11:00 p.m., and half an hour later a powerful explosion was heard. The once-dreaded Reich commissar had blown himself up.[42]

When Norway awoke on May 9, it was free. "All the bells rang, tens of thousands waved flags, and the streets teemed with people," wrote the Austrian author Heimito von Doderer, an officer stationed in Oslo at the time.[43] Before the day was over, Vidkun Quisling, the puppet prime minister installed by the German occupiers, whose name had become synonymous with craven collaboration with the enemy, was taken into custody. He was swiftly convicted of high treason and executed in Oslo's Akershus Fortress on October 24, 1945.

Numerous exiles to Sweden returned to Oslo, and one of the first was Willy Brandt, who arrived back in his adoptive homeland on May 10. He was tasked with reporting for the Swedish press on liberated

Norway. About 350,000 German soldiers remained in the country, although they were gradually sent back home. Much to the amazement of the émigré reporter, some of the former occupiers continued for weeks to sign their orders with "Heil Hitler" and "generally behaved as if nothing had changed."[44]

NEWS OF GERMANY'S UNCONDITIONAL surrender was, in the words of Winston Churchill, "the signal for the greatest outburst of joy in the history of mankind . . . weary and worn, impoverished but undaunted and now triumphant, we had a moment that was sublime."[45] In London, people flooded the streets to celebrate May 8 as VE Day, singing and dancing into the early morning. At 3:00 p.m. that afternoon, Churchill spoke on the radio, preparing his countrymen for further sacrifices: "We may allow ourselves a brief period of rejoicing; but let us not forget for a moment the toil and efforts that lie ahead. Japan, with all her treachery and greed, remains unsubdued." His radio address concluded with "Advance Britannia! Long live the cause of freedom! God save the King!"[46]

From 10 Downing Street, Churchill headed to the Lower House of Parliament. "Winston comes in—a little shy—a little flushed—but smiling boyishly," wrote the diplomat Harold Nicolson. "The House jumps to its feet and there is one long roar of applause."[47] Churchill repeated his radio address but then laid his manuscript to one side and thanked Parliament in emotional words for the support he had been given as wartime prime minister over the previous five years: "We have all of us made our mistakes, but the strength of the Parliamentary institution has been shown to enable it at the same moment to preserve all the title-deeds of democracy while waging war in the most stern and protracted form."[48]

An enormous crowd congregated that evening in front of Buckingham Palace to cheer the royal couple and their two daughters, all of whom appeared on the palace's balcony. At the same time, Churchill was improvising a speech to give to tens of thousands of Londoners from the balcony of the Ministry of Health. To his question "Were we ever downhearted?" the crowd cried out "No!" and then burst into laughter—an expression of relief that the worst was now over.[49]

There were similar scenes of jubilation in New York City. "I was standing in Times Square when the letters on the *New York Times* building announced Germany's total surrender to the tightly packed crowd," remembered Elsbeth Weichmann, who had gone into exile with her husband, Herbert, the former mayor of Hamburg, first to France in 1933 and then in 1940, after the Wehrmacht's invasion, to the United States. "A loud cheer went up. I could hardly hear it. With knees trembling, I sat down in the nearest café. Tension yielded to the certainty that as of today a new phase of life for the world and probably for us as well had begun, one which we had longed to have for years and which now had become possible. . . . That evening, after work, the excitement drove us out on Broadway into the throngs of people, into the celebration and intoxication."[50]

In his radio address to the nation on May 8, President Harry S. Truman remembered his predecessor Franklin D. Roosevelt, who had taken the country to war and led it until his death on April 12, 1945. Amid his joy over the end of the war in Europe, Truman articulated the collective pain resulting from "the terrible price we have paid to rid the world of Hitler and his evil band." He also reminded his countrymen that the war was only half-won: "The West is free, but the East is still in bondage to the treacherous tyranny of the Japanese. When the last Japanese division has surrendered unconditionally, then only will our fighting job be done."[51] In Santa Monica, the exiled German writer Bertolt Brecht noted laconically, "Nazi Germany surrenders unconditionally. At six in the morning, the president holds a radio address. Listening to it, I savor the blossoming California gardens."[52]

In Paris, although France had already celebrated its liberation in August 1944, there were outbreaks of uninhibited, triumphant joy. "[It was] an incomparable spectacle in which an entire mass of the people was united in expressing the elan of relief and liberation," observed the engineer Ferdinand Picard. "All generations joined together in this flood, which was continually augmented by crowds of people from the suburbs. . . . A moving picture of the joy of an entire people that gives its emotions free rein for a day."[53]

In Moscow, Soviet radio held off broadcasting the news of Germany's surrender until May 9. But once the people heard it, they came together in boisterous celebrations of the end of a war in which the Soviet Union had suffered and sacrificed more than any other nation. Stalin raised that fact in his radio address, which he ended by saying, "The great patriotic war has concluded with our complete victory. The period of war in Europe is at an end. The period of peaceful development has begun."[54]

A young Markus Wolf—later the head of intelligence for the East German secret police, the Stasi—attended the evening celebrations near the Kremlin with his parents. As he would later recall, "During the gun salute for the 'Day of Victory,' we felt as one with thousands of celebrating people, whose fatherland had become our second home after eleven long years of exile from Germany."[55] A large crowd also congregated in front of the American embassy in Moscow to express their cordial, enthusiastic feelings, as diplomat George F. Kennan witnessed.[56] How many of the celebrants suspected that the Soviet Union and the United States would soon be such bitter enemies?

"This evening, for the first time in six years, there was no blackout," the German author Ernst Jünger wrote on May 8. "That at least is a modest improvement for us on a day when victory celebrations radiate in all the Allied capitals from New York to Moscow, while the defeated sit deep in their basements with their heads in their hands."[57]

EPILOGUE

O n May 10, 1945, two days after the Wehrmacht's unconditional surrender, Thomas Mann addressed German radio listeners from faraway California. "This is a great hour, not just for the world of the victors but for Germany," he said. "It's the hour when the dragon is laid low. The bestial and sick monstrosity called National Socialism is in its death throes, and Germany has at last been freed from being known as the country of Hitler. Of course, if it had been able to free itself early on when there was still time or even later, at the last minute, if it had been able to celebrate its liberation, its return to humanity with the tolling of bells and the music of Beethoven, that would have been better. That would have been most desirable."[1]

As we know, what Mann thought "most desirable" did not happen. Germans were unable to muster the strength to free themselves, so Germany's liberation would have to come from the outside. Despite growing criticism of the Nazi party and its leaders, both the Wehrmacht and the civilian populace stayed the course to an astonishing extent until deep into the death agonies of the Third Reich, and even then, the myth of the Führer never completely lost its power. Hitler's aura is the only way to explain how the dictator was able to exert a hypnotic hold on those around him down to his final days. When the war had long been lost, many Germans still pinned their hopes on "miracle weapons," "final victory," or a collapse of the anti-Hitler coalition.

Most Germans, even those critical of the regime, regarded May 8, 1945, not as a day of liberation but as an unprecedented national catastrophe. "How 'harmless' the misfortune of 1918 we found so difficult to bear and considered so impossible to top actually was compared to this terrible collapse," wrote the Göttingen historian Siegfried A. Kaehler in mid-May 1945.[2] Major Karl-Günther von Hase, who became a government spokesperson under the West German chancellors Konrad Adenauer, Ludwig Erhard, and Kurt Georg Kiesinger, later recalled the emotions he felt in a Moscow prison on May 9, 1945: "[They were] predominantly ones of great mourning over the total collapse of the German Reich, doubtless . . . the greatest tragedy of our national history. The 'finis Germaniae'—I couldn't see it otherwise at the time—had arrived."[3]

Ursula von Kardorff experienced something similar in the southeastern village of Jettingen where she had sought refuge. "So this is what defeat is like," the journalist wrote on May 7, when the unconditional surrender in Reims was announced. "We foolishly imagined it would be different, that is, we didn't imagine it at all. Everything, but everything, had to be better than Hitler. But liberation? What a strange word."[4]

When the war ended, Theodor Heuss, later a president of West Germany, was in the Heidelberg suburb of Handschuhsheim, where he fled with his wife, Elly Heuss-Knapp, to escape the intensifying bombardment of Berlin. On May 9, he wrote that Germany's capitulation was "one of the most terrible days in German history." He did, however, welcome the fact that unlike in 1918—when the centrist politician Matthias Erzberger had relieved the generals of the "dirty business" of surrender—the military commanders, Keitel and Jodl, had been forced to put their names to the capitulation. In 1945, there was no chance of a "stab-in-the-back" legend.[5] Four years later, when the Parliamentary Council ratified the West German constitution, the Basic Law, Heuss retrospectively characterized May 8, 1945, as the "most tragic and dubious paradox of history for every one of us," describing his compatriots' collective reaction as "relieved and devastated at once."[6] It would be four decades until a German president, Richard von Weizsäcker, in a landmark speech on the fortieth anniversary of the end of the war, would stake out an unambiguously positive position. "May 8 was a day of liberation," Weizsäcker said. "It liberated us all from the system of National Socialist violence with its contempt for human life."[7]

One group that genuinely felt liberated in the spring of 1945 consisted of the Hitler adversaries who had survived the terror following the attempted assassination of the dictator on July 20, 1944. Another, much larger group was composed of the millions of POWs and slave laborers who had been brought against their will to the Third Reich. The same was true, above all, for the inmates of the concentration camps, even though many were too exhausted to express any joy.

The memoirs of many Germans from the period reflect a mix of ambivalent feelings and thoughts: sadness at the loss of loved ones, homes, and hometowns; relief at having survived; a sense of respite after the endless nights of air raids; happiness at being able to sleep soundly; fear of the victors' potential vengeance and their own uncertain future; and feelings of emptiness after so much misplaced idealism and disappointed faith. "All our belief, all our sacrifices were in vain," lamented the university student Lore Walb on May 8. "Six years after Hitler's seizure of power, an unparalleled rise—and six years after that, our downfall. And they always bandied about the idea of a 'thousand-year Reich.'"[8]

Two emotions seldom encountered in these memoirs, though, were shame and remorse for the crimes of National Socialism. For the author Alfred Kantorowicz, in exile in New York City, there was no question that Nazi crimes went beyond anything previously imaginable. "This is what lies behind us," he noted during the night of May 8. "Twelve years. Twelve years in which the crimes of a millennium were accumulated."[9] In the initial days and weeks after Germany's surrender, radio stations and newspapers in Germany and around the world reported extensively about the horrors of the concentration camps and death camps. The revelations shocked not just the victors but also the vanquished, even if these reports only shed light on what Germans had repressed in the years before. "It is only our just deserts . . . that the horrors of the concentration camps are now thrown in our faces every day," wrote Mathilde Wolff-Mönckeberg from Hamburg. "We all must bear responsibility for the horrific crimes, and no one should be allowed to shunt it aside."[10]

But very few Germans were prepared to confront such monstrous facts and their own complicity in them. On the contrary, most reacted with emotional frigidity and a well-practiced, reflexive look away, as radio journalist Stephan Hermlin—later one of the most famous writers in Communist East Germany—observed about a screening in Frankfurt of a documentary film about Buchenwald and Dachau. "In the half-light of the projector, I saw how most people turned their faces to one side at the start of the film and stayed in that posture until the end."[11] "We didn't know!" became the catchphrase of German denialism. *Life* correspondent Margaret Bourke-White heard these words with such "monotonous frequency" in the spring of 1945 that they sounded in her ears "like a kind of national chant for Germany."[12]

The reverse side of this emotional frigidity was the solicitousness, indeed servile devotion, Germans expressed toward representatives of the victorious powers in each of the occupation zones. "People grovel before the three flags of the occupation as they did in 1933 before the red banner with the black spider in the white circle" remarked the writer and art historian Wilhelm Hausenstein in Tutzing, Bavaria, the day after Germany's surrender. "Subservient as peasants who know how to profit from the new situation!"[13] More than a few Allied observers viewed this unexpected obsequiousness with mixed feelings. "Embarrassingly friendly" was how no less than George Orwell described people in southern Germany in a report from early May 1945.[14]

On May 10, Thomas Mann's son Klaus, also a writer, arrived in Munich with the photographer John Tewksbury. Klaus had been anxious to learn how the Bavarian capital had survived the war, but the extent of the destruction exceeded his worst fears: "What was once considered the loveliest city in Germany and one of the most attractive in Europe has been transformed into a gigantic cemetery. In the entire center, without exaggeration, not a single building remains standing. There is nothing but piles of rubble. . . . I had difficulty finding my way through streets once familiar to me. It was like a bad dream."[15] His boyhood home at Poschingerstrasse 1 had not escaped damage. From a stenographer sitting on a third-story balcony and from the neighbors, Mann was shocked to hear that after 1933, the SS had sometimes used the building for their Lebensborn organization in which "Aryan" children were sired with specially selected women. "Our poor, amputated, abused house!" he reported to his father in a long letter on May 16, in which he advised Thomas not to return to Germany. "It will take years or decades to rebuild the cities. This lamentable nation will remain stunted and crippled for generations."[16]

THE DÖNITZ GOVERNMENT persisted for two weeks after the Wehrmacht's unconditional surrender, although it had no authority. Actual power was transferred to the Allied Control Council (ACC) under the leadership of American major general Lowell W. Rooks and British brigadier general Edward J. Foord. On May 12, the two men arrived with a staff of specialists in Flensburg, taking over the ship HMS *Patria* as their headquarters. Their main task was to ensure the terms of surrender were kept. On May 17, a Russian delegation under Major General Truskov joined the Americans and British.[17]

Meanwhile a powerless Dönitz and his associates went about the

On May 10, 1945, Klaus Mann inspected his family's half-destroyed
home at Munich's Poschingerstrasse 1. The image was taken by
the American photographer John Tewksbury.

routines of government business as though nothing had changed. Every
morning, Krosigk called together his cabinet in a former classroom. For
Speer, it was as though the "directing minister" were trying to make
up for lapses during the Third Reich, as Hitler had not convened the
cabinet since February 1938.[18] The ministers and state secretaries assid-
uously drew up memos and other documents, which the ACC received
with seeming interest but which had no effect whatsoever. The Dönitz
government existed merely in an insubstantial world of appearances, in
Speer's words, of "sham activity."[19]

On May 13, Rooks summoned Dönitz to the *Patria* for their first
meeting. On behalf of the Allied Supreme Command, Rooks informed
him that Keitel had been stripped of his position as head of the Wehr-

macht High Command and would henceforth be considered a POW. Jodl was temporarily named as successor.[20] Although Dönitz had pledged not to remain in his office any longer than honor demanded, he now refused to resign. In his memoirs he would claim that his intention had been, both during and after the war, to hang on to the office he had inherited "until elections were held or the Allies removed him by force."[21]

In the days following Germany's surrender, the Dönitz government continued to prove neither willing nor able to distance itself from the fallen regime. On May 8, traditional military greetings were reintroduced to the Wehrmacht in place of the Hitler salute, but it took an explicit ACC order for the Reich war flag to be lowered from the government building and a ban on the swastika to be instituted. On May 12, Dönitz refused to have photographs of Hitler removed from public offices. Two days later he ordered them taken down, but only from rooms where meetings with the occupational authorities were held, as a precautionary measure.[22] The admiral was particularly vehement about the right of German military men to continue to wear their stripes, ribbons, and medals. The German soldier, he insisted, could be "proud of (the) achievements of the Wehrmacht and his people during the war."[23] Even as late as May 18, he still resisted Allied demands that medals and the like be abolished: "The other side's tactic is to keep tightening the screws on us until he meets with resistance. The sooner such resistance starts, the more likely it is that Germany will preserve a certain remnant of its position. If despite our protest, the other side insists that military decorations not be worn, the OKW will have acted under duress and kept face."[24]

The continuity the Dönitz government sought to maintain with the Hitler regime was evident in the conclusions it reached during a "conversation about governmental questions" on May 9: "The basis for the further existence of the German people is the popular ethnic community created by National Socialism." The minutes of the cabinet meeting on May 15 emphasized that "the true popular ethnic community created by National Socialism must be preserved. The party insanity of the period before 1933 can never be allowed to take hold again."[25] The Dönitz government could not conceive of Germany becoming a parliamentary democracy again like other western countries. In this respect, too, it did not at all represent a new beginning, but rather the end of a long tradition of pre- and anti-democratic thinking in German history, which found its most extreme form in Hitler and Nazism.[26]

On May 11 and 16, the cabinet discussed reports of the horrors of the concentration camps. Even among this circle of high-ranking Nazi officials, several of whom were directly connected to the state apparatus of terror and murder, everyone claimed to have known nothing of Nazi crimes against humanity. They agreed that the Dönitz government would argue to the ACC "that neither the German Wehrmacht nor the German people had knowledge of these things and distanced themselves from them in every form."[27] In a letter to Eisenhower on May 16, Krosigk had the temerity to declare that "the concentration camps were fully cut off from the outside world, and everything that took place in these camps was kept top secret. Even leading German figures had no opportunity to learn about the actual conditions in the concentration camps."[28]

At first, the Allies seemed uncertain about what to do with the Dönitz government. Churchill was inclined to leave Dönitz in place as a top administrator under Allied control. "There must be some kind of force which will give orders which they will obey," he told his skeptical foreign secretary, Anthony Eden, on May 14. "Do you want to have a handle with which to manipulate this people, or just have to thrust your hands into the agitated antheap?"[29] But the Americans and Soviets rejected Churchill's argument, as they wanted to get rid of the Dönitz regime as soon as possible after the military conditions of the articles of surrender were fulfilled. As the May 20 edition of *Pravda* declared, "The defeated German warmongers are adapting to their new environment and trying with help from foreign powers to evade responsibility and retain key positions in the country—in order to continue their game of political intrigue by speculating about divisions within the Allied camp."[30]

On May 17, Eisenhower's political adviser Robert Murphy arrived in Flensburg. He was tasked with evaluating Dönitz's legitimacy as head of state. In lieu of an official document naming him to the post, all the admiral could present were the three radio messages broadcast by the Nazi regime in besieged Berlin between April 30 and May 1, and Murphy was deeply skeptical about the value of such evidence. His reaction strengthened the conviction among members of the Dönitz regime that their dismissal was but a matter of time.[31]

Indeed, Murphy quickly recommended that Dönitz's regime be brought to an end, emphasizing the fact that the admiral had not expressed any regret about the crimes Germany had committed. On May 19, after consulting with the Red Army High Command and securing its approval, Eisenhower ordered the 21st British Army Group to arrest the members of the Dönitz government and the Wehrmacht High Command and secure their papers.[32]

On the afternoon of May 22, Dönitz was told to appear before the ACC at 9:45 a.m. the next morning alongside Jodl and Friedeburg. The admiral knew what was in store. "Pack my bags," he told his adjutant. Punctual to the minute, the Germans arrived on board the *Patria*. This time there was no officer to greet them at the gangway. Instead, a large group of reporters had gathered. In the ship's bar, the Germans were kept waiting for several minutes before Rooks, followed by Foord and Truskov, entered the room. With no preamble, they declared that they had received orders from Eisenhower to place the Dönitz government and the Wehrmacht High Command under arrest. The Germans were to consider themselves from that moment on prisoners of war. When asked if he had anything to add, Dönitz said that he was sure any further words would be superfluous.[33]

While Dönitz and his fellow officers aboard the *Patria* were taken into custody in an orderly fashion, the arrests of the other members of the final government of the Third Reich and the military leadership at the Flensburg naval academy were less civil. British tanks, infantry, and military police surrounded the government building, and soldiers burst into the cabinet meeting Krosigk was holding, as he did every day at 10:00 a.m., with machine pistols drawn, yelling "hands up!" After being relieved of their papers and valuables, the prisoners were paraded in front of press photographers in the courtyard with their hands clasped behind their heads. Friedeburg, who witnessed the spectacle on his way back from the *Patria*, would poison himself shortly afterward.[34]

The next morning, the British surrounded Glücksburg Castle and arrested Albert Speer. Together with the other members of the Dönitz government and the military leadership, he was brought to the Flensburg police presidium, where all of them were carefully frisked. The British were apparently looking for ampules of poison to prevent more high-profile POWs from committing suicide.[35] Late that afternoon, the prisoners were taken in trucks to a landing strip, where two cargo planes were waiting to fly them to Luxembourg. Before the day was over, they were delivered to Mondorf-les-Bains, the spa town that the Allies had made into a central collection point for top representatives of the Nazi regime and the German military.

AS SPEER WOULD WRITE in his memoirs, "We stopped in front of a large building, the Palace Hotel in Mondorf, and were led into the lobby. From outside we had been able to see Göring and other members of the leadership of the Third Reich pacing back and forth. The whole hierarchy was there: ministers, field marshals, Reichsleiters, state secretaries, and generals. It was a ghostly experience to find all those who at the end had scattered like chaff in the wind reassembled here."[36]

For the Allies, the most important prisoner was Göring, the man

On May 23, 1945, British soldiers put an end to the activities of
the Dönitz government (from left to right: Albert Speer, Karl Dönitz,
and Alfred Jodl).

whom Hitler had once named his successor but who had fallen from
grace in the final days of the Third Reich for supposedly "betraying"
the Führer. The Reich marshal had surrendered to the 36th Infantry Division of the 7th US Army in southern Bavaria on May 8 and
had been presented to the international press three days later in Augsburg. Among those who were able to get a good look at him was Klaus
Mann, who wrote in *Stars and Stripes*, "He is far from being a half-
crazy clown. . . . He is shrewd, hard-boiled and calculating . . . He is
conciliatory, moderate, and yet avoids being undignified and too defer-
ential."[37] Göring had been brought to Mondorf on May 21.

By contrast, other top Nazis taken to Mondorf had tried to go
underground using false identities. Robert Ley, whom Hitler had
confirmed in his testament of April 29 as the director of the German
Labor Front and a member of the Reich cabinet, had been appre-

hended in a mountain hut near Berchtesgaden on May 15 by troops of the 101st Airborne Division. He was passing himself off as "Dr. Ernst Distelmeyer" but was positively identified by Nazi Party treasurer Franz Xaver Schwarz. After his arrest, this fanatical worshipper of the Führer declared that "life means nothing at all to me anymore. You can torture or beat me or impale me on a stake. But I will never doubt the greater deeds of Hitler."[38]

On May 22, the 101st Airborne also caught Julius Streicher, the editor of the anti-Semitic newspaper *Der Stürmer*. A former Gauleiter in northern Bavaria, he had withdrawn to the town of Waidring in Austria when he heard the news of Hitler's death. Streicher had been living under the name "Joseph Seiler," had grown a beard, and was passing the time as an amateur painter. During routine questioning, an American officer had said half-jokingly, "You look like Julius Streicher," whereupon the "Führer of Franconia" dropped his fake identity and replied, "Yes, I am he."[39] When he learned that Streicher and Ley had been arrested, the writer Erich Kästner noted in his diary that "it's like a costume rental agency. Or a gangster film. There are no limits to the lack of dignity."[40]

One of the final high-ranking Nazis the Allies captured was Hitler's longtime foreign minister Joachim von Ribbentrop. After failing to secure a role for himself in the Dönitz government, he had fled to Hamburg, rented an apartment on Schlüterstrasse 14 under the name Johann Riese, and revived pre-1933 business connections from his days as a champagne and spirits merchant. But the son of a wine dealer with whom Ribbentrop was friendly informed on the fugitive, and on June 14 he was arrested by British military police. They came up with a clever trick to ascertain his identity, arranging a meeting between Ribbentrop and his sister Ingeborg in the city's Four Seasons hotel. That ended any remaining doubts about Ribbentrop's identity, and he was immediately brought to Mondorf.[41]

The code name for the Mondorf interrogation camp was "Ashcan," and it was strictly off-limits to the public. The grounds of the Palace Hotel were surrounded by a five-meter-tall, barbed-wire fence hung with cloth and a camouflage net. Sentries with machine guns manned the guard towers. To prevent suicide attempts, the inmates were required to turn over razor blades, neckties, suspenders, and other personal effects. They had to eat using spoons only. Their rooms were spartan, with an army cot and straw mattress, a small table, and a chair. Their rations amounted to 1,550 calories per day, the same as ordinary German civilians at the time. The prisoners were allowed to talk to one another, move freely about the grounds, and sunbathe on the terrace. A delegation from the Soviet secret police, which was granted permission in June to interrogate the German officials, was surprised at how healthy they seemed, describing them as "tanned like spa guests."[42] Göring, who had been badly addicted to the morphine substitute Paracodin when he was brought to the hotel, was able to kick his habit and regain his physical strength. He was, as Krosigk recalled, "a magnet . . . always ready to be interviewed, to tell stories and to hand out souvenirs."[43]

Cliques soon formed among the prisoners. The military leaders—Keitel, Jodl, and Kesselring, among others—mostly kept to themselves, as did the "old streetfighters" Hans Frank, Robert Ley, and Thuringia Gauleiter Fritz Sauckel, Hitler's onetime "plenipotentiary for labor details." These two groups were largely avoided by the "bureaucrats" and diplomats Krosigk, Wilhelm Stuckart, Steengracht von Moyland, and Hans Heinrich Lammers, the former head of Hitler's Reich chancellery.[44] Everyone avoided Streicher, refusing to take meals with him and closing their chairs in circles whenever he entered the dining room.[45]

There was an absurd competition for the status of top Nazi between Dönitz and Göring. The Reich marshal still considered himself Hitler's designated successor, while the admiral insisted that he was the legitimate head of state. "There was a muffled battle between the new Chief of State and the deposed successor over the question of who should take precedence in the Palace Hotel of Mondorf (which had been emptied of all persons but ourselves and our guards) and who in general was top dog of us all," wrote Speer. "No agreement could be reached. Soon the two principals avoided meeting at the door, while each took the presiding seat at two different tables in the dining room."[46]

During the interrogations the Soviets carried out under American supervision in June 1945, none of these men admitted to being personally involved in the crimes of the Nazi regime. "If there were individual acts of brutality by soldiers at the front or in occupied countries," declared Göring, "I assure you that no one from the leadership of state, the general staff, or the government and the party ordered them."[47] Keitel even went so far as to describe the extensively planned sneak attack on the Soviet Union as a "preventative war." Like almost all German military commanders, he also tried to deny responsibility by arguing that he was merely following orders. In no way did he "make either military or political decisions," he claimed, but had only "carried out the commands of the Führer."[48]

In August 1945, the Americans revealed to the international press that they were using the Palace Hotel in Mondorf as a detention center for the Nazi elite, and reporters flocked to the town. The prisoners were required to assemble on the hotel steps for a photo shoot. One resulting photograph was published in American newspapers with the subtitle "The Class of 1945."[49] The only woman allowed to see the "Big Fifty-Two" (there were fifty-two Nazi prisoners in total) was Erika Mann, Thomas Mann's eldest daughter and, like her brother Klaus, a writer and newspaper correspondent. "I can't imagine a spookier adventure," she wrote to her mother, Katia. "Göring, Papen, Rosenberg, Streicher, Ley—*tout le horreur du monde* (including Keitel, Dönitz, Jodl, etc. . . .)—confined in hotel-turned-prison, out of which the inmates have made a true asylum."[50] In a story that appeared in London's *Evening Standard* on August 13, she wrote, "Actually . . . the entire gang

The imprisoned Nazi elite on the steps of the Palace Hotel in Mondorf-les-Bains in the summer of 1945 (in the middle: Hermann Göring).

were doing one and the same thing: writing, embellishing, and brooding over the parts they were busily preparing for *Der Tag*."[51]

Der Tag—the day—was the date set for the involuntary spa guests to appear in front of a court. Beginning in mid-August 1945, they were gradually transferred from Mondorf to Nuremberg, where they were scheduled to face trial in the city's Palace of Justice as war criminals. The lone exception was Speer. Several weeks after arriving at the Palace Hotel, he was sent to Versailles and then Kransberg Castle near Frankfurt, where the top technical specialists and scientists of the Third Reich were being interrogated.[52]

Among the members of the German leadership under Dönitz, Keitel and Jodl were the two sentenced to death at Nuremberg. The admiral himself received ten years in prison while Speer escaped with twenty years. The former armaments minister and Hitler protégé had skillfully presented himself as someone who had seen the light, accepting responsibility in general terms while rejecting any suggestion of direct involvement in Nazi crimes against humanity.[53] Krosigk received a ten-year sentence at the so-called Wilhelmstrasse Trial, named after a main street in Berlin's governmental district, but he was released from Landsberg Prison early in 1951. By the time he was actually convicted, Stuckart—another of the Wilhelmstrasse Trial defendants— had already served his time of three years, ten months, and twenty days after his arrest in May 1945 and was simply set free.

Before the arrest of Dönitz and his government, Nazi transportation minister Julius Dorpmüller had been flown to Le Chesnay near Paris, where he was assigned to help rebuild the railroad system for the American occupation zone. On July 5, after returning to Malente, he died of cancer. Nazi labor minister Franz Seldte was scheduled to face trial in Nuremberg, but he died in Fürth on April 1, 1947, before charges were issued. Former head of agriculture Herbert Backe was flown to the main Allied headquarters in Reims on May 15 to make use of his expertise in the provision of food, but once there he was arrested. He hanged himself in his Nuremberg prison cell on April 6, 1947. Otto Ohlendorf, who voluntarily testified for the prosecution in January 1946 in the main Nuremberg trial, was sentenced to death by hanging on April 10, 1948, for his role as the leader of Einsatzgruppe D in the Soviet Union.[54]

WHEN THE ALLIES CONQUERED Germany in the spring of 1945, they were astonished to find that they had arrived in a country apparently free of National Socialists. "No one is a Nazi," wrote the correspondent Martha Gellhorn for *Colliers*. "No one ever was. . . . We stand around looking blank and contemptuous and listen to this story without friendliness and certainly without respect. To see a whole nation passing the buck is not an enlightening spectacle."[55]

Hitler's German opponents were likewise appalled at how quickly ardent supporters of the regime completely changed their convictions. "No one now wants to have been 'part of it,'" noted the writer Wilhelm Hausenstein on May 6, 1945. "No one intended the party pin on his uniform to be taken seriously. Such characters are blossoming everywhere. It makes you sick."[56]

Immediately after the end of the war, there was great demand for documents nicknamed "Persil certificates" after a popular brand of detergent, Allied attestations that individuals were politically unproblematic. "They show up by the dozens trying to certify their Nazi past out of existence," wrote the journalist Ruth Andreas-Friedrich, a member of a resistance group in Berlin. "Everyone has a different excuse. Everyone suddenly has a Jew to whom he gave at least two kilos of bread or ten pounds of potatoes. Everyone listened to foreign radio. Everyone helped the persecuted. 'At great risk to my own life,' the majority of these posthumous good Samaritans add with proud modesty. Attestations of good character are the order of the hour."[57]

Ordinary Germans turned their backs on Nazism with unexpected speed, and the symbols and emblems of Hitler's regime disappeared from the surface of daily life, for the most part overnight. "An iconoclastic wave such as we have never seen is currently surging through Germany," observed Marta Hillers a week after her country's surrender.[58] In August 1945, the new regional councillor of Gunzenhausen, an early Nazi stronghold, noted in his first report after the demise of the Third Reich that "although the war has only been over for a few months, National Socialism is hardly ever spoken about, and when at all, only in a negative sense. There's no sign of any emblems of the National Socialist state among people who had displayed them in their homes."[59]

Meanwhile, the once-deified Führer was now a monster, a devil in human guise, against whose demonic, enthralling power there had been no defense. In this way, Germans avoided acknowledging their own complicity in National Socialism. If anyone was at fault for the nation's crimes, the logic ran, it was Hitler—or at most Hitler and the SS. Ordinary people had nothing to do with their atrocities and now had no desire to be bothered by the memory of those crimes. In the book *Der SS-Staat* (The SS State), the first on the concentration camps, from late 1945, the former Buchenwald inmate Eugen Kogon drew a series of depressing conclusions. Most Germans had not in fact redis-covered their consciences. On the contrary, few of them wanted to hear about the horrors of Nazism. "Reports from the concentration camps usually elicit at most head-shaking amazement," Kogon wrote. "They never become a subject for the rational mind, to say nothing of stirring people's emotions."[60]

Increasingly, the defeated came to consider themselves the true victims: they had suffered terribly in the air raids, had been driven from their homes, and were now being subjected to severe treatment by the Allies. "The Germans honestly believe—each for him- or her-self and without having to conspire with each other—that their ago-nies defy description," wrote Erika Mann in the spring of 1946.[61] The previous May, her brother Klaus had been dumbfounded by the self-righteousness, self-pity, and ignorance of his former compatriots. It seemed to him they had nothing to complain about except the unfor-tunate situation in which they found themselves: "They don't see why they of all people should have to suffer so much. 'What have we done to deserve this?' they will ask you—all wild-eyed naivete and bland innocence."[62]

Most Germans showed no interest in or sympathy for the immea-surable suffering they had inflicted in the territories they conquered and occupied. Instead, they devoted themselves with grim diligence to cleaning up the rubble and rebuilding. The writer Alfred Döblin registered his astonishment when he toured southern Germany in late 1945 that "people scurry back and forth like ants in a destroyed anthill, enraged and driven to work amid the ruins."[63]

The philosopher Hannah Arendt observed something similar two years later when she first returned to the country she had reluctantly left in 1933. In the "general lack of emotion" she encountered, and the "apparent heartlessness, sometimes covered over with cheap sentiment," Arendt diagnosed "the most conspicuous outward symptom of a deep-rooted, stubborn, and at times vicious refusal to face and come to terms with what really happened." She continued, "Watching the Germans busily stumble through the ruins of a thousand years of their own history, shrugging their shoulders at the destroyed landmarks or resentful when reminded of the deeds of horror that haunt the whole surrounding world, one comes to realize that busyness has become their chief defense against reality."[64]

The postwar "economic miracle" in the western occupation zones and later the Federal Republic of Germany encouraged Germans to flee the reality of their recent history. In the second German state that coalesced after the war, the Communist German Democratic Republic, the official policy of opposing capitalism, of which fascism was considered a form, gave Germans an excuse to forgo contemplating their own participation in National Socialism. An "inability to mourn" was how the psychologists Alexander and Margarete Mitscherlich characterized this process of repression in 1967.[65] In different ways, this deficit was equally manifest in both postwar German states.

EVENTS IN EARLY MAY 1945 ended the historical episode that began on January 30, 1933, when Hitler was handed control of Germany. "Twelve years of the Hitler regime has sufficed to cast a great power into ruin," the Norwegian correspondent Theo Findahl wrote from Berlin on May 9. "It's too overwhelming to comprehend."[66] Germany's military defeat and collapse were so complete, its physical destruction so vast, and its crimes so unprecedented that more than a few contemporary observers doubted whether this vanquished nation could have any future at all.

Yet May 8, 1945, marked not only an end but a beginning. Amid the exhaustion and bitterness, and despite the general lack of self-blame concerning the past, many Germans felt reinvigorated, almost euphoric, and ready to start over. Never again, the centrist politician Hildegard Hamm-Brücher recalled, would she "feel so intensely what it meant to be allowed to live on."[67] Joy at having survived the inferno released previously unknown energies—all the more so in that minority of Germans who had resisted the lure of National Socialism and maintained a sense of common human decency and a respect for the dignity of human life. "Twelve years lie behind us—something new is beginning," remarked Ruth Andreas-Friedrich. "Every step will be a new beginning. Every time we grasp something, it will have the value and importance of an act of foundation. The motto now is to take hold of and tackle what needs to be done."[68]

Andreas-Friedrich and other like-minded Germans had no intention of repressing the recent past as they industriously set about clearing away what had been destroyed. On the contrary, their industry reflected a desire to build a new political and social order that would respect individual liberties. What is more, the young frontline soldiers and antiaircraft auxiliaries who had grown up under the propaganda of the Third Reich did not, as the Allies feared, become so-called werewolves, fanatical underground partisans. Radically disillusioned by the shock they had been through, most of them rather than stubbornly rejecting change combined the drive for achievement they had learned before 1945 with a remarkable openness toward western democratic values and culture.[69]

Despite the harshness of everyday existence, which often pushed Germans to their limits just to ensure their own survival, a powerful thirst for culture arose after twelve years of conformity and intellectual barrenness. A previously closed cosmos of books, newspapers, visual arts, and music opened. Like never before and never again, people flooded theaters, concert halls, and cinemas. Alongside the destruction, self-justification, and inability to face their monstrous past and to mourn, the first tender shoots of a new start could be seen. It would, of course, take some time before democracy, which was reimplanted under the direction of the Americans, British, and French, took root among Germans in the western occupation zones. It is crucial to remember the extent of the devastation, material and moral, to understand how unlikely this democratic revival must have seemed on May 8, 1945, and what an achievement it is that Germans today live in a nation defined by stability, freedom, and peace. Perhaps now is the right time to recall this revival, this achievement, as well.

ACKNOWLEDGMENTS

First of all I'd like to thank the chief editor of the C.H. Beck publishing house in Germany, Detlef Felken, who came up with the idea for this book and cordially and attentively supervised the writing of the manuscript. I'm also grateful to Alexander Gröller for his careful editing and Janna Rösch for coordinating the production of the German version.

I'd also like to thank Mirjam Zimmer, Kerstin Wilhelms, and their colleagues at the fact-checking department of *Zeit* newspaper as well as Dorothee Mateika and Christine Riemer at the Forschungsstelle für Zeitgeschichte research center in Hamburg. All of them were enormously helpful in procuring the literature I needed.

My greatest gratitude, though, goes out to my wife, Gudrun, and my son, Sebastian. Without our many inspiring conversations and their critical remarks, this book, too, would never have been written.

I would like to dedicate this book to my mother, who died in 2004 and who navigated with great bravura through the final years of the Second World War and the initial years thereafter with her five sons. As the bombing of Berlin began to intensify in 1942 and 1943, she left the city with us children, going to a village in the Lüneburg Heath. I can no longer remember the end of the war. I was barely two years old at the time. But I can recall a scene from 1947 or 1948 of a British military patrol driving through the village and the soldiers tossing candy to me and fellow children by the side of the street. It tasted great!

HAMBURG, NOVEMBER 2019

NOTES

PREFACE: THE LAST WEEK OF THE THIRD REICH

1 Erich Kästner, *Notabene 45 ein Tagebuch* (Munich: dtv, 1989), 130 (May 7, 1945). This book, first published in 1961, is a revised version of the author's original notes. See also the introduction by Sven Hanuschek in Erich Kästner, *Das blaue Buch: Geheimes Kriegstagebuch 1941–1945* (Zürich: Atrium, 2018), 25–31. All translations in the English edition, unless otherwise noted, are those of the present translator.

2 Martin Sabrow, "Die 'Stunde Null' als Zeiterfahrung," *Aus Politik und Zeitgeschichte* 70, no. 4–5 (2020), 31–38. On the conceit of a "zero hour" in the biographies of politicians, see Volker Depkat, *Lebenswelten und Zeitenwenden: Deutsche Politiker und die Erfahrungendes 20. Jahrhunderts* (Munich: Oldenbourg, 2007), 189–196.

3 Anonymous [Marta Hillers], *A Woman in Berlin: Diary 20 April 1945 to 22 June 1945*, trans. Philip Boehm (New York: Harcourt Grace Jovanovich, 1954), 177.

4 On temporal "no man's land," see Harald Jähner, *Wolfszeit: Deutschland und die Deutschen 1945–1955* (Berlin: Rowohlt Berlin, 2019), 20.

5 Friedrich Kellner, *My Opposition: The Diary of Friedrich Kellner: A German against the Third Reich*, trans. and ed. Robert Scott Kellner (Cambridge: Cambridge University Press, 2018), 405.

6 Reinhold Maier, *Ende und Wende: Briefe und Tagebuchaufzeichnungen 1944–1946* (Wuppertal: Fingscheidt, 2004), 232.

7 See Richard Bessel, *Germany 1945: From War to Peace* (London: Harper Perennial, 2009), 134 f.

8 Ivone Kirkpatrick, *Im inneren Kreis: Erinnerungen eines Diplomaten* (Berlin: Propyläen, 1964), 167 (English ed., *The Inner Circle: Memoirs* [London: Macmillan, 1959], 191). See Jähner, *Wolfszeit*, 61 ff. h.

9 See Stefan-Ludwig Hoffmann, "Besiegte, Besatzer, Beobachter: Das Kriegsende im Tagebuch," in *Demokratie im Schatten der Gewalt: Geschichten des Privaten im deutschen Nachkrieg*, ed. Daniel Fulda et al. (Göttingen: Wallstein, 2010), 25–55; and Susanne zur Nieden, *Alltag im Ausnahmezustand: Frauentagebücher im zerstörten Deutschland* (Berlin: Orlanda Frauenverlag, 1993).

PROLOGUE: APRIL 30, 1945

1 On the general circumstances of Hitler's suicide, see Volker Ullrich, *Hitler: Downfall 1939–1945*, trans. Jefferson Chase (London: Bodley Head, 2020), 595 ff.; Joachim Fest, *Der Untergang: Hitler und das Ende des Dritten Reiches* (Berlin: Alexander Fest, 2002), 128 ff.; and Anton Joachimsthaler, *Hitlers Ende: Legenden und Dokumente* (Munich/Berlin: Herbig, 1995), 201 ff.

2 Ernst Günther Schenck, *Patient Hitler: Eine medizinische Biographie* (Düsseldorf: Droste, 1989), 400.

3 See Joachimsthaler, *Hitlers Ende*, 205–209.

4 See ibid., 210–213; and *Das Buch Hitler: Geheimdossier des NKWD für Josef W. Stalin, zusammengestellt aufgrund der Verhörprotokolle des Persönlichen Adjutanten Hitlers, Otto Günsche, und des Kammerdieners Heinz Linge*, ed. Henrik Eberle and Matthias Uhl (original ed., Moscow, 1948–49; Bergisch-Gladbach: Lübbe, 2005), 444 f. (page reference is to the 2005 edition).

5 Traudl Junge, *Bis zur letzten Stunde: Hitlers Sekretärin erzählt ihr Leben* (Munich: Claassen, 2002), 205.

6 See the facsimile in Joachimsthaler, *Hitlers Ende*, 192.

7 Hans Baur, *Ich flog Mächtige der Erde* (Kempten: Albert Pröpste, 1956), 275 f.

8 Heinz Linge, *Bis zum Untergang: Als Chef des persönlichen Dienstes bei Hitler*, ed. Werner Maser (Munich: Herbig, 1982), 286 f. See also Eberle and Uhl, *Das Buch Hitler*, 446 f.

9 Junge, *Bis zur letzten Stunde*, 206.

10 Reproduced in Joseph Goebbels, *Tagebücher 1945: Die letzten Aufzeichnungen* (Hamburg: Hoffmann und Campe, 1977), 549 f. The letter was brought by the pilot and Hitler admirer Hanna Reitsch on April 28 from Berlin and after several detours reached Harald Quandt, who was a British POW in northern Africa. See Joachim Scholtyseck, *Der Aufstieg der Quandts: Eine deutsche Unternehmerdynastie* (Munich: Beck, 2011), 252.

11 See Joachimsthaler, *Hitlers Ende*, 221 f.

12 See the comparison of the eyewitness testimony in ibid., 230–270; and Eberle and Uhl, *Das Buch Hitler*, 447 f.

13 See Joachimsthaler, *Hitlers Ende*, 288–332; and Eberle and Uhl, *Das Buch Hitler*, 448 f.

14 See Antony Beevor, *The Fall of Berlin 1945* (New York: Viking, 2002), 370–385; and Tony Le Tissier, "Chronik der Schlacht um Berlin," in *Der Todeskampf der Reichshauptstadt*, ed. Bengt von zur Mühlen (Berlin-Kleinmachnow: Chronos, 1994), 79–86.

15 See Jörg Müllner, "Wie Russlands Fahne 1945 auf den Reichstag kam," *Die Welt*, January 18, 2008.

16 See Jewgeni Chaldej, *Der bedeutende Augenblick*, ed. Ernst Volland and Heinz Krimmer (Leipzig: Neuer Europa Verlag, 2008).

17 See the account by war reporter Konstantin Simonov in *Der Kampf um Berlin 1945 in Augenzeugenberichten*, ed. Peter Gosztony (Düsseldorf: Karl Rauch, 1970), 389.

18 A Russian major wrote to his sister on May 9, 1945, "There are numerous messages from our glorious Russian soldiers and officers written on the walls with chalk, coal, and carbon pencil. Some read: 'Here were men of Stalingrad—signatures,' 'Here stood a Russian soldier from Smolensk—signature,' 'We're at the Reichstag. Everything is fine. Ivan Petrov May 9, 1945.'" See *Rotarmisten schreiben aus Deutschland: Briefe von der Front (1945) und historische Analysen*, ed. Elke Scherstjanoi (Munich: Saur, 2004), 172.

19 Marianne Feuersenger, *Im Vorzimmer der Macht: Aufzeichnungen aus dem Wehrmachtführungsstab und Führerhauptquartier 1940–1945* (Munich: Herbig, 1999), 271.

20 Reprinted in *München und der Nationalsozialismus: Katalog des NS-Dokumentations zentrums München*, ed. Winfried Nerdinger (Munich: Beck, 2015), 298.

21 Facsimile in ibid., 301. See also David Clay Large, *Hitlers München: Aufstieg und Fall der Hauptstadt der Bewegung* (Munich: Beck, 1998), 431 f. (English ed., *Where Ghosts Walked: Munich's Road to the Third Reich* [New York: W.W. Norton, 1997], 346); and Wolfgang Görl, "Als die Amerikaner München befreiten," *Süddeutsche Zeitung*, April 24, 2015.

22 Facsimile of the program in Nerdinger, ed., *München und der Nationalsozialismus*, 297. On the FAB, see Veronika Diem, *Die Freiheitsaktion Bayern: Ein Aufstand in der Endphase des NS-Regimes* (Kallmünz: Lassleben, 2013). For a highly critical account of the "insufficiently prepared and dilettantish attempt at an uprising," see Klaus-Dietmar Henke, *Die amerikanische Besetzung Deutschlands* (Munich: Oldenbourg, 1995), 854 ff.

23 Facsimile of the appeal in Nerdinger, ed., *München und der Nationalsozialismus*, 296.

24 See Henke, *Die amerikanische Besetzung*, 859 f.; and Frederick Taylor, *Zwischen Krieg und Frieden: Die Besetzung und Entnazifizierung Deutschlands 1944–1946* (Berlin: Berlin Verlag, 2011), 137–141 (English ed., *Exorcising Hitler: The Occupation and Denazification of Germany* [New York: Bloomsbury, 2011], 89–92).

25 The Seventh United States Army, *Report of Operations France and Germany 1944–1945*, vol. 3 (Heidelberg: Aloys Graf, 1946), 837.

26 *Kriegstagebuch einer jungen Nationalsozialistin: Die Aufzeichnungen Wolfhilde von Königs 1939–1946*, ed. Sven Keller (Berlin/Boston: De Gruyter, 2015), 213.

27 See Görl, "Als die Amerikaner." As a press officer after the war, Langendorf was responsible for issuing the first newspaper licenses and was heavily involved in founding the *Süddeutsche Zeitung*, one of postwar Germany's most respected newspapers. See Knud von Harbou, *Als Deutschland seine Seele retten wollte: Die Süddeutsche Zeitung in den Gründerjahren nach 1945* (Munich: dtv, 2015), 24 f.

28 Edgar Kupfer-Koberwitz, *Dachauer Tagebücher: Die Aufzeichnungen des Häftlings 24814* (Munich: Kindler, 1997), 451 f.

29 Ludwig Eiber, "Gewalt im KZ Dachau: Vom Anfang eines Terrorsystems," in *Das Jahr 1933: Die nationalsozialistische Machteroberung und die deutsche Gesellschaft*, ed. Andreas Wirsching (Göttingen: Wallstein, 2009), 178.

30   See Gabriele Hammerstein, "Das Kriegsende in Dachau," in *Kriegsende 1945: Verbrechen, Katastrophen, Befreiungen in nationaler und internationaler Perspektive*, ed. Bernd-A. Rusinek (Göttingen: Wallstein, 2004), 27–45, on 28; *Der Ort des Terrors: Geschichte der nationalsozialistischen Konzentrationslager*, vol. 2, ed. Wolfgang Benz and Barbara Distel (Munich: Beck, 2005), 268–271; Nikolaus Wachsmann, *KL: Die Geschichte der nationalsozialistischen Konzentrationslager* (Munich: Pantheon, 2015), 682–684; and Henke, *Die amerikanische Besetzung*, 862–931.

31   Henke, *Die amerikanische Besetzung*, 905–913; Benz and Distel, eds., *Ort des Terrors*, vol. 2, 269 f.; and Daniel Blatman, *Die Todesmärsche 1944/45: Das letzte Kapitel des nationalsozialistischen Massenmords* (Hamburg: Rowohlt, 2011), 334–337 (English ed., *The Death Marches: The Final Phase of Nazi Genocide*, trans. Chaya Galai [Cambridge, MA: Belknap, 2011], 206–208).

32   Kupfer-Koberwitz, *Dachauer Tagebücher*, 444.

33   "Lt. Col. Felix Sparks Dachau Liberator's Speech," remember.org, https://remember .org/witness/sparks; and "Dachau and Liberation: Personal Account by Felix L. Sparks Brigadier General," remember.org, https://remember.org/witness/sparks2.

34   Hammerstein, "Kriegsende in Dachau," 41 f.; Henke, *Die amerikanische Besetzung*, 919–922; and Keith Lowe, *Der wilde Kontinent: Europa in den Jahren der Anarchie 1943–1950* (Stuttgart: Klett-Cotta, 2014), 113 f. (English ed., *Savage Continent: Europe in the Aftermath of World War II* [New York: Macmillan, 2012], 83). Another detailed account of events is contained in Alex Kershaw's biography of Felix Sparks, *Der Befreier: Die Geschichte eines amerikanischen Soldaten im Zweiten Weltkrieg* (Munich: dtv, 2014), 309–345 (English ed., *The Liberator: One World War II Soldier's 500-Day Odyssey from the Beaches of Sicily to the Gates of Dachau* [New York: Crown, 2012], 267–301).

35   Kupfer-Koberwitz, *Dachauer Tagebücher*, 459.

36   Reproduced in *Die Niederlage 1945: Aus dem Kriegstagebuch des Oberkommandos der Wehrmacht*, ed. Percy Ernst Schramm (Munich: dtv dokumente, 1982), 419; and Walter Lüdde-Neurath, *Regierung Dönitz die letzten Tage des Dritten Reiches*, 3rd ed. (Göttingen: Wallstein, 1964), 130.

37   See Ullrich, *Hitler: Downfall*, 592–594.

38   Karl Dönitz, *Zehn Jahre und zwanzig Tage* (Frankfurt/Bonn: Athenäum, 1963), 434. On Dönitz's final day in prison on September 30, 1956, his fellow inmate Albert Speer denied having suggested during his last visit to the "Führer bunker" on April 27, 1945, that Dönitz succeed Hitler. He had merely made positive remarks about the job Dönitz was doing in the "northern realm," Speer said. See Speer, *Spandauer Tagebücher* (Berlin/Munich: Propyläen, 2002), 445. Nonetheless, Dönitz insisted in his memoirs that Speer had recommended him.

39   Ullrich, *Hitler: Downfall*, 581 f.

40   Ibid., 589 f.

41   Lüdde-Neurath, *Regierung Dönitz*, 42 f.; and Dönitz, *Zehn Jahre*, 433.

42   Reimer Hansen, *Das Ende des Dritten Reiches: Die deutsche Kapitulation 1945* (Stutt-

gart: Klett, 1966), 103. In interrogations in Mondorf, Dönitz also declared, "Hitler was an extraordinary personality." See *Verhört: Die Befragungen deutscher Generale und Offiziere durch die sowjetischen Geheimdienste 1945–1952*, ed. Wassili S. Christoforow et al. (Berlin/Boston: de Gruyter, 2015), 66.

43 Heinrich Schwendemann, "'Deutsche Menschen vor der Vernichtung durch den Bolschewismus zu retten': Das Programm der Regierung Dönitz und der Beginn einer Legendenbildung," in *Kriegsende 1945 in Deutschland*, ed. Jörg Hillmann and John Zimmermann (Munich: Oldenbourg, 2002), 9–33, on 9.

44 Lüdde-Neurath, *Regierung Dönitz*, 29 f.

45 *"Als der Krieg zu Ende war": Erinnerungen an den 8. Mai 1945*, ed. Hans Sarkowicz (Frankfurt/Leipzig: Insel, 1995), 112 f.

46 Dönitz, *Zehn Jahre*, 436. See also Lüdde-Neurath, *Regierung Dönitz*, 89 f.; and Marlis G. Steinert, *Die 23 Tage der Regierung Dönitz* (Düsseldorf/Vienna: Econ, 1967), 88 f.

47 See "Kriegstagebuch des Führungsstabes Nord (A), 30. 4. 1945," in *Kriegstagebuch des Oberkommandos der Wehrmacht*, vol. 4, part 2, ed. Percy Ernst Schramm (Herrsching: Pawlak, 1982), 1468 (henceforth cited as *KTB-OKW*).

MAY 1, 1945

1 Hans Refior, "Mein Berliner Tagebuch 1945," in Mühlen, ed., *Todeskampf*, 132.

2 Wassilij Tschuikow, *Das Ende des Dritten Reiches* (Munich: Wilhelm Goldmann, 1966), 184 f. (English ed., *The Fall of Berlin*, trans. Ruth Kisch [New York: Holt, Rinehart and Winston, 1968], 217.) See also *Hitlers Tod: Die letzten Tage im Führerbunker*, ed. Ulrich Völklein (Göttingen: Wallstein, 1998), 48 f., which puts the time of Hitler's death at 3:30 p.m.

3 See Ullrich, *Hitler: Downfall*, 399 f., 496 f.

4 Refior, "Tagebuch," 132; and Rochus Misch, *Der letzte Zeuge: Ich war Hitlers Telefonist, Kurier und Leibwächter* (Zürich/Munich: Pendo, 2008), 225 f.

5 Artur Axmann, "Das Ende im Führerbunker," *Stern*, May 2, 1965, cited in Gosztony, ed., *Kampf um Berlin*, 350.

6 Junge, *Bis zur letzten Stunde*, 208.

7 See the account by Theodor von Dufving, "Die Kapitulationsverhandlungen vom 30. April bis zum 2. Mai 1945," in Mühlen, ed., *Todeskampf*, 168 f.

8 Tschuikow, *Ende*, 183. *The Fall of Berlin 1945*, 215.

9 See the extensive description of the negotiations in Tschuikow, *Ende*, 185–214. *The Fall of Berlin 1945*, 218–250.

10 Reproduced in Eberle and Uhl, eds., *Das Buch Hitler*, 463. See also Völklein, ed., *Hitlers Tod*, 46 f.

11 Georgy Zhukov, *The Memoirs of Marshal Zhukov*, trans. APN (London: Jonathan Cape, 1971), 619, https://archive.org/stream/in.ernet.dli.2015.110648/2015.110648 .The-Memoirs-Of-Marshal-Zhukov_djvu.txt.

12 Dufving, "Kapitulationsverhandlungen," 173–175.

13 Axmann, "Ende," 363.

14 Reproduced in Schramm, ed., *KTB-OKW*, vol. 4, part 2, 1469. See also Schramm, ed., *Niederlage*, 419. The radiogram message was sent at 3:27 p.m.

15 Facsimile of Speer's draft in Heinrich Breloer (with Rainer Zimmer), *Die Akte Speer: Spuren eines Kriegsverbrechers* (Berlin: Propyläen, 2006), 319.

16 On Speer's ambiguous role toward the end of the war, see Magnus Brechtken, *Albert Speer: Eine deutsche Karriere* (Munich: Siedler, 2017), 276–280; and Ullrich, *Hitler: Downfall*, 556–561.

17 Reprinted in Schramm, ed., *Niederlage*, 420. See also Lüdde-Neurath, *Regierung Dönitz*, 130. The telegram was sent at 7:40 a.m. from Berlin.

18 See Hansen, *Ende*, 95; and Jochen von Lang, *Der Sekretär: Martin Bormann—Der Mann, der Hitler beherrschte* (Stuttgart: DVA, 1977), 336.

19 Reprinted in Schramm, ed., *Niederlage*, 420. See also Lüdde-Neurath, *Regierung Dönitz*, 130.

20 Dönitz, *Zehn Jahre*, 444; and Albert Speer, *Erinnerungen* (Frankfurt/Berlin: Ullstein, 1993), 490.

21 Lars Lüdicke, *Constantin von Neurath: Eine politische Biographie* (Paderborn: Ferdinand Schöningh, 2014), 558.

22 Steinert, *23 Tage*, 107. See also Lüdde-Neurath, *Regierung Dönitz*, 82.

23 Lutz Graf Schwerin von Krosigk, *Es geschah in Deutschland: Menschenbilder unseres Jahrhunderts*, 3rd ed. (Tübingen/Stuttgart: Rainer Wunderlich, 1952), 366. See also Krosigk, *Memoiren* (Stuttgart: Seewald, 1977), 242 f.

24 See Steinert, *23 Tage*, 89; and Krosigk, *Es geschah*, 374.

25 See Lüdde-Neurath, *Regierung Dönitz*, 53–60; Steinert, *23 Tage*, 172 f.; and Herbert Kraus, "Karl Dönitz und das Ende des 'Dritten Reiches,'" in *Ende des Dritten Reiches—Ende des Zweiten Weltkriegs: Eine perspektivische Rückschau*, ed. Hans-Erich Volkmann (Munich/Zürich: Piper, 1995), 1–23, on 11.

26 Friedrich Karl Engel, "1. Mai 1945: Hitlers Tod in Rundfunksendungen," *Funkgeschichte* 41 (2018), pdf 1 f. https://www.abruckner.com/Data/articles/articlesgerman/engel-friedrich-hitlers-death-as-announced-on-the-/Hitlers-Tod-in-Rundfunksen Dokumentationszentrums dungen_2019-01-03.pdf.

27 All quotes from Lüdde-Neurath, *Regierung Dönitz*, 132.

28 Engel, "1. Mai 1945," 1.

29 Reprinted in Lüdde-Neurath, *Regierung Dönitz*, 133. Keitel suggested this wording because he considered it impossible under the circumstances to have the Wehrmacht swear a new oath of loyalty. See *Generalfeldmarschall Keitel: Verbrecher oder Offizier? Erinnerungen, Briefe, Dokumente des Chefs OKW*, ed. Walter Görlitz (Göttingen/Berlin/Frankfurt: S. Bublies, 1961), 372.

30 Kästner, *Notabene*, 105.

31 Sönke Neitzel, *Abgehört: Deutsche Generäle in britischer Kriegsgefangenschaft 1942–1945* (Berlin: Propyläen, 2005), 205–210.

32 Ursula von Kardorff, *Berliner Aufzeichnungen 1942 bis 1945*, ed. Peter Hartl

(Munich: Beck, 1992), 319 (English ed., *Diary of a Nightmare: Berlin 1942–1945*, trans. by Ewan Butler. [New York: John Day Company, 1966], 190).

33   Albert Speer, *Inside the Third Reich: Memoirs by Albert Speer* (New York: Macmillan, 1970), 488–489. In her pocket calendar, Kardorff simply wrote, "Hitler is dead. Most unsettling. I'm weeping." *Berliner Aufzeichnungen*, 320.

34   Brechtken, *Albert Speer*, 295 ff.; and Volker Ullrich, "Zum Dank ein Bild vom Führer," *Die Zeit*, May 16, 2016.

35   William L. Shirer, "San Francisco, Tuesday, May 1," in *End of a Berlin Diary* (New York: Rosetta Books, 2016), Kindle ed., n.p.

36   Thomas Mann, *Tagebücher 1944–1. 4. 1946*, ed. Inge Jens (Frankfurt: Fischer, 1986), 187.

37   Sebastian Haffner, *Germany Jekyll and Hyde* (London: Secker & Warburg, 1940), 24. See also Thomas Mann, *Tagebücher 1940–1943*, ed. Peter de Mendelssohn (Frankfurt: Fischer, 1982), 76: "Read with great interest in an English book called *Germany Jekyll and Hyde* by S. Haffner (pseudonym?), excellent."

38   Joseph Goebbels, *Die Tagebücher*, part II, vol. 15, ed. Elke Fröhlich (Munich: Saur, 1995), 383. See Ullrich, *Hitler: Downfall*, 550–552; and Volker Ullrich, "Seine letzte Rolle," *Die Zeit*, October 4, 2018.

39   Facsimile in Mühlen, ed., *Todeskampf*, 150.

40   Hugh R. Trevor-Roper, *Hitlers letzte Tage* (Frankfurt/Berlin: Ullstein, 1995), 181 f. (English ed., *The Last Days of Hitler* [Chicago: University of Chicago Press, 1992], 217). See also Junge, *Bis zur letzten Stunde*, 204.

41   Fest, *Untergang*, 168.

42   Axmann, "Ende," 350f.

43   Misch, *Letzte Zeuge*, 227.

44   See also the interrogation record of the administration of the intelligence organization SMERSH of the 1st Belarussian Front on May 7, 1945, reprinted in Lew A. Besymenski, "Das Ende der Familie Goebbels," *Die Zeit*, August 16, 1968, and excerpted in Völklein, ed., *Hitlers Tod*, 76–79.

45   See the interrogation record of May 19, 1945, reprinted in Besymenski, "Ende der Familie Goebbels," and excerpted in Völklein, ed., *Hitlers Tod*, 79 f.

46   Junge, *Bis zur letzten Stunde*, 212; and Baur, *Ich flog Mächtige*, 282.

47   Misch, *Letzte Zeuge*, 232.

48   Trevor-Roper, *Hitlers letzte Tage*, 203; *The Last Days of Hitler*, 242.

49   Eberle and Uhl, eds., *Das Buch Hitler*, 455. This account conforms to the recollections of master electro-mechanic Johannes Hentschel. See Misch, *Letzte Zeuge*, 233.

50   Coroner's protocol May 7 and 9, 1945. Reproduced in Völklein, ed., *Hitlers Tod*, 106–131, on 116, 121.

51   Völklein, ed., *Hitlers Tod*, 141.

52   See Scholtyseck, *Aufstieg der Quandts*, 252 f., 770. On the "Naumann circle," see Norbert Frei, *Vergangenheitspolitik: Die Anfänge der Bundesrepublik und die NS-Vergangenheit* (Munich: Beck, 1996), 361 ff.

53 Lew Besymenski, *Die letzten Notizen von Martin Bormann: Ein Dokument und sein Verfasser* (Stuttgart: DVA, 1974), 272.

54 Junge, *Bis zur letzten Stunde*, 210 f., 212.

55 Trevor-Roper, *Hitlers letzte Tage*, 203 f. See also Eberle and Uhl, eds., *Das Buch Hitler*, 454. *The Last Days of Hitler*, 243.

56 For differing accounts of the makeup of the various groups, see Trevor-Roper, *Hitlers letzte Tage*, 204; Junge, *Bis zur letzten Stunde*, 213; Eberle and Uhl, eds., *Das Buch Hitler*, 854; and Lang, *Der Sekretär*, 339. *The Last Days of Hitler*, 243–44.

57 Junge, *Bis zur letzten Stunde*, 213.

58 Lang, *Der Sekretär*, 402 ff.; and Volker Koop, *Martin Bormann: Hitlers Vollstrecker* (Vienna/Cologne: Böhlau, 2012), 314–316.

59 Florian Huber, *Kind versprich mir, dass du dich erschießt: Der Untergang der kleinen Leute*, 4th ed. (Berlin: Berlin Verlag, 2015), 139. See also 9–77.

60 See, among others, *Vernichtungskrieg: Verbrechen der Wehrmacht 1941–1944*, ed. Hannes Heer and Klaus Naumann (Hamburg: Hamburger Edition, 1995).

61 See Bernhard Fisch, *Nemmersdorf, Oktober 1944: Was in Ostpreußen tatsächlich geschah* (Berlin: Edition Ost, 1997).

62 Goebbels, *Tagebücher*, part II, vol. 14, 10.

63 Cited in Werner Zeidler, *Kriegsende im Osten: Die Rolle der Roten Armee und die Bevölkerung Deutschlands östlich der Oder und Neiße 1944/45* (Munich: de Gruyter, 1996), 138. On the behavior of the Red Army when it invaded Germany, see also Catherine Merridale, *Ivan's War: Life and Death in the Red Army, 1939–1945* (London: Faber and Faber, 2005), 259-28; and Normann N. Naimark, *Die Russen in Deutschland: Die sowjetische Besatzungszone 1945 bis 1949* (Berlin: Propyläen, 1997), 94–98.

64 Huber, *Kind versprich mir*, 51.

65 Ibid., 59 f.

66 Somewhere between five hundred and a thousand would thus be a conservative estimate. See Huber, *Kind versprich mir*, 136–138.

67 See Christian Goeschel, *Selbstmord im Dritten Reich* (Berlin: Suhrkamp, 2011), 241–255; and Richard J. Evans, *Das Dritte Reich*, vol. 3 (Munich: DVA, 2008), 907–915 (English ed., *The Third Reich at War* [New York: Penguin, 2009], 728–734).

68 *Meldungen aus dem Reich: Die geheimen Lageberichte des Sicherheitsdienstes der SS*, vol. 17, ed. Heinz Boberach (Herrsching: Pawlak, 1984), 6737.

69 *"Gruppe Ulbricht" in Berlin April bis Juni 1945: Von den Vorbereitungen im Sommer 1944 bis zur Wiedergründung der KPD im Juni 1945—Eine Dokumentation*, ed. Gerhard Keiderling (Berlin: Berlin Verlag, 1993), 348.

70 See Mario Frank, *Walter Ulbricht: Eine deutsche Biografie* (Berlin: Siedler, 2001), 137 ff.

71 Wolfgang Leonhard, "Mai 1945: Erinnerungen eines Mitglieds der 'Gruppe Ulbricht,'" in *Das Jahr 1945: Brüche und Kontinuitäten*, ed. Christine Krauss and Daniel Küchenmeister (Berlin: Dietz, 1995), 50.

72 Keiderling, ed., *Gruppe Ulbricht*, 130–134, on 131 f., also 26–28; and Frank, *Walter Ulbricht*, 174 f.

73 See Frank, *Walter Ulbricht*, 177; and Wilfried Loth, *Stalins ungeliebtes Kind: Warum Moskau die DDR nicht wollte* (Berlin: Rowohlt, 1994), 20 ff.

74 Keiderling, ed., *Gruppe Ulbricht*, 121.

75 Ibid., 29. Frank, *Walter Ulbricht*, 176.

76 Keiderling, ed., *Gruppe Ulbricht*, 182, also 30 f., 42; and Frank, *Walter Ulbricht*, 178.

77 Keiderling, ed., *Gruppe Ulbricht*, 260–265, on 260.

78 Ibid., 273.

79 Wolfgang Leonhard, *Die Revolution entlässt ihre Kinder* (Cologne: Kiepenheuer & Witsch, 1987), 297–301; and Keiderling, ed., *Gruppe Ulbricht*, 727–732.

80 Keiderling, ed., *Gruppe Ulbricht*, 277 f.

81 Leonhard, *Revolution*, 292.

82 Ibid., 301–305; Leonhard, "Im Dienste Walter Ulbrichts," in *Die Stunde Null: Erinnerungen an Kriegsende und Neuanfang*, ed. Gustav Trampe (Stuttgart: DVA, 1995), 272 f.; Keiderling, ed., *Gruppe Ulbricht*, 39; and Richard Gyptner, "Am 1. Mai 1945 nach Bruchmühle," ibid., 699 f.

83 Leonhard, *Revolution*, 308.

84 Theo Findahl, *Letzter Akt: Berlin 1933–1945* (Hamburg: Hammerich Lesser, 1946), 180, 182.

85 Peter Merseburger, *Willy Brandt 1913–1992: Visionär und Realist* (Stuttgart/Munich: DVA, 2002), 57–221.

86 Willy Brandt, *Erinnerungen* (Berlin/Frankfurt: Ullstein, 1989), 139 f. See also the slightly different version in Brandt, *Links und frei: Mein Weg 1930–1950* (Hamburg: Knaur, 1982), 375.

87 Willy Brandt, *Verbrecher und andere Deutsche: Ein Bericht aus Deutschland 1946*, rev. Einhart Lorenz (Bonn: J. H. W. Dietz Nachf. Verlag, 2007), 7–33.

88 "Thus passes the glory of the world." Astrid Lindgren, *War Diaries: 1939–1945*, trans. Sarah Death (New Haven: Yale University, 2016), 203.

MAY 2, 1945

1 Engel, "1. Mai 1945," 1.

2 Christian Graf von Krockow, "Der deutschen Grenze entgegen," in Trampe, ed., *Stunde Null*, 250.

3 Gerd Schmückle, "Mitgegangen, mitgefangen . . . ," in Trampe, ed., *Stunde Null*, 57.

4 Kardorff, *Berliner Aufzeichnungen*, 320 (May 2, 1945).

5 Ruth Andreas-Friedrich, *Schauplatz Berlin: Ein deutsches Tagebuch* (Munich: Rheinsberg/Georg Lentz, 1962), 188 f. (May 2, 1945) (English ed., *Berlin Underground 1938–1945*, trans. by Anna Boerresen [St. Paul: Paragon House, 1990], 14, 260).

6 Karla Höcker, *Die letzten und die ersten Tage: Berliner Aufzeichnungen 1945* (Berlin: Bruno Hessling, 1966), 23 (May 1, 1945).

7 *Mein Tagebuch: Geschichten vom Überleben 1939–1947*, ed. Heinrich Breloer (Cologne: Verlags Gesellschaft Schulfernsehen, 1984), 182.

8 Neitzel, ed., *Abgehört*, 210–212, 195, 197.

9 Ernst Jünger, "Die Hütte im Weinberg," in *Sämtliche Werke*, vol. 3 (Stuttgart: Klett-Cotta, 1979), 421.

10 Sarkowicz, ed., *"Als der Krieg zu Ende war,"* 79.

11 Hermann Okrass, "Farewell to Hitler," *Hamburger Zeitung*, May 2, 1945.

12 Lore Walb, *Ich, die Alte—Ich, die Junge: Konfrontation mit meinen Tagebüchern 1933–1945* (Berlin: Aufbau, 1997), 338.

13 Breloer, ed., *Mein Tagebuch*, 213 (May 2, 1945).

14 Carola Stern, *In den Netzen der Erinnerung: Lebensgeschichten zweier Menschen* (Reinbek bei Hamburg: Rowohlt, 1986), 237. See also Stern, "Dem Führer die Treue halten?" in Trampe, ed., *Stunde Null*, 261.

15 Lothar Loewe, "Der Kampf um Berlin," in Trampe, ed., *Stunde Null*, 47. Fifteen-year-old Johanna Ruf, who together with other members of the League of German Girls had been drafted as a nurse's assistant in the field hospital under the New Reich Chancellery, wrote on May 2, "We cannot write down what is on all our minds when conversation turns one last time to the Führer." Ruf, *Eine Backpfeife für den kleinen Goebbels: Berlin im Tagebuch einer 15-Jährigen—die letzten und die ersten Tage*, ed. Wieland Giebel (Berlin: BerlinStory Verlag, 2017), 29.

16 Kellner, *My Opposition*, 405.

17 Shirer, *End of a Berlin Diary*, n.p. (Kindle ed.).

18 Tschuikow, *Ende*, 219.

19 Refior, "Tagebuch," 135.

20 Dufving, "Kapitulationsverhandlungen," 177–181.

21 Facsimile of the May 2 order in Olaf Groehler, *1945: Die Neue Reichskanzlei—Das Ende* (Berlin: Brandenburgisches Verlagshaus, 1995), 72. See also Tschuikow, *Ende*, 226 f.

22 See Stefan Doernberg, *Befreiung 1945: Ein Augenzeugenbericht* (East Berlin: Dietz, 1975), 62–64.

23 See Mühlen, ed., *Todeskampf*, 254.

24 Jelena Rshewskaja, *Hitlers Ende ohne Mythos: Jelena Rshewskaja erinnert sich an ihren Einsatz im Mai 1945 in Berlin*, ed. Stefan Doernberg (Berlin: Neues Leben, 2005), 51.

25 See Mühlen, ed., *Todeskampf*, 250 f., 255–277.

26 Margret Boveri, *Tage des Überlebens: Berlin 1945* (Munich/Zürich: Piper, 1985), 97 f.

27 *Berliner Schulaufsätze aus dem Jahr 1946*, ed. Annett Gröschner (Berlin: Kontext, 1996), 244.

28 Ibid., 164. See also the diary entries of eighteen-year-old Berlin office worker Brigitte

Eicke: "The people were all crazy and plundered like hyenas. They had no consideration for one another. They lashed out and were no longer like people." Eicke, *Backfisch im Bombenkrieg: Notizen in Steno*, ed. Barbara Felsmann, Annett Gröschner, and Grischa Meyer (Berlin: Matthes & Seitz, 2013), 269. See also Höcker, *Die letzten und die ersten Tage*: "An intoxicated lust to get their hands on whatever they can has seized people. Even the moral busybody is losing his inhibition" (24).

29 Angela Martin and Claudia Schoppmann, *"Ich fürchte die Menschen mehr als die Bomben": Aus den Tagebüchern dreier Berliner Frauen 1938–1946*, Berliner Geschichtswerkstatt, http://www.berliner-geschichtswerkstatt.de/news-reader/items/tagebuchaufzeichnungen-vom-1-april-bis-zum-9-mai-1945.html (Berlin: Metropol Verlag, 1996)

30 *The Fall of Berlin 1945*, 340.

31 Vasily Grossman, *A Writer at War: A Soviet Journalist with the Red Army 1941–1945*, ed. and trans. Antony Beevor and Luba Vinogradova (New York: Random House, 2010), 340.

32 Merridale, *Ivan's War*, 287.

33 Leonhard, *Revolution*, 309.

34 Fritz Erpenbeck, "Am Anfang war das Chaos," in Keiderling, ed., *Gruppe Ulbricht*, 640.

35 Leonhard, *Revolution*, 310, 311 f.

36 Ibid., 315–317; and Leonhard, "Im Dienste Walter Ulbrichts," in Trampe, ed., *Stunde Null*, 276.

37 See Keiderling, ed., *Gruppe Ulbricht*, 348–351, on 349. See also Frank, *Walter Ulbricht*, 186 f.

38 See the protocol 2nd Meeting of Berlin KPD Functionaries of May 20, 1945, in Keiderling ed., *Gruppe Ulbricht*, 362. See also ibid., 56 f.; Leonhard, *Revolution*, 331 f.; and Naimark, *Russen in Deutschland*, 152 f., 157.

39 Keiderling, ed., *Gruppe Ulbricht*, 349. See also Frank, *Walter Ulbricht*, 195.

40 Andreas Petersen, *Die Moskauer: Wie das Stalintrauma die DDR prägte* (Frankfurt: Fischer, 2019), 29 f.; and Frank, *Walter Ulbricht*, 195 f.

41 Keiderling, ed., *Gruppe Ulbricht*, 319–321, on 320.

42 Ibid., 298–301, on 300.

43 Leonhard, *Revolution*, 335–337; Keiderling, ed., *Gruppe Ulbricht*, 57–68; and Frank, *Walter Ulbricht*, 189–191.

44 James P. O'Donnell and Uwe Bahnsen, *Die Katakombe: Das Ende in der Reichskanzlei* (Stuttgart: DVA, 1975), 376 f.

45 *The Fall of Berlin 1945*, 390.

46 Rshewskaja, *Hitlers Ende*, 47 f.

47 Völklein, ed., *Hitlers Tod*, 94.

48 Ibid., 95–98.

49 Ibid., 98 f.

50 Rshewskaja, *Hitlers Ende*, 66 f.

51 Lew Besymenski, *Der Tod des Adolf Hitler: Unbekannte Dokumente aus Moskauer*

Archiven (Hamburg: Christian Wegner, 1968), 17 f.; Völklein, ed., *Hitlers Tod*, 100 f.; and Eberle and Uhl, eds., *Das Buch Hitler*, 464.

52   Völklein, ed., *Hitlers Tod*, 54–56; and Eberle and Uhl, eds., *Das Buch Hitler*, 463.

53   The coroner's investigation report is reproduced in Besymenski, *Tod des Adolf Hitler*, 321–351; excerpts also in Völklein, ed., *Hitlers Tod*, 106–131, and see also 131–140.

54   See Joachimsthaler, *Hitlers Ende*, 373–378; Völklein, ed., *Hitlers Tod*, 125, 139, 154; and Rshewskaja, *Hitlers Ende*, 116–123. The information that the X-rays of Hitler's bridgework were found in the Reichstag (123) is erroneous.

55   Völklein, ed., *Hitlers Tod*, 101–103; and Rshewskaja, *Hitlers Ende*, 105–107.

56   Völklein, ed., *Hitlers Tod*, 140–144; and Eberle and Uhl, eds., *Das Buch Hitler*, 466 f.

57   See the notes of Stalin's interpretor Pawlow on May 26, 1945, in Völklein, ed., *Hitlers Tod*, 60.

58   Joachimsthaler, *Hitlers Ende*, 394.

59   Ibid., 395 f. See Völklein, ed., *Hitlers Tod*, 61 f.

60   Eberle and Uhl, eds., *Das Buch Hitler*, 468–477; and Völklein, ed., *Hitlers Tod*, 162–175.

61   Völklein, ed., *Hitlers Tod*, 192 f.

62   Ibid., 194 f. See also Sven Felix Kellerhoff, "Warum Hitler und Eva Braun zehn Mal begraben wurden," *Die Welt*, April 29, 2016.

63   Bradley F. Smith and Elena Agarossi, *Unternehmen "Sonnenaufgang"* (Cologne: Kiepenheuer & Witsch, 1981), 255 f. (English ed., *Operation Sunrise: The Secret Surrender* [New York: Basic Books, 1979], 179).

64   Kerstin von Lingen, *SS und Secret Service: "Verschwörung des Schweigens": Die Akte Karl Wolff* (Paderborn: Ferdinand Schöningh, 2010), 10, 24–39. See also Jochen von Lang, *Der Adjutant: Karl Wolff—der Mann zwischen Hitler und Himmler* (Munich/ Berlin: Herbig, 1985).

65   See Max Waibel, *1945: Kapitulation in Norditalien—Originalbericht des Vermittlers*, (Basel: Helbing & Lichtenhahn, 1981), 27–45.

66   Lingen, *SS und Secret Service*, 64–66; Smith and Agarossi, *Unternehmen "Sonnenaufgang*," 127–131; and Allen Dulles and Gero von Gaevernitz, *Unternehmen "Sunrise": Die geheime Geschichte des Kriegsendes in Italien* (Düsseldorf/Vienna: Econ, 1967), 113–126 (English ed., *The Secret Surrender* [New York: Harper & Row, 1966], 118–133).

67   Smith and Agarossi, *Unternehmen "Sonnenaufgang*," 148 f.; and Lingen, *SS und Secret Service*, 67 f. (English ed., *Operation Sunrise: The Secret Surrender* [New York: Basic Books, 1979], 125–129).

68   Lang, *Adjutant*, 279 f.; and Lingen, *SS und Secret Service*, 68 f.

69   Smith and Agarossi, *Unternehmen "Sonnenaufgang*," 201; Lang, *Adjutant*, 280–282; and Dulles and Gaevernitz, *Unternehmen "Sunrise*," 208–211.

70   Hansen, *Ende*, 75 f.; Lingen, *SS und Secret Service*, 71 f.; Henke, *Die amerikanische Besetzung*, 676; Smith and Agarossi, *Unternehmen "Sonnenaufgang*," 160–171, 183–

190; Winston Churchill, *The Second World War, Volume 6: Triumph and Tragedy* (New York: Houghton Mifflin, 1953), 466–468; and John Colville, *The Fringes of Power: The Downing Street Diaries 1939–1955* (New York: Norton, 1985), 582.

71 Hansen, *Ende*, 77 f.; Holger Afflerbach, *Die Kunst der Niederlage: Eine Geschichte der Kapitulation* (Munich: Beck, 2013), 238 f.; and Smith and Agarossi, *Unternehmen "Sonnenaufgang,"* 226–238.

72 Dulles and Gaevernitz, *Unternehmen "Sunrise,"* 251.

73 Schramm, ed., *KTB-OKW*, vol. 4, part 2, 1663 f.

74 Hansen, *Ende*, 78 f.; Lingen, *SS und Secret Service*, 75–77; Smith and Agarossi, *Unternehmen "Sonnenaufgang,"* 245–255; and Albert Kesselring, *Soldat bis zum letzten Tag* (Bonn: Athenäum, 1953), 418–420.

75 *1945: Das Jahr der endgültigen Niederlage der faschistischen Wehrmacht*, ed. Gerhard Förster and Richard Lakowski (East Berlin: Deutscher Militärverlag, 1975), 364 f.

76 Lüdde-Neurath, *Regierung Dönitz*, 61; and Steinert, *23 Tage*, 188.

77 See Wilhelm Neumann's diary entry on May 1, 1945, https://www.moz.de/land kreise/oder-spree/frankfurt-oder/artikel9/dg/0/1/1109539/.

78 Dönitz, *Zehn Jahre*, 440 f.; Hansen, *Ende*, 114 f.; and Steinert, *23 Tage*, 170 f.

79 Schramm, ed., *Niederlage*, 421.

80 Schramm, ed., *KTB-OKW*, vol. 4, part 2, 1470.

81 Reproduced in Lüdde-Neurath, *Regierung Dönitz*, 135 f., on 135.

82 Joseph Goebbels, "Das Jahr 2000," *Das Reich*, February 25, 1945.

83 Volker Ullrich, "Eiserner Vorhang: Wie die NS-Propaganda Churchills Schlagwort prägte," *ZEIT-Geschichte* 5 (2019), 33; and Rainer Blasius, "Politisches Schlagwort: Nicht Churchill prägte den Begriff 'Eiserner Vorhang,'" *Frankfurter Allgemeine Zeitung*, February 19, 2015.

84 Lüdde-Neurath, *Regierung Dönitz*, 136.

85 Schramm, ed., *Niederlage*, 423.

86 Schramm, ed., *KTB-OKW*, vol. 4, part 2, 1471. See also Dönitz, *Zehn Jahre*, 445 f.; Lüdde-Neurath, *Regierung Dönitz*, 61 f.; and Steinert, *23 Tage*, 173 f.

87 Lüdde-Neurath, *Regierung Dönitz*, 63 f.

88 Michael J. Neufeld, *Wernher von Braun: Visionär des Weltraums, Ingenieur des Krieges* (Munich: Siedler, 2009), 241 f.

89 Ibid., 242.

90 On the following, see in addition to Neufeld Rainer Eisfeld, *Mondsüchtig: Wernher von Braun und die Geburt der Raumfahrt aus dem Geist der Barbarei* (Reinbek bei Hamburg: Rowohlt, 1996). See also the summary in Jens-Christian Wagner, "Ingenieur und Blender," *ZEIT-Geschichte* 3 (2019), 78 f.

91 Eisfeld, *Mondsüchtig*, 153.

92 Henke, *Die amerikanische Besetzung*, 742–776; Tom Bower, *Verschwörung Paperclip: NS-Wissenschaftler im Dienst der Siegermächte* (Munich: List, 1987), 87 ff. (English ed., *The Paperclip Conspiracy: The Hunt for the Nazi Scientists* [New York: Little, Brown and Company, 1987], 91).

93 Eisfeld, *Mondsüchtig*, 157.

94 Victor Klemperer, *I Will Bear Witness: A Diary of the Nazi Years 1942–1945*, trans. Martin Chalmers (New York: Modern Library, 1999), 470.

95 See Volker Ullrich, "Victor Klemperer: Ich will Zeugnis ablegen bis zum letzten—Tagebücher 1933–1945," in *Holocaust Zeugnis Literatur: 20 Werke wieder gelesen*, ed. Markus Roth and Sascha Feuchert (Göttingen: Wallstein, 2018), 211–222.

96 Klemperer, *Witness*, 448 (April 15, 1945).

97 Ibid., 468 (April 28, 1945), 470 (May 1, 1945), 474 (May 5, 1945).

98 Ibid., 470 (May 2, 1945).

99 For other examples, see Hermann Glaser, *1945: Ein Lesebuch* (Frankfurt: Fischer, 1995), 62 f.

100 Kardorff, *Berliner Aufzeichnungen*, 317 (April 28, 1945).

MAY 3, 1945

1 Schramm, ed., *Niederlage*, 423. See also Lüdde-Neurath, *Regierung Dönitz*, 64; and Schramm, ed., *KTB-OKW*, vol. 4, part 2, 1471. The order to redeploy all available forces to the Kaiser Wilhelm Canal was issued to the battle commandant of Schleswig at 11:20 a.m. Further communication determined, however, that there were not sufficient quantities of heavy weaponry, hand weapons, and armor.

2 René Küpper, *Karl Hermann Frank (1896–1946): Politische Biographie eines sudetendeutschen Nationalsozialisten* (Munich: Oldenbourg, 2010), 129 ff., 268 ff.

3 Walter Manoschek, *"Serbien ist judenfrei": Militärische Besatzungspolitik und Judenvernichtung in Serbien 1941–42* (Munich: Oldenbourg, 1993), 12, 55 ff.

4 Robert Bohn, *Reichskommissariat Norwegen: "Nationalsozialistische Neuordnung" und Kriegswirtschaft* (Munich: Oldenbourg, 2000), 79 ff., 423 ff.

5 Ulrich Herbert, *Best: Biographische Studien über Radikalismus, Weltanschauung und Vernunft 1903–1989* (Bonn: Dietz, 1996), 323–398.

6 Johannes Koll, *Arthur Seyß-Inquart und die deutsche Besatzungspolitik in den Niederlanden (1940–1945)* (Vienna: Böhlau, 2015), 37 ff., 69 ff., 321 ff., 383 ff., 411 ff.

7 Schramm, ed., *Niederlage*, 423 f. See also Dönitz, *Zehn Jahre*, 447; Lüdde-Neurath, *Regierung Dönitz*, 76 f.; and Steinert, *23 Tage*, 190 f.

8 Schramm, ed., *Niederlage*, 424. See also Lüdde-Neurath, *Regierung Dönitz*, 78 f.; Steinert, *23 Tage*, 179; and Herbert, *Best*, 400.

9 Koll, *Seyß-Inquart*, 556–565.

10 Schramm, ed., *Niederlage*, 424 f. See also Lüdde-Neurath, *Die Regierung Dönitz*, 78; and Steinert, *23 Tage*, 176.

11 Koll, *Seyß-Inquart*, 572 f.

12 Dönitz, *Zehn Jahre*, 448 f. See also Schramm, ed., *Niederlage*, 425 f.; and Lüdde-Neurath, *Regierung Dönitz*, 79 f.

13 For the text of Speer's speech, see Breloer, *Akte Speer*, 322–325. See also Speer, *Inside the Third Reich*, 495, 497; and Brechtken, *Albert Speer*, 290.

14   Facsimile in *Kriegsende in Hamburg: Eine Stadt erinnert sich,* ed. Ortwin Pelc with Christiane Zwick (Hamburg: Ellert und Richter, 2005), 164.

15   Ibid., 18–20. See also Uwe Bahnsen and Kerstin von Stürmer, *Die Stadt, die leben Wollte: Hamburg und die Stunde Null* (Hamburg: Convent, 2004), 16–20.

16   Frank Bajohr, "Hamburgs 'Führer': Zur Person und Tätigkeit des Hamburger NSDAP-Gauleiters Karl Kaufmann (1900–1969)," in *Hamburg in der NS-Zeit: Ergebnisse neuerer Forschungen,* ed. Bajohr and Joachim Szodrzynski (Hamburg: Ergebnisse-Verlag, 1995), 59–91.

17   Ursula Büttner, " 'Gomorrha' und die Folgen: Der Bombenkrieg," in *Hamburg im "Dritten Reich,"* ed. Forschungsstelle für Zeitgeschichte in Hamburg (Göttingen: Wallstein, 2005), 613–632.

18   Joachim Szodrzynski, "Die 'Heimatfront' zwischen Stalingrad und Kriegsende," in *Hamburg im "Dritten Reich,"* 633–682, on 673.

19   See testimony by Karl Kaufmann in Manfred Asendorf, *1945: Besiegt und befreit* (Hamburg: Landeszentrale für politische Bildung, 1995), 19. See also Bahnsen and von Stürmer, *Die Stadt, die leben wollte,* 31 f.

20   Mathilde Wolff-Mönckeberg, *Briefe, die sie nicht erreichten Briefe einer Mutter an ihre fernen Kinder in den Jahren 1940–1946* (Hamburg: Hoffmann und Campe, 1980), 151.

21   Pelc, ed., *Kriegsende in Hamburg,* 94. On the initial establishment of contact with the British, see ibid., 34–36; and Bahnsen and von Stürmer, *Die Stadt, die leben wollte,* 73–84.

22   Lüdde-Neurath, *Regierung Dönitz,* 36 f., 129.

23   Bahnsen and von Stürmer, *Die Stadt, die leben wollte,* 92.

24   Pelc, ed., *Kriegsende in Hamburg,* 46.

25   Szodrzynski, "Heimatfront," 677.

26   Pelc, ed., *Kriegsende in Hamburg,* 41; and Bahnsen and von Stürmer, *Die Stadt, die leben wollte,* 102 f.

27   "Gauleiter Karl Kaufmann spricht zu den Hamburgern," archived radio recording, May 3, 1945 (3:59 minutes), NDR-Mediathek.

28   Wolff-Mönckeberg, *Briefe,* 160.

29   Bajohr, "Hamburgs 'Führer,' " 59–61.

30   Pelc, ed., *Kriegsende in Hamburg,* 41 f.; and Bahnsen and von Stürmer, *Die Stadt, die leben wollte,* 104–109.

31   Pelc, ed., *Kriegsende in Hamburg,* 46 f.; and Bahnsen and von Stürmer, *Die Stadt, die leben wollte,* 110 f.

32   Wolff-Mönckeberg, *Briefe,* 161.

33   Hans-Ulrich Wagner, "Radio Hamburg: Der erste Sender nach dem Zweiten Weltkrieg," television documentary (January 21, 2014), NDR-Mediathek.

34   Ralph Giordano, *Erinnerungen eines Davongekommenen: Die Autobiographie* (Cologne: Kiepenheuer und Witsch, 2007), 244.

35   Bajohr, "Hamburgs 'Führer,' " 84.

36   Günther Schwarberg, *Angriffsziel Cap Arcona* (Göttingen: Wallstein, 1998), 42–47; and Bahnsen and von Stürmer, *Die Stadt, die leben wollte*, 118.

37   Wachsmann, *KL*, 667.

38   Detlef Garbe, "Eine Stadt und ihr KZ: Die Hansestadt Hamburg und ihr Konzentrationslager Neuengamme," *Jahrbuch Zeitgeschichte in Hamburg 2018* (2019), 12–31, here 26–28. See also Hermann Kaienburg, *Das Konzentrationslager Neuengamme 1938–1945* (Bonn: Dietz, 1997).

39   This thesis is advanced by Wilhelm Lange in his book *Cap Arcona: Das tragische Ende einiger Konzentrationslager-Evakuierungen im Raum der Stadt Neustadt in Holstein* (Eutin-Neustadt: Eutin, 2005). See also Lange, "Neueste Erkenntnisse zur Bombardierung der KZ-Schiffe in der Neustädter Bucht am 3. Mai 1945: Vorgeschichte, Verlauf, Verantwortlichkeiten," in *Häftlinge zwischen Befreiung und Vernichtung: Die Auflösung des KZ Neuengamme und seiner Außenlager durch die SS im Frühjahr 1945*, ed. Detlef Garbe and Carmen Lange (Bremen: Edition Temmen, 2005), 217–229, on 226.

40   Schwarberg, *Angriffsziel*, 56 f.; and Rudi Goguel, *"Cap Arcona": Report über den Untergang der Häftlingsflotte in der Lübecker Bucht am 3. Mai 1945* (Frankfurt: Röderberg, 1972), 26 f.

41   Goguel, *"Cap Arcona,"* 29 f.

42   Lange, "Neueste Erkenntnisse," 225.

43   Erwin Geschonneck, "Der Untergang der 'Cap Arcona,'" in Trampe, ed., *Stunde Null*, 128–133, on 130 f. See also Schwarberg, *Angriffsziel*, 86 f.

44   Geschonneck, "Untergang," 131–133. See also Garbe, "Eine Stadt," 29; and Schwarberg, *Angriffsziel*, 89 ff.

45   Anonymous, *Woman in Berlin*, 146, 83.

46   On the history of the text, see Yuliya von Saal, "Anonyma—'Eine Frau in Berlin': Geschichte eines Bestsellers," *Vierteljahrshefte für Zeitgeschichte* 67 (2019), 343–376, on 344, 351–359.

47   See Jens Bisky, "Wenn Jungen Weltgeschichte spielen, haben Mädchen stumme Rollen: Wer war die Anonyma in Berlin? Fragen, Fakten und Fiktionen—Anmerkungen zu einem großen Bucherfolg dieses Sommers," *Süddeutsche Zeitung*, September 24, 2003; and Matthias Sträßner, *"Erzähl mir vom Krieg!" Ruth Andreas-Friedrich, Ursula von Kardorff, Margret Boveri und Anonyma: Wie vier Journalistinnen ihre Berliner Tagebücher schrieben* (Würzburg: Königshausen & Neumann, 2014), 153–188, on 173.

48   Anonymous, *Woman in Berlin*, 197.

49   Volker Ullrich, "Authentisch? Vielleicht, vielleicht auch nicht: Wie der Versuch scheiterte, Einblick in das Original-Tagebuch der 'Anonyma' aus dem Jahr 1945 zu nehmen," *Die Zeit*, October 9, 2003; and Götz Aly, "Ein Fall für Historiker: Offene Fragen um das Buch 'Eine Frau in Berlin,'" *Süddeutsche Zeitung*, October 18–19, 2003.

50   Volker Ullrich, "Die Zweifel bleiben: Walter Kempowskis Gutachten zum Buch

der Anonyma," *Die Zeit*, January 22, 2004; and Gustav Seibt, "Kieselsteine zählen: Walter Kempowskis Gutachten zum Tagebuch der Anonyma," *Süddeutsche Zeitung*, January 21, 2004.

51   Saal, "Anonyma," 368–376. See also Volker Ullrich, "Was von der Anonyma bleibt: Zweifel an den Tagebüchern der Marta Hillers gab es immer—in Teilen haben sie sich nun bestätigt," *Die Zeit*, July 4, 2019. There were similar questions about the authenticity of the diaries of Ursula von Kardorff and Karla Höcker. See Volker Ullrich, "Geschönt und darum nicht mehr authentisch," *Die Zeit*, July 3, 1992; and Hoffmann, "Besiegte," in Fulda et al., eds., *Demokratie*, 31–33.

52   Saal, "Anonyma," 376.

53   Anonymous, *Woman in Berlin*, 84.

54   Ibid., 85.

55   Ibid., 140.

56   Ibid., 99.

57   Ibid., 62.

58   Ibid., 96.

59   Erich Kuby, *Die Russen in Berlin 1945* (Rastatt: Moewig, 1965), 313. See also the report by the military prosecutor of the 1st Belarussian Front to the front's military council on May 2, 1945: "The cases of arbitrary and (unjustified) shooting of Germans, of marauding and rapes of German women have significantly declined, even though a series of such cases has been recorded after the issuance of the directive of the Supreme Command's main headquarters and the front's military council." Scherstjanoi, ed., *Rotarmisten schreiben aus Deutschland*, 166.

60   Naimark, *Russen in Deutschland*, 100 f.

61   Andreas-Friedrich, *Schauplatz Berlin*, 189 f. (May 6, 1945). On the rapes as a topic of conversation in Berlin, see Jens Bisky, *Berlin: Biographie einer großen Stadt* (Berlin: Rowohlt, 2019), 636 f.

62   Naimark, *Russen in Deutschland*, 102.

63   Kuby, *Russen in Berlin*, 317.

64   Loewe, "Kampf um Berlin," in Trampe, ed., *Stunde Null*, 51.

65   Gröschner, ed., *Berliner Schulaufsätze aus dem Jahr 1946*, 90.

66   Ingrid Schmidt-Harzbach, "Eine Woche im April. Berlin 1945: Vergewaltigung als Massenschicksal," in *Befreier und Befreite: Krieg, Vergewaltigungen, Kinder*, ed. Helke Sander and Barbara John (Munich: Antje, Kunstmann, 1992), 25–27, 40 f.

67   Boveri, *Tage des Überlebens*, 119 (May 6, 1945).

68   Naimark, *Russen in Deutschland*, 169 f.

69   Ibid., 108–125.

70   Bertolt Brecht, *Arbeitsjournal 1941–1955*, vol. 2 (Frankfurt: Suhrkamp, 1973), 850.

71   Naimark, *Russen in Deutschland*, 170 f.

72   Miriam Gebhardt, *Als die Soldaten kamen: Die Vergewaltigung deutscher Frauen am Ende des Zweiten Weltkriegs* (Munich: DVA, 2015), 32–38. Gebhardt estimates that there were roughly 860,000 German rape victims between 1944 and 1955, with

190,000 being carried out by American soldiers; 50,000 by French; and 45,000 by British. That would dramatically reduce the number of rapes carried out by the Red Army while raising the number committed by the western Allies. On the difficulty of estimating these crimes, see Klaus-Dieter Henke, "Rechenfehler und Ungere-imtheiten," *Frankfurter Allgemeine Zeitung*, May 18, 2015.

73   Taylor, *Zwischen Krieg und Frieden*, 200–203 (*Exorcising Hitler*, 146–147); Thomas Faltin, "Dreifurchtbare Tage," *Stuttgarter Zeitung*, April 18, 2015.

74   See the case study by Herfried Münkler, *Machtzerfall: Die letzten Tage des Drit-ten Reiches, dargestellt am Beispiel der hessischen Kreisstadt Friedberg* (Berlin: Siedler, 1985), 238 f. In early May 1945, American lieutenant Melvin L. Lasky described seeing German women on the street smoking American-made ciga-rettes and his driver saying with a knowing grin, "One pack per trick." See Lasky, *Und alles war still: Deutsches Tagebuch 1945* (Berlin: Rowohlt Berlin, 2014), 208. Munich cardinal Michael Faulhaber noted with outrage on May 7, 1945, "The behavior of many women is scandalous. They accept gifts of chocolate," https://www.faulhaber-edition.de/dokument.html?idno=09265_1945-05-07 _T01&searchterm=Chokolade.

75   *The Memoirs of Field-Marshal the Viscount Montgomery of Alamein, K.G.* (Cleve-land/New York: World Publishing, 1958), 300, https://archive.org/stream/memoirs offieldma000362mbp/memoirsoffieldma000362mbp_djvu.txt.

76   Lüdde-Neurath, *Regierung Dönitz*, 65.

77   *Memoirs of Montgomery*, 300.

78   Ibid., 301 f.

79   Ibid., 302 f.; and Lüdde-Neurath, *Regierung Dönitz*, 138.

MAY 4, 1945

1   Schramm, ed., *Niederlage*, 426.

2   Schramm, ed., *KTB-OKW*, vol. 4, part 2, 1472.

3   Dönitz, *Zehn Jahre*, 449 f.; and Lüdde-Neurath, *Regierung Dönitz*, 65.

4   Dönitz, *Zehn Jahre*, 450 f.; Lüdde-Neurath, *Regierung Dönitz*, 66 f.; and Steinert, *23 Tage*, 184 f.

5   Schramm, ed., *Niederlage*, 426f.

6   *Memoirs of Montgomery*, 303.

7   Ibid., 303 f. Facsimile of the capitulation declaration is found in Lüdde-Neurath, *Regierung Dönitz*, 139.

8   Schramm, ed., *KTB-OKW*, vol. 4, part 2, 1278.

9   Herbert, *Best*, 408, 429–434.

10   Schramm, ed., *KTB-OKW*, vol. 4, part 2, 1674 f.; Kesselring, *Soldat bis zum letzten Tag*, 420 f.; Hansen, *Ende*, 134 f.; and Henke, *Die amerikanische Besetzung*, 936 f.

11   Henke, *Die amerikanische Besetzung*, 679–683, on 682. Resident Ruth Bodensieck from a village called Klietznick near the Elbe noted in her diary on May 4, 1945, "Soldiers rolled through here, taking whatever they though useful for their flight

across the Elbe to the Americans. Rafts were made from the walls and doors of barns. Whoever can save himself does, without regard for anyone else." https://www .volksstimme.de/nachrichten/lokal/genthin/1472844_Auf-dem-Weinberg-wird-die -weisse-Fahne-gehisst.html.

12 Albert A. Feiber, "Der lange Schatten Adolf Hitlers: Der Obersalzberg 1945–2005," in *Die tödliche Utopie: Bilder, Texte, Dokumente—Daten zum Dritten Reich*, 6th ed., ed. Volker Dahm, Albert A. Feiber, Hartmut Mehringer, and Horst Möller (Berlin: Stiftung zur wissenschaftlichen Erforschung der Zeitgeschichte, 2011), 672; and Florian M. Beierl, *Hitlers Berg: Licht ins Dunkel der Geschichte—Geschichte des Obersalzbergs und seiner geheimen Bunkeranlagen*, 4th ed. (Berchtesgaden: Plenk, 2015), 142.

13 Ulrich Chaussy and Christoph Püschner, *Nachbar Hitler: Führerkult und Heimatzerstörung am Obersalzberg* (Berlin: Ch. Links, 1995), 163; Beierl, *Hitlers Berg*, 142; and Feiber, "Der lange Schatten," 672. On Jean Gabin, see Karin Wieland, *Dietrich und Riefenstahl: Der Traum von der neuen Frau* (Munich: Hanser, 2011), 411.

14 See Volker Ullrich, *Hitler: Ascent 1889–1939*, trans. Jefferson Chase (London: Bodley Head, 2016), 608–623; Ullrich, *Hitler: Downfall*, 435–448; and Heike Görtemaker, *Hitlers Hofstaat: Der innere Kreis im Dritten Reich und danach* (Munich: Beck, 2019), 156 ff.

15 Henke, *Die amerikanische Besetzung*, 937–943; *Die verhinderte Alpenfestung: Das Ende des Zweiten Weltkriegs im Raum Berchtesgaden-Bad Reichenhall-Salzburg*, ed. Hellmut Schöner (Berchtesgaden: Plenk, 1996), 5–75; and Dwight D. Eisenhower, *Crusade in Europe* (London: William Heinemann, 1948), 452, 458.

16 Christa Schroeder, *Er war mein Chef: Aus dem Nachlass der Sekretärin von Adolf Hitler*, 3rd ed. (Munich: Herbig, 1985), 212.

17 Beierl, *Hitlers Berg*, 123–129; and Feiber, "Der lange Schatten," 663. See also Karl Koller, *Der letzte Monat: 14. April bis 27. Mai 1945—Tagebuchaufzeichnungen des ehemaligen Chefs des Generalstabs der deutschen Luftwaffe* (Esslingen/Munich: Bechtle, 1985): "According to information from [SS commandant] Frank, Obersalzberg looks like a lunar landscape. Göring's house almost completely gone. Same for half of the Führerbau. Bormann's house also bombed" (85).

18 Schroeder, *Er war mein Chef*, 213.

19 Josef Geiß, *Obersalzberg: Die Geschichte eines Berges von Judith Platter bis heute*, 20th ed. (Berchtesgaden: Plenk, 2016), 158. See also Feiber, "Der lange Schatten," 676 f.; and Chaussy and Püschner, *Nachbar Hitler*, 162.

20 Schroeder, *Er war mein Chef*, 214–216.

21 Lee Miller, *Krieg—Mit den Alliierten in Europa 1944–1945: Reportagen und Fotos*, ed. Antony Penrose (Berlin: Edition Tiamat, 2013), 229–233 (photo on 232). See also *Lee Miller's War: Photographer and Correspondent with the Allies in Europe 1944–45*, ed. Antony Penrose (Boston: Little, Brown, 1992), 188–192; and *Eine Amerikanerin in Hitlers Badewanne: Drei Frauen berichten über den Krieg—Margaret*

Bourke-White, Lee Miller und Martha Gellhorn, ed. Elisabeth Bronfen and Daniel Kampa (Hamburg: Hoffmann und Campe, 2015), 132, 297 f.

22 Miller, *Krieg*, 246.

23 Ibid., 247 f.; and Despina Stratigakos, *Hitler at Home* (New Haven: Yale University Press, 2015), 266.

24 Klaus Mann, *Tagebücher 1944 bis 1949*, ed. Joachim Heimannsberg, Peter Laemmle, and Wilfried F. Schoeller (Munich: Rowohlt, 1991), 82 (May 8, 1945).

25 Klaus Mann, "Hitler ist tot," in K. Mann, *Auf verlorenem Posten: Aufsätze, Reden, Kritiken 1942–1949*, ed. Uwe Naumann and Michael Töteberg (Reinbek bei Hamburg: Rowohlt, 1994), 211–215. See also *"Ruhe gibt es nicht bis zum Schluss": Klaus Mann (1906–1949)—Bilder und Dokumente*, ed. Uwe Naumann (Reinbek bei Hamburg: Rowohlt, 1999), 272–294.

26 Klaus Mann to Thomas Mann, May 16, 1945, in Klaus Mann, *Der Wendepunkt: Ein Lebensbericht* (Frankfurt: Fischer, 1963), 429.

27 Feiber, "Der lange Schatten," 679 f. (quote on 680), 699 f.; and Chaussy and Püschner, *Nachbar Hitler*, 167, 171–174.

28 Anneliese Poppinga, *Meine Erinnerungen an Konrad Adenauer* (Stuttgart: DVA, 1970), 253.

29 Hans-Peter Schwarz, *Adenauer, Bd. 1: Der Aufstieg 1876–1952* (Munich: DVA, 1994), 343–424. See also the sizable collection of documents in *Adenauer im Dritten Reich*, ed. Hans Peter Mensing (Berlin: Siedler, 1991).

30 Schwarz, *Adenauer 1*, 428–434. On Oppenhoff's murder, see Taylor, *Zwischen Krieg und Frieden*, 73–75, 79–87 (*Exorcising Hitler*, 32–33, 37–45).

31 Konrad Adenauer, *Erinnerungen 1945–1953* (Stuttgart: DVA, 1965), 21. See also the moving report about destruction in Cologne by Stephen Spender, *Deutschland in Ruinen: Ein Bericht* (Heidelberg: Matthes, 1995), 36–39. For a portrait of Adenauer, see ibid., 71–73: "He seemed astonishingly young and had the calm, self-assured manner of a successful and polite man" (71).

32 Konrad Adenauer to Hans Rörig, July 5, 1945, cited in Schwarz, *Adenauer 1*, 447.

33 Schwarz, *Adenauer 1*, 430, 442–444, 472.

34 Adenauer, *Erinnerungen 1945–1953*, 34–37. See also Schwarz, *Adenauer 1*, 469–471.

35 Schwarz, *Adenauer 1*, 477.

36 Jacob Kronika, *Der Untergang Berlins* (Flensburg/Hamburg: Verlagshaus Christian Wolff, 1946), 188. See also Findahl, *Letzter Akt*: "The Russians continue to refuse to touch German bodies, but they take all the greater care of their own dead, who are given proper graves with red stars and other adornments, flowers and large nameplates" (184).

37 See Hans Mahle's recollections in Krauss and Küchenmeister, eds., *Das Jahr 1945*, 65–77, on 70. See also Kronika, *Untergang Berlins*, 200.

38 Höcker, *Die letzten und die ersten Tage*, 31 (May 7, 1945).

39 Boveri, *Tage des Überlebens*, 107 (May 4, 1945). See Felsmann et al., eds., *Backfisch im Bombenkrieg* (May 6, 1945): "Having to schlep water is a curse" (272).

40 Andreas-Friedrich, *Schauplatz Berlin*, 189 (May 4, 1945).

41 Kronika, *Der Untergang Berlins*, 189 (May 4, 1945).

42 Andreas-Friedrich, *Schauplatz Berlin*, 189 (May 4, 1945). See also Boveri, *Tage des Überlebens* (May 6, 1945): "Most Russians don't know how to ride bicycles, and they take comical practice runs on the street, during which a large portion of the bikes emerge partially or completely wrecked" (118).

43 Anonymous, *Woman in Berlin*, 209. See also Findahl, *Letzter Akt* (May 11, 1945): "Hardly have the Russians left a building than the Germans are in position to cart off whatever they can get their hands on" (194).

44 *Neuanfang auf Trümmern: Die Tagebücher des Bremer Bürgermeisters Theodor Spitta 1945–1947*, ed. Ursula Büttner and Angelika Voß-Louis (Munich: Oldenbourg, 1992), 100 (May 2, 1945). See also p. 140 (May 27, 1945): "The sense of yours and mine has completely disappeared."

45 Findahl, *Letzter Akt*, 187 (May 6, 1945).

46 Höcker, *Die letzten und die ersten Tage*, 29 (May 4, 1945).

47 Erik Reger, *Zeit des Überlebens: Tagebuch April bis Juni 1945* (Berlin: Transit, 2014), 76 (May 2, 1945), 102 (May 20, 1945).

48 Boveri, *Tage des Überlebens*, 117 (May 6, 1945). See also Höcker, *Die letzten und die ersten Tage* (May 3, 1945): "Objectively speaking, we still don't know what's going on. Where is Goebbels? Where's Göring? From where is Dönitz 'issuing orders'? Who actually surrendered in Berlin? We're not told anything" (26).

49 Fritz Klein, *Drinnen und draußen: Ein Historiker in der DDR—Erinnerungen* (Frankfurt: Fischer, 2000), 97.

50 Anonymous, *Woman in Berlin*, 135 (May 2, 1945).

51 Andreas-Friedrich, *Schauplatz Berlin*, 188 (May 2, 1945).

52 Höcker, *Die letzten und die ersten Tage*, 32 f. (May 15, 1945), 36 f. (May 17, 1945), 40 (June 8, 1945), 41 (June 28, 1945). See Boveri, *Tage des Überlebens* (May 12, 1945): "It's astonishing how quickly everything gets back up and running. . . . In Friedenau, many streets already have water and light. It's said that parts of four streetcar lines are also running again" (135).

53 Helmut Schmidt's pocket calendar on May 3, 1945, cited in Hartmut Soell, *Helmut Schmidt 1918–1969: Vernunft und Leidenschaft* (Munich: DVA, 2003), 166.

54 Helmut Schmidt, *Kindheit und Jugend unter Hitler* (Berlin: Siedler, 1992), 214.

55 Ibid., 219.

56 Sabine Pamperrien, *Helmut Schmidt und der Scheißkrieg: Die Biographie 1918–1945* (Munich/Zürich: Piper, 2014), 247 f. See ibid., 161, 221, 261.

57 Schmidt, *Kindheit*, 221.

58 Jörg Ganzenmüller, *Das belagerte Leningrad 1941–1944*, 2nd ed. (Paderborn: Ferdinand Schöningh, 2007), 32 ff., 64 ff.

59 Soell, *Helmut Schmidt*, 105. See Pamperrien, *Helmut Schmidt*, 219.

60   Helmut Schmidt and Fritz Stern, *Unser Jahrhundert: Ein Gespräch* (Munich: Beck, 2010), 79.

61   Soell, *Helmut Schmidt*, 152–159; and Pamperrien, *Helmut Schmidt*, 259–267.

62   Soell, *Helmut Schmidt*, 159 f., 166.

63   This explains Schmidt's fierce resistance in the 1990s to the Hamburg Institute of Social Research's exhibition on the Wehrmacht's war crimes. See the protocol of the round-table discussion with the creator of the exhibition, Hannes Heer: "We thought we could remain upstanding." ("Deutschstunde: Die Wehrmachtsausstellung und ihre historische Bedeutung – eine Streitgespräch mit Helmut Schmidt, Ausstellungsmacher Hannes Heer und dem Historiker Habbo Knoch. Interview: Christian Staas und Volker Ullrich, *Die Zeit*, May 3, 1995.)

64   Soell, *Helmut Schmidt*, 163.

65   Schmidt, *Kindheit*, 234.

66   Soell, *Helmut Schmidt*, 161.

67   See Rüdiger Overmans, "'Ein untergeordneter Eintrag im Leidensbuch der jüngeren Geschichte'? Die Rheinwiesenlager 1945," in *Ende des Dritten Reiches, Ende des Zweiten Weltkriegs*, ed. Hans-Erich Volksmann (Munich: Piper, 1995), 259–291; Overmans, "Das Schicksal der deutschen Kriegsgefangenen des Zweiten Weltkriegs," in *Das Deutsche Reich und der Zweite Weltkrieg*, vol. 10, part 2 (München: DVA, 2008), 417–421; Lowe, *Wilde Kontinent*, 149–152 (*Savage Continent*, 113–116). On the Remagen camp, see Winfried Becker, "Die Brücke und die Gefangenenlager von Remagen: Über die Interdependenz eines Massenschicksals im Jahre 1945," in Becker, *Die Kapitulation von 1945 und der Neubeginn in Deutschland* (Cologne/Vienna: Böhlau, 1987), 44–71.

68   Hansheinrich Thomas and Hans Hofmeister, *Das war Wickrathberg: Erinnerungen aus den Kriegsgefangenenlagern des Rheinlands* (Minden: Bruns, 1950), 15.

69   Marzell Oberneder, *Wir waren in Kreuznach: Eindrücke und Bilder aus den Kriegsgefangenenlagern Kreuznach und St. Avold* (Straubing: Attenkofer, 1954), 102.

70   Fritz von Hellweg, *Rheinwiesen 1945* (Wuppertal: Eugen Huth, 1951), 81.

71   In his sensationalist 1989 book *Other Losses*, Canadian journalist James Bacque claimed that the Americans and French had purposely allowed hundreds of thousands of German prisoners to die. Professional historians have rejected such numbers as grotesquely exaggerated. See Bacque, *Other Losses: An Investigation into the Mass Deaths of German Prisoners at the Hands of the French and Americans after World War II* (Toronto: Stoddart, 1989).

72   Arthur L. Smith, *Die "vermißte Million": Zum Schicksal deutscher Kriegsgefangener nach dem Zweiten Weltkrieg* (Munich: Oldenbourg, 1992), 86. For the Remagen camp, which took in 169,036 prisoners by the end of April 1945, the number of dead is estimated at around 1,200. See Becker, "Die Brücke," 56, 70.

73   Ulrich Herbert, *Geschichte Deutschlands im 20. Jahrhundert* (Munich: Beck, 2014), 445.

74   Hans Frank, *Im Angesicht des Galgens: Deutung Hitlers und seiner Zeit aufgrund eige-*

ner Erlebnisse und Erkenntnisse (Munich: Beck, 1953), 428. See also Dieter Schenk, *Hans Frank: Hitlers Kronjurist und Generalgouverneur* (Frankfurt: Fischer, 2006), 370 f.

75 Frank, *Im Angesicht des Galgens*, 39 f. See also Schenk, *Hans Frank*, 48.

76 Ulrich von Hassell, *Vom andern Deutschland: Aus den nachgelassenen Tagebüchern 1938–1944* (Frankfurt: Hamburg Fischer Bücherei, 1964), 99 (December 25, 1939).

77 Schenk, *Hans Frank*, 158.

78 Ibid., 232 f.

79 Stephan Lehnstaedt, *Der Kern des Holocaust: Bełżec, Sobibór, Treblinka und die Aktion Reinhardt* (Munich: Beck, 2017).

80 Schenk, *Hans Frank*, 243–253.

81 Ibid., 360–369.

82 Ibid., 372 f.

83 Kurt von Schuschnigg, *Ein Requiem in Rot-Weiß-Rot* (Zürich: Verlag Amstutz, Herdeg & Co., 1946), 503.

84 Henke, *Die amerikanische Besetzung*, 875.

85 Ibid., 875; Benz and Distel, eds., *Ort des Terrors*, vol. 2, 268 f., 353 f.; Hans Otto Eglau, *Fritz Thyssen: Hitlers Gönner und Geisel* (Berlin: Siedler, 2003), 259 f.; and Christopher Kopper, *Hjalmar Schacht: Aufstieg und Fall von Hitlers mächtigstem Bankier* (Munich/Vienna: Hanser, 2006), 353.

86 Hermann Pünder, *Von Preußen nach Europa: Lebenserinnerungen* (Stuttgart: DVA, 1968), 175.

87 Benz and Distel, eds., *Ort des Terrors*, vol. 2, 353 f.

88 Isa Vermehren, *Reise durch den letzten Akt: Ein Bericht (10. 2. 44 bis 29. 6. 45)* (Hamburg: Wegner, 1948), 181 f.

89 Pünder, *Von Preußen nach Europa*, 176.

90 Vermehren, *Reise durch den letzten Akt*, 187.

91 Ibid., 187–189; and Eglau, *Fritz Thyssen*, 261 f.

92 Vermehren, *Reise durch den letzten Akt*, 205.

93 Ibid., 230.

MAY 5, 1945

1 Schramm, ed., *Niederlage*, 429.

2 Lüdde-Neurath, *Regierung Dönitz*, 83 f.; and Hansen, *Ende*, 167 f. On the formation of a "caretaker Reich government," see Steinert, *23 Tage*, 142–159.

3 Eckart Conze, Norbert Frei, Peter Hayes, and Moshe Zimmermann, *Das Amt und die Vergangenheit: Deutsche Diplomaten im Dritten Reich und in der Bundesrepublik* (Munich: Blessing, 2010), 153 f.

4 Hans-Christian Jasch, *Staatssekretär Wilhelm Stuckart und die Judenpolitik: Der Mythos von der sauberen Verwaltung* (Munich: de Gruyter, 2012).

5 Ullrich, *Hitler: Downfall*, 611.

6 Götz Aly and Susanne Heim, *Vordenker der Vernichtung: Auschwitz und die deutschen*

Pläne für eine neue europäische Ordnung (Hamburg: Hoffmann und Campe, 1991), 366–374; Joachim Lehmann, "Herbert Backe—Technokrat und Agrarideologe," in *Die braune Elite II: 21 weitere biographische Skizzen,* ed. Ronald Smelser, Enrico Syring, and Rainer Zitelmann (Darmstadt: Wissenschaftliche Buchgesellschaft, 1993), 1–12.

7 Wigbert Benz, *Hans-Joachim Riecke: NS-Staatssekretär—Vom Hungerplaner vor, zum "Welternährer" nach 1945* (Berlin: WVB, 2014).

8 Heiner Lichtenstein, *Mit der Reichsbahn in den Tod: Massentransporte in den Holocaust 1941 bis 1945* (Cologne: Bund, 1985), 48 (facsimile of letter 32). See also Alfred Gottwaldt, *Dorpmüllers Reichsbahn: Die Ära des Reichsverkehrsministers Julius Dorpmüller 1920–1945* (Freiburg: Eisenbahn Kurier, 2009).

9 *Das Reichsarbeitsministerium im Nationalsozialismus: Verwaltung-Politik-Verbrechen,* ed. Alexander Nützenadel (Göttingen: Wallstein, 2017).

10 Sereny, *Albert Speer,* 632; and Brechtken, *Albert Speer,* 289 (Gitta Sereny, *Albert Speer: His Battle with Truth* (New York: Knopf, 1995).

11 Andrej Angrick, *Besatzungspolitik und Massenmord: Die Einsatzgruppe D in der südlichen Sowjetunion 1941–1943* (Hamburg: Hamburger Edition, 2003).

12 Stephan Linck: "'Festung Nord' und 'Alpenfestung': Das Ende des NS-Sicherheitsapparates," in *Die Gestapo im Zweiten Weltkrieg: "Heimatfront" und besetztes Europa,* ed. Gerhard Paul and Klaus-Michael Mallmann (Darmstadt: Primus, 2000), 569–597, on 588.

13 Stanislav Kokoška, *Prag im Mai 1945: Die Geschichte eines Aufstands* (Göttingen: V&R Unipress, 2009), 153; and Rudolf Ströbinger, *Poker um Prag: Die frühen Folgen von Jalta* (Zürich/Osnabrück: Edition Interfrom/A. Fromm, 1985), 62.

14 Küpper, *Karl Hermann Frank,* 376–380, on 380. See also Kokoška, *Prag im Mai,* 95–97.

15 Küpper, *Karl Hermann Frank,* 381; and Kokoška, *Prag im Mai,* 144.

16 Schramm, ed., *Niederlage,* 423.

17 Kokoška, *Prag im Mai,* 153–159, on 153; and Ströbinger, *Poker um Prag,* 62 f.

18 Kokoška, *Prag im Mai,* 169.

19 Ibid., 188–192.

20 Ströbinger, *Poker um Prag,* 67.

21 Ibid., 68; and Kokoška, *Prag im Mai,* 195–200.

22 Schramm, ed., *Niederlage,* 431.

23 Roland Kaltenegger, *Schörner: Feldmarschall der letzten Stunde—Biographie* (Munich/Berlin: Herbig, 1994), 297.

24 Ströbinger, *Poker um Prag,* 79.

25 Kokoška, *Prag im Mai,* 215.

26 Ibid., 232; and Ströbinger, *Poker um Prag,* 75 f.

27 Ströbinger, *Poker um Prag,* 81–83; and Kokoška, *Prag am Mai,* 287–293.

28 Küpper, *Karl Hermann Frank,* 396–402.

29 Kokoška, *Prag im Mai,* 297 f.

30 Peter Steinkamp, "Generalfeldmarschall Ferdinand Schörner," in *Hitlers militärische Elite, Bd. 2: Vom Kriegsbeginn bis zum Weltkriegsende*, ed. Gerd R. Ueberschär (Darmstadt: Wissenschaftliche Buchgesellschaft, 1998), 236–255, esp. 238.

31 Ströbinger, *Poker um Prag*, 94 f.

32 Peter Demetz, *Prague in Danger: The Years of German Occupation, 1939-1945* (New York: Farrar, Straus and Giroux, 2009), 32 f. Peter Demetz, *Mein Prag: Erinnerungen 1939 bis 1945* (Vienna: Zsolnay, 2007), 373 f. On the fate of the city's German population during the Prague uprising and afterward, see *Dokumentation der Vertreibung der Deutschen aus Ost-Mitteleuropa*, ed. Bundesministerium für Vertriebene, Flüchtlinge und Kriegsbeschädigte (Berlin: DTV, 1957), 60–64, 107–206; and Lowe, *Wilde Kontinent*, 165–169 (*Savage Continent*, 126–130).

33 Mathias Beer, *Flucht und Vertreibung der Deutschen: Voraussetzungen, Verlauf, Folgen* (Munich: Beck, 2011), 80.

34 R. M. Douglas, *"Ordnungsgemäße Überführung": Die Vertreibung der Deutschen nach dem Zweiten Weltkrieg* (Munich: Beck, 2012), 124 f. (English ed., *Orderly and Humane: The Expulsion of the Germans after the Second World War* [New Haven: Yale University Press, 2013], 93).

35 Emilia Hrabovec, *Vertreibung und Abschub: Deutsche in Mähren 1945–1947* (Frankfurt: Peter Lang, 1995), 96–101; and Douglas, *"Ordnungsgemäße Überführung,"* 129–131.

36 Hrabovec, *Vertreibung und Abschub*, 115 f., on 116.

37 Ulrich Herbert, *Fremdarbeiter: Politik und Praxis des "Ausländer-Einsatzes" in der Kriegswirtschaft des Dritten Reiches* (Berlin/Bonn: Dietz, 1985), 341.

38 See Susan L. Carruthers, *The Good Occupation: American Soldiers and the Hazards of Peace* (Cambridge, MA: Harvard University Press, 2016), 157. See also Wolfgang Jacobmeyer, *Vom Zwangsarbeiter zum heimatlosen Ausländer: Die Displaced Persons in Westdeutschland 1945–1951* (Göttingen: Wallstein, 1985), 16.

39 Jacobmeyer, *Zwangsarbeiter*, 42.

40 Ulrich Herbert, *Geschichte der Ausländerpolitik in Deutschland: Saisonarbeiter, Zwangsarbeiter, Gastarbeiter, Flüchtlinge* (Munich: Beck, 2001), 146 f.

41 Ibid., 154–157.

42 Ibid., 336–340; and Andreas Heusler, "Die Eskalation des Terrors: Gewalt gegen ausländische Zwangsarbeiter in der Endphase des Zweiten Weltkrieges," in *Terror nach innen: Verbrechen am Ende des Zweiten Weltkrieges*, ed. Cord Arendes, Edgar Wolfrum, and Jörg Zedler (Göttingen: Wallstein, 2006), 172–182.

43 Herbert, *Fremdarbeiter*, 342. On acts of revenge by slave laborers, see Lowe, *Wilde Kontinent*, 129–134 (*Savage Continent*, 94–98).

44 Jacobmeyer, *Zwangsarbeiter*, 39.

45 Ibid., 47. See also the diary of school principal Heinfried Niedermeyer from the town of Mellendorf near Hanover on May 3, 1945: "The prisoners from all the peoples of Europe, who were brought to this country in such great numbers, have now become a horrible danger. They are terrorizing the German lands and people and

feel like lords. . . . They spend all their days robbing and looting, and because they're armed, we cannot defend ourselves and can only watch on with clenched teeth as they continue their disgraceful activities day by day." *Mellendorfer Kriegstagebuch* (Hanover: self-published, 1996), 59.

46 Werner Borgsen and Klaus Volland, *Stalag X B Sandborstel: Zur Geschichte eines Kriegsgefangenen- und KZ-Auffanglagers in Norddeutschland 1939–1945* (Bremen: Edition Temmen, 1991), 218. For more on Bremen, see the diaries of Theodor Spittas, in Büttner and Voß-Louis, eds., *Neuanfang auf Trümmern* (April 30, 1945): "Looting by foreigners is increasing, street for street and systematically" (98).

47 Jacobmeyer, *Zwangsarbeiter*, 48–50; Herbert: *Fremdarbeiter*, 342–344; and Michael Pegel, *Fremdarbeiter, Displaced Persons, Heimatlose Ausländer: Konstanten eines Randgruppenschicksals nach 1945* (Münster: LIT, 1997), 76 f.

48 Jacobmeyer, *Zwangsarbeiter*, 37 f.

49 Findahl, *Letzter Akt*, 185 (May 3, 1945). See also Kronika, *Untergang Berlins* (May 6, 1945): "Long columns of foreign slave laborers move down Tiergartenstrasse. They want to go home! They aren't afraid of the long march on foot" (192).

50 Bettina Greiner, "Warten auf das wirkliche Leben," *ZEIT-Geschichte* 1 (2015), 42–47. On confiscation of people's homes in Haren, see Ulrich Müller, *Fremde in der Nachkriegszeit: Displaced Persons—zwangsverschleppte Personen—in Stuttgart und Württemberg-Baden 1945–1951* (Stuttgart: Klett-Cotta, 1990), 19–39.

51 Jacobmeyer, *Zwangsarbeiter*, 42–46; and Herbert, *Fremdarbeiter*, 342.

52 Jacobmeyer, *Zwangsarbeiter*, 82–84.

53 Patrick Wagner, *Displaced Persons in Hamburg: Stationen einer halbherzigen Integration 1945 bis 1958* (Hamburg: Dölling und Galitz, 1997), 21.

54 Jacobmeyer, *Zwangsarbeiter*, 126 f.

55 Ibid., 132. See also Bernd Bonwetsch, "Sowjetische Zwangsarbeiter vor und nach 1945: Ein doppelter Leidensweg," *Jahrbücher für die Geschichte Osteuropas* 41 (1993), 533–546, on 538 f.; Herbert, *Fremdarbeiter*, 344 f.; and Herbert, *Geschichte der Ausländerpolitik in Deutschland*, 182 f.

56 Werner Sollors, *The Temptation of Despair: Tales of the 1940s* (Cambridge, MA: Harvard University Press, 2014), 140. See also Jacobmeyer, *Zwangsarbeiter*, 134.

57 Bonwetsch, "Sowjetische Zwangsarbeiter," 540–543; and *Für immer gezeichnet: Die Geschichte der Ostarbeiter in Briefen, Erinnerungen und Interviews*, ed. Memorial Moskau and Heinrich Böll-Stiftung (Berlin: Ch. Links, 2019).

58 Edgar Wolfrum, *Rot-Grün an der Macht: Deutschland 1998–2005* (Munich: Beck, 2013), 603–607.

59 Jay Howard Geller, *Jews in Post-Holocaust German Society 1943–1953* (New York: Cambridge University Press, 2005), 24. See also *Lebensmut im Wartesaal: Die jüdischen DPs (Displaced Persons) im Nachkriegsdeutschland*, ed. Angelika Königseder and Juliane Wetzel (Frankfurt: Fischer, 1994), 18–31, 35–37, on 37.

60 Jay Howard Geller's *Jews in Post-Holocaust German Society 1943–1953*, 41.

61 Ruth Klüger, *Still Alive: A Holocaust Girlhood Remembered* (New York: Feminist Press, 2009), 150, [Munich: Anaconda Verlag, 2010], 196.

62 Königseder and Wetzel, *Lebensmut im Wartesaal*, 47, 48–53.

63 Ibid., 56 f., 148–154, 169–172.

64 Tom Segev, *Simon Wiesenthal: The Life and Legends* (New York: Doubleday, 2012), 63, 83. See also Benz and Distel, eds., *Ort des Terrors*, 322 f.

65 Segev, *Simon Wiesenthal*, 43–80.

66 Benz and Distel, eds., *Ort des Terrors*, 314 f., 324.

67 Segev, *Simon Wiesenthal*, 83.

68 Ibid., 85–95.

69 Ibid., 123–129, 213–219, 248–262.

70 Ibid., 21.

MAY 6, 1945

1 Schramm, ed., *Niederlage*, 427.

2 Ibid., 81.

3 Eisenhower, *Crusade in Europe*, 462. See also *Papers of Dwight David Eisenhower: The War Years*, vol. 4, ed. Alfred D. Chandler and Stephen Ambrose (Baltimore: Johns Hopkins University Press, 1976), 2615 f.

4 Henke, *Die amerikanische Besetzung*, 966.

5 Eisenhower, *Crusade in Europe*, 446.

6 See Walter Bedell Smith, *Eisenhower's Six Great Decisions* (New York/London/Toronto: Longmans, 1956), 204 f.; and Steinert, *23 Tage*, 195 f.

7 Schramm, ed., *Niederlage*, 430 f.

8 Dönitz, *Zehn Jahre*, 454.

9 See Alfred Jodl's notes on his meeting with Walter Bedell Smith on May 6, 1945, in Schramm, ed., *KTB-OKW*, vol. 4, part 2, 1479–1481. See also Smith, *Eisenhower's Six Great Decisions*, 205 f.; and Eisenhower, *Crusade in Europe*, 464 f.

10 Schramm, ed., *KTB-OKW*, vol. 4, part 2, 1481 f.; and Schramm, ed., *Niederlage*, 432.

11 Hansen, *Ende*, 165.

12 Rudolf Höß, *Kommandant in Auschwitz: Autobiographische Aufzeichnungen*, 4th ed., ed. Martin Broszat (Munich: dtv, 1978), 148. See also Wachsmann, *KL*, 672 f.

13 Lüdde-Neurath, *Regierung Dönitz*, 90.

14 Hansen, *Ende*, 165. See also Steinert, *23 Tage*, 143.

15 Hansen, *Ende*, 165; Steinert, *23 Tage*, 144; and Michael Wildt, *Generation des Unbedingten: Das Führungskorps des Reichssicherheitshauptamtes* (Hamburg: Hamburger Edition, 2002), 733 f.

16 Schramm, ed., *Niederlage*, 431 f.

17 Görlitz, ed., *Generalfeldmarschall Keitel*, 375. On May 7, 1945, Keitel announced simply, "All responsibilities of the Reichsführer SS are discontinued." See John Zimmermann, "Die Eroberung und Besetzung des Deutschen Reiches," in *Das Deutsche*

Reich im Zweiten Weltkrieg, vol. 10/1, ed. Militärgeschichtliches Forschungsamt (Munich: DVA, 2008), 481.

18 Lüdde-Neurath, *Regierung Dönitz*, 91.

19 Peter Longerich, *Heinrich Himmler: Biographie* (Munich: Siedler, 2008), 7–9, 756 f.

20 Sara Rubenstein, "Yad Vashem Features Death March Survivors for Women's History Day," *Jerusalem Post*, March 7, 2019, https://www.jpost.com/Diaspora /Yad-Vashem-features-Death-March-survivors-for-Womens-History-Day-582747. See also Blatman, *Todesmärsche*, 312; and Daniel Jonah Goldhagen, *Hitler's Willing Executioners: Ordinary Germans and the Holocaust* (New York: Vintage, 1997), 331 ff.

21 See Goldhagen, *Willing Executioners*, 334–346; and Blatman, *Todesmärsche*, 292 f.

22 Blatman, *Todesmärsche*, 302, 296–301; and Goldhagen, *Willing Executioners*, 347.

23 Blatman, *Todesmärsche*, 303 f.

24 Goldhagen, *Willing Executioners*, 350. On the Goldhagen debate, see Volker Ullrich, "Eine produktive Provokation: Die Rolle der Medien in der Goldhagen-Kontroverse," in *Zeitgeschichte als Streitgeschichte: Große Kontroversen nach 1945*, ed. Martin Sabrow, Ralph Jessen, and Klaus Große Kracht (Munich: Beck'sche Reihe, 2003), 152–170.

25 Peter Engelbrecht, *Der Krieg ist aus: Frühjahr 1945 in Oberfranken* (Weißenstadt: Heinz Späthling, 2015), 84.

26 See Blatman, *Todesmärsche*, 305–313, statistics on 312 f.

27 This is the main accusation made by Blatman against Goldhagen, who interprets the death marches as the final act in the intended destruction of European Jews and an expression of a fanatic, German "eliminatory" anti-Semitism; Blatman, *Todesmärsche*, 313–319.

28 Blatman, *Todesmärsche*, 11 f.

29 Ibid., 196–202; and Benedikt Erenz, "Apokalypse in Ostpreußen," *Die Zeit*, March 1, 2007.

30 On the reaction of "ordinary Germans," see Wachsmann, *KL*, 676 f.; Katrin Greiser, *Die Todesmärsche von Buchenwald: Räumung, Befreiung und Spuren der Erinnerung* (Göttingen: Wallstein, 2008), 257–277; and Martin C. Winter, *Gewalt und Erinnerung im ländlichen Raum: Die deutsche Bevölkerung und die Todesmärsche* (Berlin: Metropol, 2018), esp. 154–199.

31 Bernhard Strebel, *Celle April 1945 Revisited* (Bielefeld: Verlag für Regionalgeschichte, 2008), 52–123; Strebel, "Celle, 5. April 1945," *Die Zeit*, April 23, 2009; and Blatman, *Todesmärsche*, 435–443.

32 Blatman, *Todesmärsche*, 499–568.

33 Horst G. W. Gleiss, *Breslauer Apokalypse 1945: Dokumentarchronik vom Todeskampf und Untergang einer deutschen Stadt und Festung am Ende des Zweiten Weltkrieges*, vol. 5 (Wedel: Natura et Patria, 1988), 326.

34 Ibid., 433.

35 See Gregor Thum, *Die fremde Stadt: Breslau 1945* (Berlin: Siedler, 2003), 18–30, on

19; and Norman Davies and Roger Moorhouse, *Microcosm: A Portrait of a Central European City* (London: Jonathan Cape, 2002), 15.

36　Paul Peikert, "Festung Breslau," in *Den Berichten eines Pfarrers, 22. Januar bis 6. Mai 1945*, ed. Karol Jonca and Alfred Konieczny (Berlin: Union, 1970), 26.

37　Gleiss, *Breslauer Apokalypse*, vol. 1, 204.

38　Davies and Moorhouse, *Microcosm*, 15.

39　Ibid., 33.

40　Speer, *Inside the Third Reich*, 423.

41　Goebbels, *Tagebücher*, part II, vol. 15, 209.

42　Ibid., 274, see also 267 f.

43　Thum, *Fremde Stadt*, 21; and Davies and Moorhouse, *Microcosm*, 36-37, 404.

44　See Gregor Thum, "Stalingrad an der Oder," *Die Zeit*, March 3, 2005; and Davies and Moorhouse, *Microcosm*, 24.

45　Gleiss, *Breslauer Apokalypse*, vol. 3, 651. See also Thum, *Fremde Stadt*, 24.

46　*Völkischer Beobachter*, March 4, 1945; and Gleiss, *Breslauer Apokalypse*, vol. 3, 128 f.

47　Goebbels, *Tagebücher*, part II, vol. 15, 416, 421.

48　*Schlesische Tageszeitung: Frontzeitung der Festung Breslau*, March 7, 1945; and Gleiss, *Breslauer Apokalypse*, vol. 3, 230.

49　Davies and Moorhouse, *Microcosm*, 28; and Thum, *Fremde Stadt*, 25.

50　Goebbels, *Tagebücher*, part II, vol. 15, 640.

51　Peikert, "Festung Breslau," 284.

52　*Schlesische Tageszeitung: Frontzeitung der Festung Breslau*, April 20, 1945; and Gleiss, *Breslauer Apokalypse*, vol. 4, 864.

53　Breloer, *Akte Speer*, 315.

54　Joachimsthaler, *Hitlers Ende*, 191. On the awarding of the German Order in Gold, see Goebbels, *Tagebücher*, part II, vol. 15, 692 f.

55　*Schlesische Tageszeitung: Frontzeitung der Festung Breslau*, May 4, 1945; and Gleiss, *Breslauer Apokalypse*, vol. 5, 156.

56　Gleiss, *Apokalypse*, 181 f. See also the article by Breslau's last church dean, Joachim Konrad, "Das Ende von Breslau," *Vierteljahrshefte für Zeitgeschichte* 4 (1956), 387–390.

57　Gleiss, *Breslauer Apokalypse*, vol. 5, 233.

58　Thum, *Fremde Stadt*, vol. 30, 533 (note 31).

59　Hans von Ahlfen and Hermann Niehoff, *So kämpfte Breslau: Verteidigung und Untergang von Schlesien* (Munich: Gräfe und Unzer, 1959).

60　Davies and Moorhouse, *Microcosm*, 37.

61　Ibid., 419.

62　Ibid., 420 f.

63　Hugo Hartung, *Schlesien 1944/45: Aufzeichnungen und Tagebücher* (Munich: dtv, 1956), 131.

64　Peter Merseburger, *Der schwierige Deutsche: Kurt Schumacher—Eine Biographie*, (Stuttgart: DVA, 1995), 11–193, on 119 f.

65   Albrecht Kaden, *Einheit oder Freiheit: Die Wiedergründung der SPD 1945/46* (Hanover: Dietz Nachf., 1964), 17.

66   See Schumacher's speech on May 6, 1945, in *Kurt Schumacher: Reden—Schriften—Korrespondenzen 1945–1952*, ed. Willy Albrecht (Berlin/Bonn: Dietz, 1985), 203–236. See also the summaries in Kaden, *Einheit oder Freiheit*, 17–21; and Kristina Meyer, *Die SPD und die NS-Vergangenheit 1945–1990* (Göttingen: Wallstein, 2015), 32–34.

67   Annemarie Renger, "Die Trümmer in den Köpfen der Menschen," in Trampe, ed., *Stunde Null*, 225–233, on 233. See also Annemarie Renger, *Ein politisches Leben: Erinnerungen* (Stuttgart: DVA, 1993), 65–69.

68   Renger, *Ein politisches Leben*, 70 f.

69   Meyer, *SPD und die NS-Vergangenheit*, 35.

70   Albrecht, ed., *Kurt Schumacher*, 241.

71   Kaden, *Einheit oder Freiheit*, 69; and Kurt Klotzbach, *Der Weg zur Staatspartei, Programmatik, praktische Politik und Organisation der deutschen Sozialdemokratie 1945 bis 1965* (Berlin/Bonn: Dietz, 1982), 43.

72   "Politische Richtlinien der SPD in ihrem Verhältnis zu anderen politischen Faktoren," in Albrecht, ed., *Kurt Schumacher*, 256–286. See also the summary in Kaden, *Einheit oder Freiheit*, 70–74.

73   Brigitte Seebacher-Brandt, *Ollenhauer: Biedermann und Patriot* (Berlin: Siedler, 1984), 287.

74   Ibid., 291.

75   Albrecht, ed., *Kurt Schumacher*, 301–319, on 318.

76   Ibid., 320.

77   Ibid., 387–418, on 418. On the development of the SPD between October 1945 and April 1946, see Kaden, *Einheit oder Freiheit*, 233–280; and Klotzbach, *Der Weg zur Staatspartei*, 73–81.

78   Hartmut Peters, "Das Kriegsende in Jever 1945 und der Massenprotest gegen die Verteidigung der Stadt," Gröschler Haus, https://www.groeschlerhaus.eu/das-kriegsende-in-jever-1945-und-der-massenprotest-gegen-die-verteigungder-stadt/.

79   Ibid.

MAY 7, 1945

1   Schramm, ed., *Niederlage*, 432. See also Dönitz, *Zehn Jahre*, 455.

2   Smith, *Eisenhower's Six Great Decisions*, 210.

3   Steinert, *23 Tage*, 200.

4   See Harry C. Butcher, *My Three Years with Eisenhower: The Personal Diary of Captain Harry C. Butcher* (New York: Simon & Schuster, 1946), 833; and Eisenhower, *Crusade in Europe*, 465.

5   For a facsimile of the original articles of surrender, see Wikipedia, "German Instrument of Surrender," https://en.wikipedia.org/wiki/German_Instrument

_of_Surrender; German version in Lüdde-Neurath, *Regierung Dönitz*, 144 f.; and Schramm, ed., *KTB-OKW*, vol. 4, part 2, 1676 f.

6　Lüdde-Neurath, *Regierung Dönitz*, 70.

7　Ibid., 152 f.; and Krosigk, *Memoiren*, 247 f.

8　Schramm, ed., *Niederlage*, 433.

9　On Dietrich and her family, see Heinrich Thies, *Fesche Lola, brave Liesel: Marlene Dietrich und ihre verleugnete Schwester* (Hamburg: Campe und Campe, 2017), 9 ff.; and Thies, "Im Schatten des Blauen Engels," *Die Zeit*, September 27, 2017.

10　Wachsmann, *KL*, 651–653, 668.

11　Thies, *Fesche Lola*, 9, 14–18, 214 f.

12　Wieland, *Dietrich und Riefenstahl*, 9–13, 38–85, on 52; Thies, *Fesche Lola*, 19–42, 49–56; and Eva Gesine Baur, *Einsame Klasse: Das Leben der Marlene Dietrich* (Munich: Beck, 2017), 7–67.

13　Wieland, *Dietrich und Riefenstahl*, 183 ff.; and Baur, *Einsame Klasse*, 110 ff.

14　Thies, *Fesche Lola*, 57–64, 110–118, on 116.

15　Goebbels, *Tagebücher*, part I, vol. 3, art. II, 55. See also ibid., vol. 3, art. II, 341: "After that with Hitler. 'Shanghai Express.' Marlene Dietrich is really good."

16　Goebbels, *Tagebücher*, part III, vol. 2, 393.

17　Thies, *Fesche Lola*, 132, 135–139, 153–159.

18　Quoted in Renate Seydel, *Marlene Dietrich: Eine Chronik ihres Lebens in Bildern und Dokumenten* (Berlin: Henschel, 1990), 223. See also Marlene Dietrich, *Nehmt nur mein Leben . . .* (Munich: Goldmann, 1979), 143. Dietrich's autobiography in English is out of print.

19　*New York Herald Tribune*, August 13, 1944, cited in Wieland, *Dietrich und Riefenstahl*, 380–409; see also Baur, *Einsame Klasse*, 254–296.

20　Dietrich, *Nehmt nur mein Leben*, 171.

21　Thies, *Fesche Lola*, 201; and Baur, *Einsame Klasse*, 304 f.

22　Thies, *Fesche Lola*, 216.

23　Marlene Dietrich to Rudolf Sieber, September 27, 1945, in Wieland, *Dietrich und Riefenstahl*, 412. See also Thies, *Fesche Lola*, 226; and Baur, *Einsame Klasse*, 309 f.

24　Thies, *Fesche Lola*, 245–256.

25　Wieland, *Dietrich und Riefenstahl*, 424–429, 482–488, 496–500; and Baur, *Einsame Klasse*, 360 f., 389 ff.

26　Thies, *Fesche Lola*, 285–292, 357–361.

27　Ibid., 369. See also Wieland, *Dietrich und Riefenstahl*, 503 f., 529–543; and Baur, *Einsame Klasse*, 404 f., 472–474.

28　See Barbara Beuys, *Leben mit dem Feind: Amsterdam unter deutscher Besatzung 1940–1945* (Munich: Hanser, 2012), 350.

29　Ibid., 103.

30　Ibid., 109–150, on 149.

31　Ibid., 152–191, on 191.

32　Anne Frank, *The Diary of a Young Girl*, ed. Otto H. Frank and Mirjam Pressler, trans. Susan Massotty, https://archive.org/stream/AnneFrankTheDiaryOfAYoung Girl_201606/Anne-Frank-The-Diary-Of-A-Young-Girl_djvu.txt, quote in June 12, 1942. See also Melissa Müller, *Das Mädchen Anne Frank: Die Biographie* (Frankfurt: Fischer, 2013), 213 f.; and Matthias Heyl, *Anne Frank* (Reinbek bei Hamburg: Rowohlt, 2002), 52.

33 Frank, *Diary*, June 20, 1942.

34 Ibid., July 8, 1942. See also Beuys, *Leben mit dem Feind*, 192–198; Heyl, *Anne Frank*, 60–66; and Müller, *Das Mädchen Anne Frank*, 244–248.

35 Frank, *Diary*, October 9, 1942. See Beuys, *Leben mit dem Feind*, 204–207, 227–236.

36 Beuys, *Leben mit dem Feind*, 255, 285 f.

37 Frank, *Diary*, June 6, 1944.

38 Beuys, *Leben mit dem Feind*, 302 f., 313 f.; Heyl, *Anne Frank*, 111–115, 118–123, 126–131, on 131; and Müller, *Das Mädchen Anne Frank*, 345–348, 358–361, 364–378, 380–383. On the dates of the Frank sisters' death, see Stephanie Pappas, "Anne Frank Likely Died Earlier Than Believed," LiveScience, April 2, 2015, https://www.livescience.com/50360-anne-frank-died-earlier.html.

39 Beuys, *Leben mit dem Feind*, 304 f.; and Heyl, *Anne Frank*, 124 f.

40 Max Beckmann, *Tagebücher 1940–1950*, collected by Mathilde Q. Beckmann, ed. Erhard Göpel (Munich/Vienna: Langen/Müller, 1979), 97.

41 Beuys, *Leben mit dem Feind*, 305–312, 316–342.

42 Carry Ulreich, *Nachts träum ich vom Frieden: Tagebuch 1941 bis 1945* (Berlin: Aufbau, 2018), 286.

43 Koll, *Seyß-Inquart*, 574. See also Beuys, *Leben mit dem Feind*, 344–352.

MAY 8, 1945

1 *The Papers of Dwight David Eisenhower: Occupation, 1945*, vol. 6, ed. Alfred D. Chandler Jr. and Louis Galambos (Baltimore: Johns Hopkins University Press, 1978), 5–8; Steinert, *23 Tage*, 203 f.; and Karl-Heinz Janßen, "Der 8. Mai 1945: Die deutsche Kapitulation in Karlshorst," in Janßen, *Und morgen die ganze Welt . . . : Deutsche Geschichte 1871–1945* (Bremen: Donat, 2003), 485–492, on 487.

2 Eisenhower, *Crusade in Europe*, 466; and Steinert: *23 Tage*, 206 f.

3 See Konstantin Simonov's diary entry in Walter Kempowski, *Das Echolot: Abgesang '45—Ein kollektives Tagebuch* (Munich: Knaus, 2005), 439. See also Görlitz, ed., *Generalfeldmarschall Keitel*, 376.

4 Janßen, "Der 8. Mai 1945," 488.

5 Martin Sabrow, *Erich Honecker: Das Leben davor 1912–1945* (Munich: Beck, 2016), 441; see also 425–432.

6 Steinert, *23 Tage*, 207 f. For the German version of the surrender of May 8, 1945, see Lüdde-Neurath, *Regierung Dönitz*, 207 f.; and Schramm, ed., *KTB-OKW*, vol. 4, part 2, 1679 f.

7 Zhukov, *Memoirs*, 627.

8   Butcher, *Three Years with Eisenhower*, 843.

9   Zhukov, *Memoirs*, 629.

10 Ibid., 630.

11 Ibid., 29; and Janßen, "Der 8. Mai 1945," 486.

12 Quoted in Kempowski, *Echolot*, 442.

13 Zhukov, *Memoirs*, 630 f.

14 Görlitz, ed., *Generalfeldmarschall Keitel*, 378.

15 Hansen, *Ende*, 177 f. See also Speer, *Inside the Third Reich*, 497.

16 Breloer, *Akte Speer*, 329–336; and Brechtken, *Albert Speer*, 295 f.

17 Schramm, ed., *Niederlage*, 435. See also Dönitz, *Zehn Jahre*, 463; and Hansen, *Ende*, 178.

18 Lüdde-Neurath, *Regierung Dönitz*, 157 f.

19 Steinert, *23 Tage*, 213.

20 Schramm, ed., *KTB-OKW*, vol. 4, part 2, 1484 f.

21 Ibid., 1495; and *1945: Das Ende des Krieges*, ed. Gerd R. Ueberschär and Rolf-Dieter Müller (Darmstadt: Primus, 2005), 112.

22 Wilhelm Wintgen's diary entry of May 9, 1945, in "Tagebuch Wintgen," Aule Mettmanner, https://aulemettmanner.de/index.php/erzaehlungen-von-frueher/110 -tagebuch-eines-mettmanner-soldaten.

23 Steinert, *23 Tage*, 230 f.

24 Hansen, *Ende*, 161 f.

25 Schramm, ed., *KTB-OKW*, vol. 4, part 2, 1281 f.; and Ueberschär and Müller, eds., *1945*, 112 f. In his memoirs, Dönitz wrote, "I still think the fundamental thrust of these words is correct today." *Zehn Jahre*, 458.

26 Förster and Lakowski, eds., *1945*, 382–388, on 387.

27 Ernst Kubin, *Sonderauftrag Linz: Die Kunstsammlung Adolf Hitler—Aufbau, Vernichtungsplan, Rettung, Ein Thriller der Kulturgeschichte* (Vienna: Orac, 1989), 141–143.

28 Birgit Schwarz, *Auf Befehl des Führers: Hitler und der NS-Kunstraub* (Darmstadt: Theiss, 2014), 39–45; and Schwarz, *Geniewahn: Hitler und die Kunst* (Vienna/Cologne/Weimar: Böhlau, 2009), 221–228.

29 Schwarz, *Auf Befehl des Führers*, 49–55, 81–83, on 82, 83; Schwarz, *Geniewahn*, 228–235; and Kubin, *Sonderauftrag Linz*, 14–18.

30 Schwarz, *Auf Befehl des Führers*, 16–18; Schwarz, *Geniewahn*, 238 f.; and Kubin, *Sonderauftrag Linz*, 19 f.

31 Schwarz, *Auf Befehl des Führers*, 218–221, 230–232.

32 Goebbels, *Tagebücher*, part II, vol. 6, 430 f.; Schwarz, *Auf Befehl des Führers*, 235 f., 239 f.; Kubin, *Sonderauftrag Linz*, 61–64; and Meike Hoffmann and Nicola Kuhn, *Hitlers Kunsthändler: Hildebrand Gurlitt 1895–1956—Die Biographie* (Munich: Beck, 2016), 213 ff.

33 Schwarz, *Auf Befehl des Führers*, 237, 248–253; and Kubin, *Sonderauftrag Linz*, 79–89.

34 Ullrich, *Adolf Hitler: Downfall*, 547–549.

35 Kubin, *Sonderauftrag Linz*, 99–102; Schwarz, *Auf Befehl des Führers*, 256; and Konrad Kramar, *Mission Michelangelo: Wie die Bergleute in Altaussee Hitlers Raubkunst vor der Vernichtung retteten* (St. Pölten/Salzburg/Vienna: Residenz, 2013), 99–117.

36 Joachimsthaler, *Hitlers Ende*, 192.

37 Kubin, *Sonderauftrag Linz*, 115.

38 Ibid., 114–130; Kramar, *Mission Michelangelo*, 120–147; Schwarz, *Auf Befehl des Führers*, 257; and Peter Black, *Ernst Kaltenbrunner: Vasall Himmlers—Eine SS-Karriere* (Paderborn: Schöningh, 1991), 276 f.

39 Kubin, *Sonderauftrag Linz*, 146–160; and Schwarz, *Auf Befehl des Führers*, 272–279.

40 Bohn, *Reichskommissariat Norwegen*, 1–3.

41 Ibid., 97.

42 Ibid., 3.

43 Kempowski, *Echolot*, 353.

44 Brandt, *Erinnerungen*, 141. See also Brandt, *Links und frei*, 381 f.

45 Churchill, *Second World War*, vol. 6, 477.

46 Audio at bbc.com, On This Day, "Victory Europe," http://news.bbc.co.uk/onthisday /spl/pop_ups/04/all_world_war_ii/html/14.stm. See also Lindgren, *War Diaries*: "How must it feel to that vigorous old man of over 70 to announce that to the British empire? He spoke like a man in his prime, in resounding tones, and I liked him more than ever" (206).

47 See Walter Kempowski, "VE Day: What the End of the War Was Like for Those Who Were There," *Guardian*, May 8, 2015, https://www.theguardian.com/books/2015/ may/08/ve-day-what-the-end-of-the-war-was-like-for-those-who-were-there.

48 International Churchill Society, "End of the War in Europe: May 8, 1945," https:// winstonchurchill.org/resources/speeches/1941-1945-war-leader/end-of-the-war-in -europe/.

49 See the description by Joan Widham, a member of the Women's Auxiliary Air Forces, in Kempowski, *Echolot*, 322–324; and Janßen, "Der 8. Mai 1945," 491.

50 Elsbeth Weichmann, *Zuflucht: Jahre des Exils* (Munich: Knaus, 1983), quote in Kempowski, *Echolot*, 313 f.

51 University of Michigan Digital Library, Public Papers of the Presidents of the United States, "Harry S. Truman: 1945," https://quod.lib.umich.edu/p/ppotpus/4728442 .1945.001?rgn=main;view=fulltext.

52 Werner Hecht, *Brecht Chronik 1898–1956* (Frankfurt: Suhrkamp, 1997), 754. Thomas Mann noted in his diary, "In the evening French champagne to celebrate V-E Day. Listened to the speeches by Truman and Churchill" (*Tagebücher 1944–1. 4. 1946*, 202).

53 Kempowski, *Echolot*, 315 f.

54 *Ursachen und Folgen: Vom deutschen Zusammenbruch 1918 bis zur staatlichen Neuordnung Deutschlands in der Gegenwart*, vol. 23, ed. Herbert Michaelis and Ernst Schraepler (Berlin: Herbert Wendler, 1958), 258 f.

55 Markus Wolf, "Sozialismus stand nicht auf der Tagesordnung," in Trampe, ed., *Stunde Null*, 281–290, on 281.

56 See the description of Kennan in Kempowski, *Echolot*, 334.

57 Jünger, "Die Hütte im Weinberg," 434.

EPILOGUE

1   Thomas Mann, *An die gesittete Welt: Politische Schriften und Reden im Exil* (Frankfurt: Fischer, 1980), 616.

2   See letter from Siegfried A. Kaehler to Martin Kaehler, May 19, 1945, in Kaehler, *Briefe: 1900–1963*, ed. Walter Bußmann and Günther Grünthal with Joachim Stemmler (Boppard: Harald Boldt, 1993), 299.

3   Karl-Günther von Hase, "Düstere Gedanken im Moskauer Gefängnis," in Trampe, ed., *Stunde Null*, 147–151, on 148.

4   Kardorff, *Berliner Aufzeichnungen*, 324.

5   See Peter Merseburger, *Theodor Heuss: Der Bürger als Präsident* (Munich: DVA, 2012), 364. See also Heinrich Krone, *Tagebücher, 1. Bd.: 1945–1961*, ed. Hans-Otto Kleinmann (Düsseldorf: Droste, 1995): "The names of the generals are at the bottom of the ceasefire document and not, as in 1918, the name of a private citizen. Those who reaped should now sow so that there won't be another legend about how they were stabbed in the back" (8).

6   Merseburger, *Theodor Heuss*, 367 f.

7   See Gunter Hofmann, *Richard von Weizsäcker: Ein deutsches Leben* (Munich: Beck, 2010), 188. On the conflicts in West Germany over how to interpret May 8, 1945, see Sebastian Ullrich, "Wir sind, was wir erinnern: Es hat lange gedauert, bis sich ein selbstkritischer Umgang mit der Vergangenheit durchsetzen konnte," *ZEIT-Geschichte* 1 (2005), 27–34.

8   Walb, *Ich, die Alte*, 345. See also Keller, ed., *Kriegstagebuch*: "Can it be true that everything we believed in and lived for is over? Has all our sacrifice been in vain? I can't believe it" (211).

9   Alfred Kantorowicz, *Deutsches Tagebuch, 1. Teil* (Berlin: Verlag Anpassung und Widerstand, 1978), 80.

10 Wolff-Mönckeberg, *Briefe*, 171.

11 Stephan Hermlin, *Bestimmungsorte* (Berlin: Aufbau, 1985), 46.

12 Margaret Bourke-White, *"Dear Fatherland, Rest Quietly": A Report on the Collapse of Hitler's Thousand Years* (New York: Simon and Schuster, 1946), 103.

13 Wilhelm Hausenstein, *Licht unter dem Horizont: Tagebücher von 1942 bis 1946* (Munich: Bruckmann, 1967), 348.

14 George Orwell, "Now Germany Faces Hunger," *Manchester Evening News*, May 4, 1945.

15 Klaus Mann, "Es gibt keine Heimkehr," in K. Mann, *Auf verlorenem Posten*, 224–230, on 227. See also Wilhelm Hoegner, *Der schwierige Außenseiter: Erinnerungen eines Abgeordneten, Emigranten und Ministerpräsidenten* (Munich:

Isar, 1959): "To my eyes, incinerated Pompeii looks well preserved compared to Munich" (190 f.).

16 See *Die Briefe der Manns: Ein Familienporträt*, ed. Tilman Lahme, Holger Pils, and Kerstin Klein (Frankfurt: Fischer, 2016), 308–314, on 309, 314. See also Naumann, *Klaus Mann*, 300 f. (with John Tewksbury's photos of the Manns' house on Poschingerstrasse).

17 Lüdde-Neurath, *Regierung Dönitz*, 106; Hansen, *Ende*, 187; and Steinert, *23 Tage*, 239.

18 See Speer, *Inside the Third Reich*, 498.

19 Hansen, *Ende*, 189 f. See also Speer, *Inside the Third Reich*: "We composed memoranda in a vacuum, trying to offset our unimportance by sham activity" (498).

20 See the notes on the meeting between Rooks and Dönitz on May 13, 1945, in Förster and Lakowski, eds., *1945*, 400–402, on 400. See also Schramm, ed., *Niederlage*, 443 f.; and Görlitz, ed., *Generalfeldmarschall Keitel*, 379 f.

21 Dönitz, *Zehn Jahre*, 463.

22 See Schramm, ed., *KTB-OKW*, vol. 4, part 2, 1484; and Schramm, ed., *Niederlage*, 437 f., 440 f., 445.

23 Schramm, ed., *Niederlage*, 446.

24 See note by Dönitz on May 18, 1945, in Förster and Lakowski, eds., *1945*, 411–413, 412.

25 Schramm, ed., *Niederlage*, 436, 446.

26 For an overview, see Heinrich August Winkler, *Der lange Weg nach Westen*, 2 vols. (Munich: Beck, 2000).

27 Schramm, ed., *Niederlage*, 439, 447. See also Dönitz, *Zehn Jahre*: "We asked ourselves how we could have missed things that were going on in the center of Germany" (458).

28 See letter from Schwerin von Krosigk to Eisenhower on May 16, 1945, in Förster and Lakowski, eds., *1945*, 408 f., on 409.

29 Winston Churchill, *The Second World War Volume VI: Triumph and Tragedy 1956* (Boston: Houghton Mifflin, 1953), 646. See also Hansen, *Ende*, 193; and Marlies Steinert, "Die alliierte Entscheidung zur Verhaftung der Regierung Dönitz," *Militärgeschichtliche Mitteilungen* 2 (1986), 85–99, on 89.

30 Hansen, *Ende*, 195.

31 Robert Murphy, *Diplomat among Warriors* (Garden City, NJ: Doubleday, 1964), 242 f. See also Lüdde-Neurath, *Regierung Dönitz*, 107, 112; and Krosigk, *Memoiren*, 251.

32 Hansen, *Ende*, 200; and Steinert, "Die alliierte Entscheidung," 92 f.

33 Lüdde-Neurath, *Regierung Dönitz*, 113; and Dönitz, *Zehn Jahre*, 465.

34 Lüdde-Neurath, *Regierung Dönitz*, 114, 115 f.; and Krosigk, *Es geschah*, 379.

35 Speer, *Inside the Third Reich*, 501; and Sereny, *Albert Speer*, 640 f. One of the men arrested with Speer and taken to the Flensburg police presidium was Hitler's physician Karl Brandt, one of the main organizers of the infamous Nazi euthanasia

program. See Ulf Schmidt, *Hitlers Arzt Karl Brandt: Medizin und Macht im Dritten Reich* (Berlin: Aufbau, 2009), 514.

36 Speer, *Inside the Third Reich*, 502.

37 Frederic Spotts, *Cursed Legacy: The Tragic Life of Klaus Mann* (New Haven: Yale University Press, 2016), 231.

38 Ronald Smelser, *Robert Ley: Hitlers Mann an der "Arbeitsfront"—Eine Biographie* (Paderborn: Schöningh, 1989), 286.

39 Daniel Roos, *Julius Streicher und "Der Stürmer" 1923–1945* (Paderborn: Schöningh, 2014), 467. See also Richard Overy, *Verhöre: Die NS-Elite in den Händen der Alliierten* (Munich/Berlin: Propyläen, 2001), 41.

40 Kästner, *Notabene*, 148. See also Kästner, *Blaue Buch*: "The whole thing is ending somewhat like a costume rental agency. It's beneath the dignity of even these craven loudmouths" (213).

41 See "Hamburg-Journal," NDR broadcast, June 14, 2015. See also Conze et al., *Das Amt*, 332; and Theo Sommer, *1945: Die Biographie eines Jahres* (Reinbek bei Hamburg: Rowohlt, 2005), 83.

42 Christoforow et al., eds., *Verhört*, 48–57, on 51. On the conditions in Mondorf, see Overy, *Verhöre*, 65–67; Conze et al., *Das Amt*, 332 f.; Kirkpatrick, *Im inneren Kreis*, 171 f. (*The Inner Circle*, 193); and Philipp Schnee, "Hotel der Kriegsverbrecher," *Der Spiegel*, October 28, 2009.

43 Krosigk, *Memoiren*, 57.

44 Conze et al., *Das Amt*, 333; and Mark Mazower, *Hitlers Imperium: Europa unter der Herrschaft des Nationalsozialismus* (Munich: Beck, 2009), 486 (English ed., *Hitler's Empire: How the Nazis Ruled Europe* [New York: Penguin, 2008], 536).

45 Roos, *Julius Streicher*, 471.

46 Speer, *Inside the Third Reich*, 502.

47 See the interrogation of Göring on June 17, 1945, in Christoforow et al., eds., *Verhört*, 78–95, on 91. In conversation with the British diplomat Ivone Kirkpatrick in June 1945, Göring also showed no remorse for Nazi crimes against humanity or his part in them. See Kirkpatrick, *Im inneren Kreis*, 174 (*The Inner Circle*, 195).

48 See interrogation of Keitel on May 17, 1945, in Christoforow et al., eds., *Verhört*, 95–121, on 97, 103.

49 Mazower, *Hitlers Imperium*, 487 (*Hitler's Empire*, 536).

50 Lahme et al., eds., *Briefe der Manns*, 322–324, on 323. See also *Die Kinder der Manns: Ein Familienalbum*, ed. Uwe Naumann (Reinbek bei Hamburg: Rohwolt, 2005), 200 f.

51 See the facsimile of the article at Munich Stadtbibliothek, "Familie Mann: Erika Mann," http://www.monacensia-digital.de/mann/content/pageview/117776.

52 See Speer, *Inside the Third Reich*, 502–505.

53 Volker Ullrich, "Speers Erfindung," *Die Zeit*, May 4, 2005; and Brechtken, *Albert Speer*, 299–310.

54 Hansen, *Ende*, 200 f.; and Angrick, *Besatzungspolitik und Massenmord*, 716–719.

55   Martha Gellhorn, *The Face of War* (New York: Atlantic Monthly Press, 1994), 162–163. See also Saul K. Padover, *Lügendetektor: Vernehmungen im besiegten Deutschland 1944/45* (Frankfurt: Die andere Bibliothek/Eichborn, 1999), 46 (English ed., *Experiment in Germany: The Story of an American Intelligence Officer* [New York: Duell, Sloane and Pearce, 1946], xxx). Padover, a member of the US Army's division of psychological warfare, interrogated people in occupied Germany.

56   Hausenstein, *Licht unter dem Horizont*, 347. See also Kellner, *My Opposition*, 406–407.

57   Andreas-Friedrich, *Schauplatz Berlin*, 194.

58   Anonymous, *Woman in Berlin*, 211.

59   Ian Kershaw, *The Hitler Myth: Image and Reality in the Third Reich* (Oxford: Oxford University Press, 1987), 225. See also Klemperer, *Witness*: "The 3rd Reich is already almost as good as forgotten" (478); and Kardorff, *Berliner Aufzeichnungen*: "The war is over. The Nazis have been swept away like in the 73rd psalm. They've collapsed. They're already so much in the past they're no longer of interest" (326).

60   Eugen Kogon, *Der SS-Staat: Das System der deutschen Konzentrationslager* (Munich: Karl Alber, 1974), 393. Padover also described Germans placing all the blame on Hitler in an attempt to avoid their own moral responsibility.

61   Erika Mann, "German State of Mind," Munich Stadtbibliothek, "Familie Mann: Erika Mann," http://www.monacensia-digital.de/mann/content/pageview/60149.

62   Klaus Mann, "The Job ahead in Germany," *Stars and Stripes*, May 13, 1945. For illustrations of this attitude, see Niedermeyer, *Mellendorfer Kriegstagebuch*: "We will now have to start along our own Via Dolorosa without any hope at all," and "We are now more helplessly delivered up to our enemies than any other people of this earth in the preceding centuries" (both on 59).

63   Quoted in Hans Magnus Enzensberger, ed., *Europa in Ruinen: Augenzeugenberichte aus den Jahren 1944-1948* (Munich: dtv, 1995) 188.

64   Hannah Arendt, "The Aftermath of Nazi Rule," *Commentary*, October 1950, 342, 345.

65   Alexander and Margarete Mitscherlich, *Die Unfähigkeit zu trauern: Grundlagen kollektiven Verhaltens* (Munich: Piper, 1967).

66   Findahl, *Letzter Akt*, 190.

67   Sarkowicz, ed., *"Als der Krieg zu Ende war,"* 173.

68   Andreas-Friedrich, *Schauplatz Berlin*, 196, 203.

69   Norbert Frei, "Große Gefühle: Das Kriegsende war eine Zeit voll widerstreitender Emotionen," *ZEIT-Geschichte* 1 (2015), 16–23, on 23.

IMAGE CREDITS

INDEX

Note: page numbers in italics refer to maps and photos and accompanying captions